The Headmaster

The Headmaster

Roxburgh of Stowe and His Influence
in English Education

Noel Annan

SCHOCKEN BOOKS · NEW YORK

Published in U.S.A. 1966
by Schocken Books Inc.
67 Park Avenue, New York, N.Y. 10016

Published in Great Britain under
the title ROXBURGH OF STOWE.

Manufactured in the United States of America

To Lucy and Juliet

Contents

Acknowledgements

I am grateful to Mr Evelyn Waugh for permission to quote from *A Little Learning*, published by Chapman and Hall (London) and Little, Brown (Boston); to Messrs Allen & Unwin from *Public Schools and Private Practice* by John Wilson; to Mr Hugh Heckstall-Smith from *Doubtful Schoolmaster*, published by Peter Davies.

I must thank my colleagues at King's, Professor Meyer Fortes, Dr Royston Lambert, Mr George Rylands and Professor Edward Shils for reading the whole or part of this book in draft and proof and making innumerable helpful suggestions; Miss Eileen Hayman and Mrs Josephine Gould for typing the manuscript; and my wife who also read many drafts with patience and solicitude.

N. A.

Introduction

The English public schools hold a quite extraordinary position in British life. If an American parent cares to pay large fees to send his son to a New England prep school, that is regarded as his concern: no one imagines he has bought a passport to success or even a secure chance of a place at Harvard. But the English public schools are different. They are, of course, the reverse of public. They are private establishments independent of the local councils who control the State schools in Britain. They are religious in the sense that Christian worship, usually that of the Anglican Church, forms part of their way of life. Most of them are boarding schools. They vary so greatly that it is almost misleading to talk of "the public schools". Some have immense prestige, some are ancient, some have from 500 to over 1,000 boys, quite a number are small, obscure and less well known than famous grammar schools. But boys from the great public schools still fill an astonishing number of positions of influence and power in diplomacy, the City, the professions—and in politics. In Harold Macmillan's Cabinet of 1959, six out of 26 were Etonians. Slightly under half of the directors of the Bank of England, the joint stock banks, the leading merchant banks and the eight largest insurance companies came at that time from the leading *six* public schools. At the end of the war a sample survey showed that of 830 people in high office 76 per cent came from public schools and 48 per cent from twelve public schools. Forty per cent of the students at Oxford and Cambridge come from these independent schools. This is not because the ancient universities are governed by snobbery in their admission policy: it is simply a reflection of the fact that the public schools are able to provide smaller classes and more hand-picked teachers. Their headmasters know that they are on the inside track and they naturally intend to keep there.

How long can they keep there and what is the future of these schools? People have asked this question ever since the days before the First World War. Then, and even more in the years between the wars, the public schools came under attack: less because they were citadels of privilege than because they were obsessed by athleticism, by a tradition of savage discipline inflicted partly by the elder upon the younger boys, and by the virtue of Latin and Greek grammar to the exclusion of science and literature. But as the years passed the criticism of privilege grew louder; and the public schools began to wonder whether they should admit solely those whose parents were rich enough to afford the fees.

The Second World War made them think even harder. They feared that few would be able to afford such expensive schools; and accordingly a scheme was put forward by which the public schools would offer places to boys in the State system of education paid for by the local councils. The scheme was a failure. Local councils could not see why they should pay $1,400–1,800 a year to finance the education of one boy when their ratepayers' money could be spent more profitably on their own schools. Not only local councils; the headmasters of the State schools were up in arms. Why should their cleverest boys be creamed off and sent to the public schools, leaving the State schools the poorer? In 1945 no one foresaw that the public schools were in fact about to enter a new era of prosperity. The rise in the birthrate, post-war prosperity which enabled many parents to pay fees out of capital gains and by certain methods of tax avoidance, fund raising by alumni and a massive grant by British industry to rebuild the schools' laboratories and provide scientific equipment—all these gave the public schools new confidence.

They were, of course, haunted by the bogey of a left-wing government; and officially the Labour Party was hostile to them. But was the bogey all that terrifying? In 1945–50 when a Labour Government was in power it had the aftermath of the war to cope with. What money was available for education was used to improve and multiply the State schools. Curiously enough, the trade union-ists who are the backbone of the Labour Party and might have been expected most to resent the public schools, were usually indifferent to the issue. Indeed they sometimes even spoke up for them. When Birley left the British Control Commission in Germany to become headmaster of Eton, Ernest Bevin told him to keep on sending Etonians to the Foreign Office because he could not get on without them. The Labour Party was in a dilemma. If they attacked the public schools head on and tried to take them over, they would not only have to spend vast sums of money which most of their sup-porters would have preferred to spend on the State schools; they would start a fearful row about religious education and run up against the principle that parents should be free to send their children to the school of their choice. On the other hand, if a Labour Government did nothing about the public schools, not only its left-wing supporters but many of its outstanding members would feel betrayed on what seems to them to be an important social issue.

Paradoxically enough, the Labour Party's best allies are the headmasters of the public schools themselves. The majority want intensely to be brought somehow into the State system. No doubt self-interest influences them. A serious recession, or a downswing in the birthrate which fifteen years later would leave them with empty places, could cripple many schools. But it is not only self-interest. The teachers at these schools are inspired by a special sense of duty towards society. They like to believe that they are turning out boys who will serve the community, and that in turn the community respects them for so doing. At the beginning of this century, they could believe that they were educating the country's ruling class. But Britain has become more democratic since those days, and no one any longer pictures it as being governed by a small elite consciously leading their inferiors and shouldering the white man's burden in the Empire. Today the ideal of service which inspires public school masters is sometimes muddled and out of date. But it exists, and they want to make it again a reality. They are unhappy when they see not merely Labour supporters, but Conservatives and people of all kinds of political persuasion, asking whether it is right that the public schools should be open almost entirely to the sons of those who have inherited wealth or have just made their fortune.

When, therefore, the Labour Government of 1964 was formed, inevitably it would have to face the issue. But what was it to do? It has announced that it intends to set up a Public Schools Commission. No one yet knows how this Commission will operate, but probably it will negotiate with individual schools and consider how each can be integrated within the State system. Some may be asked to provide places for boys whose parents can prove that their sons *need* boarding education—boys whose parents live abroad, boys from rural districts which provide inadequate schools, boys who for one reason or another have difficulty in going to day schools. Other public schools may be asked to specialise in certain types of teaching or cater for boys with special gifts. Still others may be asked to become Sixth Form colleges, i.e., to educate boys between sixteen and eighteen and prepare them for university entrance. Some change in their ethos and their curriculum seems likely, and though the process of change may take many years, it looks as if a new chapter in their long history is opening.

But do not let me mislead the reader. This book is not about politics or high policy on education. It is not a justification of the public schools as they are or as they were in the past. It simply accepts them as an historical fact with all their faults and merits. It is about something which, in a sense, is more important. It is about a teacher. J. F. Roxburgh started teaching in the public schools when the questions that today are so hotly debated were scarcely ever asked. When he retired, they had at last become practical politics. The question he was concerned with was just as important in his time. How were the English public schools to be made less brutal and Philistine?

To my good fortune, this question made sense to my parents. Although they were not rich, they were well-to-do and it seemed natural for them in those days to send me to a public school. But they chose to send me to the new school of Stowe under Roxburgh, partly because my father had been unhappy at his Victorian public school and partly because my mother, who was an American from New York City, was not taken in by British snobbery and respect for the traditions of the upper classes. Stowe was a new school, and they liked Roxburgh because he seemed to like boys. He seemed to think of them as individuals, not as Empire builders. That is why I came to write this book.

NOEL ANNAN

The Headmaster

Chapter I

The Public Schools &
The Foundation of Stowe

Among the Victorian biographies which illuminate that age
stand the lives of the great public school headmasters. They are
exceedingly oppressive to read. Written by reverential colleagues
or devoted pupils they portray figures of overpowering rectitude,
piety, singleness of purpose and ruthlessness in the exercise of
power over their assistant masters and boys. But the headmasters
deserve this memorial because they created an institution which
has been of remarkable influence in the social history of this
country in the past hundred and fifty years.

That race has vanished and the schools over which they
reigned have changed with the passing of time. These changes
were bound to occur because the manners, knowledge and ideas
of our culture have shifted. But change is sometimes symbolised
by a personality who helps to effect it; and the headmasters who

become a footnote in history are those who by their character or their innovations somehow catch the spirit of their times and transmit it to the coming generation.

J. F. Roxburgh was such a headmaster. His life was passed in the public schools. As a boy he went to Charterhouse, as a young man he taught at Lancing and in his maturity he created a new school at Stowe when in the early nineteen-twenties the great house of the Dukes of Buckingham was put up for sale and bought by an educational trust. He was something more than a successful headmaster. For he sensed the inadequacy of the public schools of his boyhood and tried to develop new qualities in them — qualities which came to be specially prized in the period between the two wars. What were these qualities? What did he want to change in the old régime and achieve in his own? To answer these questions we must look at the public schools as they were when Roxburgh first knew them as a boy.

Roxburgh went to Charterhouse in 1901 in the middle of an era which is usually described as the golden age of the public schools. So in a sense it was. Between 1830 and 1870 close on fifty had been founded, and these together with the seven ancient foundations which had been reformed by the Public Schools Act of 1868 dominated secondary education. In educating Britain's élite they were well aware that it was a power in the world. It ruled the nation unchallenged and was admired, satirised and feared abroad. The élite was expanding, and as more and more people demanded the education the public schools supplied the schools became convinced that the form of intellectual and social training they gave could not be bettered. At the beginning of the nineteenth century the élite had consisted of the nobility, the gentry and the upper ranks of the older professions such as the Church and the Army. By the end of the century it also included men from new professions which had not previously been considered as such, for instance the civil and colonial servant, the don and (significantly) the public school master; and those who worked in a few of the new occupations created by the industrial revolution. When Englishmen asked, as they did in those days, whether someone was a gentleman, they more often than not asked what kind of an education he had received. A gentleman was one who had been to a public school or to the ancient universities. He need not have been to both, but unless he had been to one or the other he needed exceptional personal qualities to be treated as such. The professions, moreover, reinforced the prestige of the schools by requiring as a condition of entry the kind of education that the schools provided. Just before the Duke of Wellington died, he ordained that no one should receive a commission in the army unless he had received the education of a gentleman. Other professions followed his lead.[1] Nonconformist manufacturers hastened to send their sons to these Anglican foundations which would grant them the status that they themselves could never hope to achieve. By the eighteen-eighties a public school education had become the common denominator of most of the rulers of the country.

At the same time the public schools also reflected an unease which was beginning to steal over this class. For although the British upper classes appeared supremely self-confident they were in fact ridden with anxieties. There were the anxieties arising from the struggle for power over Africa and Asia, from the depression of the 'eighties and the challenge abroad to British exports, but nearer at home were the nagging doubts concerning social status and the justice of the existing social order. Upper-middle-class families had begun to practise birth control, partly for fear that the expense of bringing up a large family would depress their prosperity and lower their standing in society; and an era of bitter class warfare was beginning. The war extended not merely between the working classes and the middle classes but all through the middle and upper classes themselves. The extension of the élite had made many of its older members determined to differentiate themselves from the flood of newer entrants, and most of the newer entrants were eager to disguise their parvenu origins. Birth scored off worth and wealth off both. As the old Victorian definitions of a gentleman dissolved into the more varied Edwardian categories, the public schools got involved in the process. They had always considered themselves as schools for the sons of gentlemen. Tom Brown assumed without argument

[1] G. Kitson Clark, *The Making of Victorian England* (London and Cambridge, Mass., 1962), p. 266.

that this was what Rugby was for and he was untroubled by the problem of class. But the problem obsessed Vachell, and his novel *The Hill*, published in Edwardian times but describing Harrow in the 'eighties, is almost wholly concerned with distinguishing gentlemen from bounders and preserving Harrow for the former. The whole accent was on preservation, not change; the classical curriculum must be preserved, the social customs that the schools taught must be preserved, their traditions embalmed and a strict peck-order of precedence among the schools established. It was a golden age but the sun shone on an organism that was beginning to petrify.

In describing public school education historians have paid tribute to the schemes of the great reforming headmasters and to the Clarendon and Taunton Commissioners in the 'sixties; and one of them has shown how the early Victorian ideal of combining classical scholarship and Christian virtue changed in late Victorian times to the ideal of combining Godliness with Manliness.[1] Arnold's revolution changed the system of entry, established scholarly standards in classics for sixth-form work and transformed schoolmasters from ushers governing their charges by the birch, if at all, to the awe-inspiring figures in billowing gowns that stare at us from Victorian photographs. The first generation of reforming headmasters had to hew a system of government out of a thicket of customs and abuses. But they were often foiled in making necessary reforms by the traditionalism both of the governing bodies and of the boys. The second generation of headmasters was even more important than the first. They extended the machinery of government that the older generation had set up and were far more powerful and effective administrators. Whereas their predecessors had concentrated on the Sixth Forms and the senior boys, they recognised that their mission was to the whole school. They were autocratic and overweening. They had to be. Will-power of no ordinary degree was needed to tame the boys, to create and control their staff and to frustrate the opposition of their governing bodies most of which were antiquated. Perhaps that was why they were so often humourless. Ridding completed the work that Moberly had begun at Winchester; Warre at Eton consolidated the reforms of Hawtrey and

[1] David Newsome, *Godliness and Good Learning* (London, 1963).

4

Hornby; Butler and Kennedy at Shrewsbury were succeeded by
Moss; Cotton's foundations at Marlborough were built on by
Bradley and Bell. Similarly at Charterhouse, where reforms had
begun in the last years of its existence in London under Russell
and Saunders, a powerful successor was found. William Haig-
Brown reigned for thirty-four years, planned and supervised the
move of the school to Godalming, and raised the number of boys
from a hundred and twenty to five hundred and of masters from
eight to twenty-eight.

Yet great as the influence of these men was, the form of education which developed in the public schools was as much a product
of the *structure* of the schools as of the imperfectly realised ideals
of their headmasters. Two institutions in particular gave the public
schools their peculiar character. These were the prefectorial
system and the house system, both of which antedated the Victorian reforms and both of which were used to solve the problem
that had to be solved if the schools were to survive. That problem
was discipline.

In the eighteenth and early nineteenth centuries there had been
an astonishing series of riots by the boys, riots so severe that in
several cases the troops had to be called out.[1] Maddened by
neglect, half-starved, affronted by reforms which removed
cherished privileges or by abuses left untouched by distant
ushers, or by restrictions imposed by corrupt and indolent
governing bodies, the boys had revolted. They went down in
defeat but in defeat achieved their object of being treated as
human beings with rights. It was as if a treaty had been concluded
by two High Contracting Powers. In the details of their daily lives
the boys were allowed to govern themselves, and for many years
even the most autocratic headmasters, if they were wise, negotiated with the boys many of the changes that they wished to make,
especially when those changes necessitated the abolition of
beloved customs. The system of rewards and punishments —
caps, scarves, variations on school uniform, beating, lines, extra
drill; the rules concerning fagging; the allocation of places at
meals, in dormitories or in Chapel; a multitude of restrictions,
regulations, procedures and privileges: these were in great part

[1] Five at Winchester, three at Eton and at Rugby and two at Harrow. The
last rebellion was at Marlborough in 1851.

administered by the boys and were part of the franchise entrusted to prefects which the masters used in order to create firmer discipline.

It was this mixture of ritual and tradition that was regarded as the chief glory of the public schools. A boy had to learn how to get on with his fellows. Popularity was at a premium, eccentricity at a discount. For underneath the self-conscious moral code expounded in Chapel and by the masters there was another code of behaviour set up by the boys. In that subversive book *Stalky & Co.* Kipling praised the public schools, but he did not hold up to admiration the heavy priggish housemasters or the good form herd schoolboys, the swots or the games players, who were taken in by exhortations about 'the honour of the house'. What he praised was the underground code of the boys who, leading a life of debonair cribbing, smoking and drinking, learnt to harden their shell, to submit to being crammed if cramming enabled one to enter the army, to see facts as they were, never to expect fairness, not to betray their emotions or their comrades. There was always an interplay between the official *mores* of the school and the boys' own code of conduct, and a master who had character could achieve marvels by appealing to the boys' better instincts; but it was the way of life created by the boys themselves that admirers of the public schools especially praised. The prefectorial system was the bridge between the magisterial morality and the underground code practised by the boys.

Just as the masters maintained discipline by delegating authority upon prefects, so headmasters decentralised authority to their housemasters. Decentralisation was forced on them by the schools' increasing size. The establishment of separate houses broke up the problem of discipline and moral influence into units of manageable proportions. The influence of the house system on the development of the public schools can hardly be over-emphasised. The housemaster and the house loomed over every boy. A great headmaster could always make his influence felt in the school, but once the numbers in the school had grown he had to work directly on the staff rather than on the boys, most of whom had little to do with him until their last year. The housemaster on the other hand became the most important single master in the school for the boys in his house. He was the symbol

of moral authority and watched the development of the personalities of the forty or so boys in his charge. He governed them
through the house prefects or monitors and stood up for them
against the headmaster or their form masters. He took precedence
over the form master especially when forms ceased to be units and
were divided into sets and streams and sides. In many schools the
Sixth, though it might be taken for certain periods by the headmaster, lost its sense of pre-eminence. Indeed, the housemaster was
often in opposition to the bright intellectual teachers whom he regarded as encouraging his boys to indulge in dangerous thoughts
or unorthodox behaviour. His ideal boy was one who was trained
by meticulous routine duties and Spartan living conditions to
serve his little community and learn self-restraint, conformity and
modesty. He justified the complex rules that the boys made as
giving a sense of security to thirteen-year-olds; he justified prefectorial rule by arguing that without it masters would have been
forced to become snooping inquisitors and boys sneaking prigs or
rebels; he justified the time and energy spent on games, organised
almost entirely in houses, by declaring that they taught boys to
fuse competition with sportsmanship and individual achievement
with team spirit. He believed that a good house was one in which
routine was never broken and every leisure moment was taken up
with some form of socialised activity. This habit of finding an
ethical justification for all canonised activities spread to the
curriculum itself. It was not enough to argue that the grammatical
study of Latin and Greek trained the mind; they 'formed the one
bulwark against that purely utilitarian tendency to-day which
deprecates any study that has no practical value';[1] they were a
rebuke to German materialism; they were even said to produce
the inventiveness and resourcefulness that won the Battle of Jutland.[2] Indeed the writings of the classical authors were somehow transmuted into a secular expression of the Christian morality
that was preached in Chapel — a morality which took its tone
from the Old Testament. A misdemeanour was a sin; what better
remedy than to cane the child hard and often? Sin made the tribe

[1] *Public Schools from Within. A Collection of Essays Written Chiefly by Schoolmasters* (London, 1906), pp. 5–8.
[2] E. C. Mack, *Public Schools and Public Opinion* (New York, 1941), II,
p. 310.

unclean; what better propitiation of Jehovah than to exact mass punishment?[1]

There were nearly always to be found one or two housemasters, such as Oscar Browning at Eton or Trant Bramston at Winchester, who were humane and did much to bring out their boys and cultivate their minds: just as there were always one or two brilliant teachers on the staff whom not only the clever but some of the ordinary boys looked back to in after years as a formative influence in their life. But for the most part Victorian housemasters were not on intimate terms with any but the most senior boys and carried delegation of authority to remarkable lengths. A Marlborough housemaster once roared at his head of house who had come to report a fire: 'That part of the House is your department not mine.'[2] It was indeed part of the unwritten code that a housemaster should not interfere officiously in affairs which were traditionally within the jurisdiction of the boys. As a result the prefects and the bloods often beat or abused their juniors unchecked, sometimes in the name of discipline and the maintenance of good tone in the house, sometimes because they used their position to lead a gay or squalid life of schoolboy crime. The history of most houses was of oscillation between a 'good house' where a young housemaster exerted his influence and swept with a new broom and a 'bad house' where sex, drink, bullying and misery became rampant because an old housemaster who was under no compulsion to retire had lost his vitality.

The long tenure of housemasters was undoubtedly a reason why by the end of the nineteenth century headmasters, even if they were so inclined, found reform so difficult to effect — why indeed the crop of famous headmasters became so thin. By that time the housemasters had gained their own sphere of power. They settled sometimes through a housemasters' committee many domestic and disciplinary matters not only in their own houses but throughout the school. As oligarchies they were so well entrenched that they loomed over the rest of the staff and the boys. They were not, as now, required to retire from their housemasterships after a tenure of fifteen years. Nor did they retire as now from the staff

---

[1] cf. David Newsome, *A History of Wellington College 1859–1959* (London, 1959), p. 390.

[2] Rupert Wilkinson, *The Prefects* (Oxford, 1964), p. 30.

at the age of sixty or thereabouts. Headmasters might come and go but the housemasters and the senior staff flourished interminably. When in 1914 Preston went as headmaster at the age of forty to Malvern he was the youngest member of the staff and faced housemasters of thirty to thirty-five years' standing.[1] A headmaster is bound to leave the day-to-day management of the boys to his housemasters: and the power that he could therefore exercise was limited.

The price paid for the enhanced individuality of the houses was the loss of individuality among the boys. Community living destroyed their hobbies; games and conformity their intellectual freedom. It was a community, surpassed only in rigour by a monastery, working to an unvarying time-table with a corporate religion, corporate morality and corporate tradition; in which authority was minutely defined and everyone knew exactly where and how far he could step; and where the daily round began and ended in the house.[2] The house system was far more restrictive than appeared at first sight. It often happened that boys were discouraged from making friends in other houses and rarely spoke to anyone outside the house except in form. Furthermore custom usually decreed that within the house they did not mix with those senior or junior to them. As a result a boy who entered a house of forty to fifty strong would spend most of his life in the school in the company of his ten contemporaries. Almost every aspect of his life seemed to be controlled by the house: with whom was he to sit at meals, in common room or study; whom he fagged for; what group he belonged to or games he played. The systems of privilege and authority, each boy's order of precedence, and his means of achieving status and popularity, were determined mainly in the house. The most certain way to escape from the monastic cell of the house was to excel at games; you were then elevated to the peerage of the school bloods. Otherwise there was little to break the unvarying daily routine which kept a boy perpetually on the run, at any rate in his first two years, moving from one activity to the next so that he should not be led into temptation by the luxury of leisure. The devices that had been evolved to produce

---

[1] Ralph Blumenau, *A History of Malvern College 1865–1945* (London, 1965), pp. 81, 83–5, 118–20.

[2] John Wilson, *Public Schools and Private Practice* (London, 1962), p. 56.

order in the schools and to inculcate the public school spirit came to be treated as sacrosanct. What had been sensible modifications of existing institutions in mid-Victorian times became in the twentieth century constricting and stifling practices.

Of course the spirit of the public schools was not merely the product of their structure. The ideals of the Victorian head-masters counted for much. They were the ideals of high-minded clergymen of the Established Church whose mission was to educate the sons of the governing class and of those aspiring to enter it. 'I want you, Sir, to assure me that the boys who come to your school are the sons of gentlemen,' said a pompous prospective parent to Haig-Brown at Charterhouse. 'Well, they always leave gentlemen,' was the headmaster's enigmatic reply. The pressure of public opinion and custom in the school hammered the boys into shape. The Anglican ideology of the masters, and the no less important ideology of the boys, were inculcated with self-conscious thoroughness and all institutions of the school were tuned to sing their praise. The process of indoctrination and reorientation took place at every level; informally by senior and super-senior years over their juniors; more formally by the prefects; explicitly by housemasters and their assistants; and *coram populo* by the headmaster. Self-importance and conceit among the young were deadly sins; new bugs were kicked around and at Charterhouse were made in their first fortnight to learn the school language which was almost as formidable as that of Winchester; and a premium was put upon good form.

Yet the most striking characteristic of the public school ideology at the beginning of this century was the way in which the playing fields and team spirit had become exalted into an educational mystique. The schoolboys of the eighteen-forties, who went birds'-nesting or poaching or who took exercise by fighting as often as in playing cricket or primitive football, had been replaced by boys whose ambitions centred almost solely upon competition in games between the houses in their schools. Cotton was the first at Marlborough in the fifties to realise that games could be organised to eliminate the pastimes and the idleness that got boys into trouble; and great housemasters such as Bowen at Harrow glorified the fiercely competitive struggles at games between houses. The early Victorian Moberly at Winchester spoke of 'the idle boys, I mean the boys who play cricket'; but his mid-Victorian successor Ridding declared: 'Give me a boy who is a cricketer and I can make something of him.'[1] The hierarchy in the house from prefects and monitors to new boys was practically coterminous with the hierarchy of caps and colours awarded to the bloods. The school prefects were chosen from among the bloods and at many schools the Sixth Form's prestige was minimal. Roxburgh ended his career at Charterhouse as head of his house, a Trinity Exhibitioner and a member of the Sixth, but being indifferent at games he never became a school monitor. He was not, and never could be, a blood. Charterhouse was the school where the rules of Association football were codified and which treasured the memory of 1880 when an Old Carthusian side won the F.A. Cup. The bloods of the Eleven ruled the school and dictated school customs. Only in your second term could you wear a knitted tie, only in your second year coloured socks, only in your third year a turned down collar, and only bloods could blossom into light grey trousers and butterfly collars and walk arm-in-arm across sacred grass. The Sixth had no such privileges and did not dare to claim them until six years after Roxburgh had left when some of them took the precaution of becoming school boxing champions. The Aristophanic parody was more truthful than mocking:

> *Oh, we are the bloods of the place,*
> *We shine with superior grace*
> *At the goal or the wicket, at footer or cricket,*
> *And nothing our pride can efface.*
> *The worms of the Sixth we despise . . .*
> *We count them as dirt in our eyes.*

Intellectuals often speak as if schools and universities ought to be the beacons lighting society on its way to the future. They seldom are. Like other social institutions they usually reflect current public opinion and sometimes even lag behind it. The public schools reflected the fact that all classes in England at that time were obsessed by sport which became in the upper ranges of

---

[1] J. D'E. Firth, *Winchester College* (London, 1949), p. 174.

the middle class a passport to worldly success.[1] But what was especially deplorable about the cult of athleticism was the implication that intellectual endeavour was a selfish pursuit and that the highest activities were those that heightened team spirit in the school. Intellect, culture, the curriculum — especially such subjects as science which could be sneered at as utilitarian and fit only for lower middle-class technicians — were despised by the boys and were far from taking first place in the hearts of the masters.

There was much talk of modifying the curriculum but Latin remained the staple diet. Haig-Brown, for instance, was a man of wide learning. He spoke French and German, knew Italian, taught Hebrew to the Sixth Form and was a first-class mathematician: but Classics was to him the heart of education. At Charterhouse there were twice as many classical masters as mathematicians or modern linguists and at one time they were paid two-thirds more than their colleagues. English was a matter of repetition taught in the interstices of time between classical composition and translation; History was the arbitrary record of odd unrelated epochs; Geography spelt place names; French and German were entrusted to hapless foreigners who were ragged by the boys beyond endurance; and Science was taught at first by a master who transported his apparatus in a green bag. The end of the century brought some improvement and a museum of Archaeology and Natural History had been built in 1891. But the real difficulty lay in creating a tradition of work throughout the school. In Old Charterhouse there had been fierce antipathy to any boy who exerted himself, and although under the new régime at Godalming scholars were elected by examination instead of being nominated, they formed no nucleus. The institution of College at Eton and Winchester meant that at any rate in one part of the school a place existed where intellectual achievement was respected, but Charterhouse followed the usual practice of public schools and spread scholars among the houses. R. H. Eckersley, a contemporary of Roxburgh, wrote that in his time work was

[1] In the eighteen-thirties Gaisford, the Dean of Christ Church, justified the study of Greek by observing that it 'not only elevates above the vulgar herd, but leads not infrequently to positions of considerable emolument'. Eighty years later the same could have been said about the playing of games.

despised by nearly everyone except those who had submitted to the four-year classical grind for a scholarship at Oxford or Cambridge.[1] Nor is this surprising as the average boy had no public examination to tackle such as the General Certificate to-day. As a result while most boys learnt to write hexameters and pentameters without a Gradus, what they really knew by heart were the batting averages of the Surrey and Yorkshire elevens.[2]

Before 1914 the public schools were ill-disposed to change. Like a fleet which has undergone an arduous period of refitting and retraining at sea, they settled down after the mid-Victorian reforms to enjoy the delights of life in port and the plaudits of their countrymen. Each school now had its watchdog: an Old Boys' Association, pious, retrospective, nursing adolescent memories, suspicious of innovation. Why indeed should they change? What was wrong with their scholastic achievement when the brilliant coteries of scholars from Rugby, Eton and Winchester and from the Sixth Forms of other public schools continued to dazzle the examiners at Oxford and Cambridge? Did they really inhibit individuality when they continued to throw up some notable radicals? And did not the mass of their boys turn out to be men of physical courage, unflustered confidence and ease of

[1] *The Charterhouse We Knew*, ed. W. H. Holden (London, 1950), p. 48.

[2] A contemporary account of Charterhouse reinforces this impression. In 1903 the *Saturday Review* was publishing a series of articles on schools. The correspondent found the average Carthusian 'sociable and controlled' and agreed that the régime eliminated selfishness and strengthened 'moral fibre'. But he added that 'it is a pity that the type of strong, virile, good-humoured manhood for which Charterhouse is famous does not take up and absorb a little more tense intellectual activity'. He noted the existence of a good library, a brass band and an orchestra, a carpenter's shop and a Photographic Society. There was also a Fire Brigade in which the boys wore resplendent helmets. He commended the Saturday night entertainments and commendable they were: they owed their existence to the efforts of a single master, F. W. K. Girdlestone. But although a new music master, E. D. Rendall, had arrived in the same term as Roxburgh, the *Messiah* was performed only once when he was a boy and then only by the school choir. Twice the O.U.D.S. performed a Shakespeare play to raise funds for the school Mission; normally the entertainments were a military band, pierrots, a conjuror, glee-singers or a primitive cinema show. But what did this matter when the school won nine Ashburtons and produced incomparable football elevens? (*Saturday Review*, XCV, No. 2,470, 28 February 1903, pp. 255-7.)

manner, loyal to the State, a stable and incorruptible élite? In 1913 Alington, then headmaster of Shrewsbury and soon to return to Eton, maintained in his reply to sympathetic critics that the schools had made far more progress than was generally allowed.[1] There were, it is true, unsympathetic critics; but Shaw and Wells, whose denunciations contained many unwelcome truths, would have been satisfied with nothing less than razing the public schools to the ground and sowing their playing fields with salt, and as a result they were ignored. The test was at hand which to the minds of the masters and alumni was sent by Providence to prove the superlative quality of the schools. In August 1914 the response of the public schools was immediate. They visualised the war in terms of their own ideals. Here was the long-awaited call to self-sacrifice, duty and honour, here the leaders that had been hardened and tempered would show their worth. They provided the officers for Kitchener's new armies; they formed a Public Schools battalion; their O.T.C.'s were sanctified. A few years later they were mourning the flower of five generations of public school boys killed in France and Flanders.

They were to mourn their ideals as well. They had been so sure that in the sacred struggle between British virtue and German turpitude breed would tell. But as the dull brutal slaughter dragged on, it seemed to be caused by lack of that very leadership that the public schools claimed to provide. Doubts began to rise — and the most disturbing were expressed by a boy. Alec Waugh wrote his famous novel, *The Loom of Youth*, immediately on leaving Sherborne, in the intervals of military training. It enraged and injured authority; but it reads to-day less like an attack upon the public schools than an acceptance of their worth and a plea for moderate change. Waugh was disillusioned but not embittered: he wanted to destroy philistinism and the worship of games and to contrast, as Kipling had done, the reality of the boys' code of behaviour with the myth of the official ethos of the school. But whereas Kipling believed with justice that a public schoolboy's cunning and resourcefulness could pacify the North West Frontier, Waugh denied that it was adequate for fighting or living in twentieth-century industrial Europe.

The bitter mood of post-war disillusionment, which lasted

[1] C. A. Alington, *A Schoolmaster's Apology* (London, 1914).

through the whole deflationary period of the inter-war years, was to sweep over nearly every established institution, in particular those like the public schools which were associated with authority and government. In the nineteen-twenties the intelligent public began seriously to doubt whether the public school goals were adequate and right. Once the ends were called in question the means by which they were achieved — the worship of games and the value of beating — inevitably were challenged. The intelligentsia cursed the places that had despised their minds and frozen their hearts. *The Loom of Youth* was the first of a flood of public school novels and autobiographical fragments which poured from the presses during the inter-war years delivering attacks that were often wild, usually resentful but frequently telling. They blamed the schools for being insular, class-conscious and insufferably superior; for stifling the emotions, over-strengthening the will and neglecting the brain; for promoting homosexuality by their monasticism and then treating offenders as monsters who polluted the community with their sin; for permitting the bloods to beat boys for trivial or trumped-up offences; for sowing compulsion everywhere so that 'voluntary' activities such as the cadet corps or fielding practice were voluntary only in name, and for degrading a solemn religious rite such as Confirmation to an obligatory perfunctory ritual. The future of the public schools became a well-worn topic in the press. One sign of the revolt was the foundation of boarding schools which were explicitly inspired by other educational ideals. Rendcomb, a school of eighty boys of widely differing class, was opened in 1920: others such as Bembridge and Dartington Hall were experimental and some followed Bedales (founded as long ago as 1893) in being co-educational. Never again were the public schools to bask in unclouded adulation.

But they remained unruffled and obdurate. They were unimpressed by the new foundations which were of varying quality, some being undeniably cranky. Moreover, although the younger generation might be critical of the schools, the older, in particular those too old to have fought in the war but who had lost their kinsmen, were fanatical in their defence and sometimes spoke as if public schoolboys alone had fought and died. The peculiar quality of the sentimentalism with which they expressed their devotion to their old school can be savoured by a connoisseur of school songs and stories at the turn of the century; and the devotion was to be murderously satirised during the inter-war years. But the satire deflected attention from the most fundamental question: why was it that in Britain alone among European nations men were so attached to and obsessed by their schools? Certainly one reason was that from the age of eight boys were separated from their families. The public school became the substitute for family; the boys sought among their contemporaries affection which they associated with the school; and reciprocated by giving their hearts to the place. An affront to the school was similar to an insult to the family. Indeed the severity of the Victorian public school reflected the *mores* of the Victorian patriarchal family. Another reason was that the boys were made to feel that they were of use to the school and were in no way excluded from school life if they were unable to cope with academic work. In a French *lycée* there was only one criterion — scholastic ability: if one failed to get a good *note*, still worse if one failed an examination, the teachers had no word but condemnation. Indeed both the parents and children themselves accepted this inexorable code and would judge a school-fellow a failure if he could not compete on equal terms. In Germany this was not so, and boys judged each other more in terms of ordinary human qualities; but the teachers in the *Gymnasium* by and large were at one with their French colleagues. In England, however, boys who were apparently incapable of understanding Latin prose or sums were accepted without question by the masters as having equal rights and status with those who could learn — indeed they often were given precedence over their intellectually superior contemporaries.

That this was so was due to the advocacy of Thring of Uppingham as much as to any single man. Thring urged that the school must be moulded to suit the needs of the individual boy and that if he were not a scholar then the school curriculum should be adapted to help him. He ended his days with a sense of failure and the public schools had certainly not developed a curriculum or teaching methods appropriate to the non-scholarly boy. They preferred to sanction a system whereby the non-scholar, so long as he avoided gross and persistent idleness and from time to time got his remove, could coast through the school without undue exertion. Nevertheless the fact that the average boy was accepted and scholastic ability was not obligatory for success at school produced unparalleled loyalty to the schools; and this in turn gave the schools the self-esteem and confidence which impeded any movement for reform.

During the inter-war years change slowly came. The curriculum began to alter and boys were able to exercise their minds on something other than classical prose and translations. But the general culture propagated by the schools remained meagre. Political and social questions were handled gingerly. Since the eighteen-eighties French contemporary culture in all the arts had influenced Britain, but French art was labelled dangerous or more usually ignored. The Russian novel — the novel as a form of art — was neglected. The revolution in painting was scarcely spoken of. The extreme of modernity was the work of Shaw, Wells and Chesterton, offered with a caution that they were brilliant but unsound. So much of the literature or science that is done at school acquires new meaning if it is taught in the context of what is emerging in the larger world outside the school, but for the most part the schools were content to let literature expire with Victoria and treat science as a subject devoid of cultural content. Generalisation on this topic is always difficult, partly because the clever boys created for themselves a contemporary cultural background, sometimes highly original, of their own devising; and partly because a great deal depended on the initiative of a handful of masters. So much did circumstances dictate different judgments that three contemporaries in the same school could give widely differing accounts of the education they received. A Wykehamist in Cyril Robinson's house could recall in post-war years a vigorous and gifted Archaeological Society in the school and in the house a sizeable orchestra, an ephemeral magazine, expeditions, and contacts with the W.E.A. Another in a different house described the school at the same time as insular, philistine, repressive and unaware of any social problems in the outside world. A third declared that French was taught by classics masters proudly using an English accent, that English was not taught at all, science despised and the study of the two dead classical languages dominated the teaching and dehydrated the minds of the able boys who uncritically accepted the school's version of the morality of the ancient world. It is no wonder that there existed between the passionate defenders and deadly critics of the schools a sizeable body of prospective parents, unwilling to break with the system when so many of its qualities were admirable but disturbed by the unwillingness of the schools to reform and nursing sometimes none too happy memories of their own schooldays. It was to those parents that Roxburgh was to appeal.

He was to appeal to them because he shared both their faith and their doubts. When Robert Graves, who entered Charterhouse at about the time Roxburgh left, pilloried the school, Roxburgh was displeased by his indictment because it lacked a quality to which he attached special importance: it lacked a sense of proportion and hence of truthfulness. 'He describes nothing but the unpleasant boys and masters,' Roxburgh wrote, 'omitting all the decent people who lived decent lives around him but whom he does not appear to have noticed at all.' Despite his belief that much needed to be changed he was not wholly ironical when he assured the Parents' Association that he had 'taken the greatest possible pleasure in making toast for the Captain of the school Cricket Eleven'; at one time he nursed the hope of returning to Charterhouse as headmaster and it is even possible that he would have taken it when Fletcher[1] retired in 1935 and was succeeded by Robert Birley.[2]

But he also carried with him a perfectly clear picture of the changes he would make if he ever returned to Charterhouse. He wanted a change of heart among the boys towards their work and towards each other. 'Looking back on my own schooldays,' he once said, 'I realise that what I remember about most boys is whether they were kind or not.' When in 1931 he visited Charterhouse to preach he was disappointed with what he saw and told Mrs Radice,[3] 'I do not think that anything of the slightest importance has changed at Charterhouse since I left there in 1907 though there have been very great changes in the things that do

[1] Sir Frank Fletcher, Master of Marlborough College 1903, Headmaster of Charterhouse 1911–35.

[2] Robert Birley, Headmaster of Charterhouse 1935–47, Headmaster of Eton 1949–63.

[3] Sheila Radice, Assistant Editor of *The Times Educational Supplement* 1918–1940.

not matter a scrap.' At Charterhouse there was a feeling that Roxburgh did not appreciate how much Frank Fletcher had modified
in the post-war years school rules and the relationship between
masters and boys. But Fletcher clearly did not hurry. One of his
great admirers on the staff declared: 'He did nothing until it had
to be done; it simmered long and peacefully in his mind, and
when the time came he was ready.' As for the boys: 'The great
merit of the able Carthusian was that he was so seldom bookish
or sophisticated.'[1] Roxburgh would not have deemed that a
merit. The changes that Roxburgh wanted to see in the public
schools did not begin to occur until the nineteen-forties when
the ideas which he was putting into effect at Stowe came to be
widely known. These ideas had developed in his mind by reflecting on his schooldays at Charterhouse, and on his sense of libera-
tion at Cambridge, and from his experience as a master at Lancing.
They were tempered by his Scots ancestry and the family circle in
which he grew up. These are the influences which we must now
examine.

[1] A. L. Irvine, *Sixty Years at School* (London, 1959), pp. 99, 107.

Chapter II

Growing up

Everyone who knew Roxburgh thought of him as J.F., and it comes as a mild surprise to realise that his own family called him by his Christian name. The initials stood for John Fergusson and it was as Fergusson or Fergie that he was known at home.

The name came from far back in his Scottish ancestry. Roxburgh's mother was the great-granddaughter of an Agnes Fergusson who in 1762 had married Elias Cathcart when he was sixty and she twenty-nine. His paternal grandfather, the Reverend John Roxburgh, a man framed in granite and lightning, guided Free St John's in Glasgow: for he had gone out among the Wee Frees in the Disruption of the Scottish Kirk in 1843. But though the manse was his heritage and both his father and mother were born and bred Scots, Roxburgh himself was brought up in

England. His father had not followed in the minister's footsteps. A trader in Liverpool, Alexander Balfour, had married Archibald Roxburgh's sister and a year later his brother-in-law gave him an opening: it was to join the import-export business and go out to Valparaiso where the firm had a subsidiary. After nearly twenty years there, Archibald Roxburgh considered himself rich enough to support a wife, and in July 1884 he married a girl twenty years younger than himself, Janet, or as he called her Jenty, the second daughter of John Fergusson Cathcart. Their first son, Archie, was born in Chile, but two years later they visited Britain and in the Cathcart's house in Edinburgh, 19 Belgrave Crescent, John Fergusson was born on 5 May 1888.

A year or so later the family finally settled in England. Archibald Roxburgh, who had been made a director of a recently founded concern, the Pacific Loan and Investment Company, which had been financing the development of the west coast of America, took a house in Liverpool. In 1896 they moved to 15 Kirby Park (now called Devonshire Road), West Kirby, Cheshire, where a third son, Robert, was born to them. At this time the family fortunes shifted. Some disagreement about policy led Archibald Roxburgh to sever connections with his former colleagues and for some time the family had to draw in their horns financially until new directorships restored their prosperity.

As the boys grew up they were first taught by a Miss Mabel Eley of Chiswick. But once his elder brother had gone to school, Fergie became too much for his poor governess and at nine years old he was sent as a boarder to a prep school five miles farther up the Dee Valley. The school was Moorland House and the founder and first headmaster, L. J. Dobie, ran it for forty-five years. It was a good school and Roxburgh and his headmaster liked each other. It was to Roxburgh that he turned in May 1930 at some crisis in the school's fortune and his pupil wrote his obituary when he died in 1937. He learned there to practise two of the delights of his life — photography and manipulation of the English language. 'Fergie took two photos of the church yesterday,' wrote his brother on one occasion; and on another, 'He is going in for a Sunlight Soap competition in which you have to write a Humorous Description of a Washing Day without

Sunlight Soap.' These sunlit days lasted until the summer of 1901 when he followed his elder brother to Charterhouse.

Roxburgh had the misfortune to enter the school four years after Haig-Brown retired. Above the chimneypiece of the new headmaster, G. H. Rendall, hung a text of Marcus Aurelius, 'Live as on a mountain.' He did so. It is not surprising that work and discipline declined. Rendall had, it must be admitted, an impossibly heavy job. Not only was he housemaster of a large house as well as being headmaster, but he was his own school bursar, a task for which he had few qualifications. Nor was Roxburgh's housemaster, W. Moss, much different. Although he was of the inner group of important assistant masters, he turned a blind eye to conduct in his house that even he should have found disturbing. Roxburgh's readiness to join in whatever was going on, whether or not it was his line, saved him from total misery. Soon after arrival he won a house sweepstake on the Cesarewitch by drawing Black Sand. A year or so later gaiety outran discretion. Electric light had recently been installed in some of the class-rooms, and when Roxburgh passed one of them he could not resist the temptation of performing the miracle that was impossible to perform with gas lighting: he ran his hand over the switches and plunged the class-room into darkness. The din became ear-splitting; the master's lamentations and expostulations fell upon heedless ears; and the upshot was that the culprit was beaten by the headmaster.

But it was hard for anyone to be happy at Charterhouse if he was inept at games. On arrival he had been nicknamed the Spider because he was all legs and arms on the football field. Nor was he outstanding at work. He was not a scholar and took Upper Four A (below which there were three levels) where he worked under a master called Bode who was much given to what he called 'righteous anger' when he would hand out 'swingeing blows'. After one term, however, Roxburgh got his remove into the form in which scholars were placed on entry. Moss's prim reports showed that he realised that the boy had ability and later in the Upper Fifth he benefited in particular from Radcliffe's teaching. At the age of sixteen and a half he was made a junior house

monitor. It is one thing to win your housemaster's approval; it is
another to carry your contemporaries with you, particularly when
they do not see in you anything particularly to admire. A house
monitor was responsible among other things for supervising
'banco', the period of evening preparation in 'Longroom', when
total silence was supposed to reign. Roxburgh was mercilessly
ragged. He was so unable to gain control that his brother, Archie,
had to come to the rescue and on occasions took his 'banco' for
him.[1] He learnt the hard way. The next term, when as head monitor
he walked into Longroom and shouted 'Sit down', the row went
on as in time past. Suddenly Longroom was astonished to see the
ringleader singled out and beaten on the spot. From that time he
never had any trouble and used subtler means of influencing
others. When years later in November 1939 Birley circulated to
old members of this house his intention of closing it down,
Roxburgh told him that he felt no particular loyalty to it. 'It was
a rotten house in my time.' But according to his friend W. H. C.
Romanis[2] Roxburgh transformed it. The readiness with which his
contemporaries sent their sons to be educated by him at Stowe is
evidence of the impression he made on them. Meanwhile school
prizes began to come his way. Three years running he won the
prize for English Literature, twice he was runner up for the prize
in Classical Literature, winning it in his last year, and prizes for
Divinity and Natural History (one of his hobbies) also fell to him.
Spirited encounters took place between him and Romanis in the
Debating Society on such topics as the Channel Tunnel; and in his
last year he inevitably edited the *Carthusian*. The final distinction
came when he won an Exhibition for Classics at Trinity, Cambridge.

Carthusians might be dedicated to games but there were always
some able and clever ones who swam against the tide of opinion
and became good classical scholars. In 1904–5 the list of those who

[1] Archie Roxburgh was to marry the sister of A. F. Lambert, a fellow new-
boy of his brother. Lambert, who witnessed the total eclipse of the master,
when Roxburgh extinguished the electric lights, declared that the action was
'quite out of character'.

[2] Romanis was head boy of Charterhouse the term after Roxburgh left and
his contemporary at Trinity. After winning a double first at Cambridge and
practising as a surgeon, he retired in his sixties, read law and was called to the
Bar.

got awards to Oxford and Cambridge was exceptionally long. There were in fact two excellent sixth-form teachers at Charterhouse. A. H. Tod, who taught the Under Sixth, became a legendary figure: when at a much later date his house caught fire he was heard to remark among the debris: 'Me house is on fire and I can't get a light for me cigarette.' In form he was a stickler for accuracy and a man of volcanic temper: the room resounded to the bellow of his admonitions and imprecations. 'When I remember,' Roxburgh wrote years later to a fellow Carthusian before he was to give a lunch party for Tod at Stowe, 'the terror in which I lived while I was in Tod's form, the idea of being his host even for a few hours seems highly amusing.' The headmaster who taught in the form above was a contrast. 'Not quite crisp, I think,' was the limit of his courteous criticism.

The other remarkable teacher, to whom Roxburgh owed far more, was T. E. Page. Page is known to generations of English schoolboys as the editor of the small light blue elementary school edition of the books of the *Aeneid* and the odes of Horace, but his reputation as a scholar rested on his full annotated texts used in sixth forms and on his general editorship of the great Loeb translation of the classics. In those days there were a number of public school masters who were scholars in their own right, men such as H. G. Dakyns at Clifton, the friend of Henry Sidgwick and John Addington Symonds. Such men became schoolmasters either because they had wished to marry and were therefore excluded from the celibate fellowships of Oxford and Cambridge, or because — and it is an insight into the remoteness of many masters from boys — they expected to spend most of their time out of school, when not correcting exercise books, in pressing on with their own research hoping that eventually — as happened in the case of G. G. Coulton — publication would qualify them for appointment to a university post. Masters of this kind were the nearest thing in England to *professeurs aggrégés* in a French *lycée*. Page himself had been a Fellow of St John's before going to Charterhouse and he ended his life a Companion of Honour, holding a unique position among schoolmasters. Tall and long-haired he always wore curious enveloping trousers made of shaggy white wool woven on the island of St Kilda: the story was that finding them comfortable he had bought a roll of the stuff and

from time to time had another pair hewn out of it. His house was
the most undisciplined in the school, but he was unrivalled in the
art of translation; the richness of his speech sprang from his
perpetual search for more exact words to express the subtleties
of Horace or Vergil. Tod intimidated, Page inspired: he showed,
so it was said, just enough of his own enjoyment to make his
pupils feel that they had discovered the point of the passage themselves. He would encourage the inept: 'Well, it scans, boy, it
really does, please.' He would pardon the thick-headed and quote
Schiller: 'Against stupidity the gods themselves strive in vain.'
The intelligent were fortunate. 'I was in Page's form,' wrote
Roxburgh, 'and he did more for my real education than is often
done nowadays for that of any boy.' Page gave his mind a cutting-
edge so that precision was added to natural mental energy; and he
never forgot to acknowledge his debt to him in later life.

Just as all his school attainments, including the dubious rank of
Second Lieutenant in the Rifle Corps, did not entitle him to
become a school monitor, so his literary accomplishments did
not bring him scholastic supremacy. He never won the Talbot,
the top classical prize, and even after his Trinity Exhibition he
was only for one term in the highest division of the Sixth. Page
who termed him 'a capable fellow' deplored his 'fatal fluency',
and the truth was that excellence in classics was judged by one
single criterion: the ability to produce faultless translations and
to compose elegant Latin hexameters and Greek iambics. Nor
did this change when he went up to Cambridge. Here again he
was fortunate in the fact that Trinity possessed by far the most
able classical staff in the university. Cornford was lecturing on the
Republic, the unorthodox Verrall on Greek literature, and the dry
and precise Harrison was there to correct composition and translation; outside Trinity he heard the lectures of two King's dons,
Waldstein on Greek sculpture and Sheppard on Aeschylus and
Euripides. But of the fifteen papers in Part I of the Classical Tripos
(which Roxburgh sat for in 1910 and which in those days qualified
those who passed for the B.A. degree)[1] nine were purely linguistic
and concerned with translating or composing Latin and Greek
poetry and prose; one was devoted entirely to the analysis of
syntax and grammatical forms; and of the four papers on

[1] He proceeded to his M.A. degree in 1914.

history, philosophy, sculpture and architecture two contained passages for translation as well as comment. A premium was therefore put upon exact knowledge of the languages and the texts; there was correspondingly less scope for someone with Roxburgh's breadth of interests and power of literary appreciation. He got a First but was placed in the third division of that class.

Nevertheless it was at Trinity that he found himself. There he experienced the blessed relief from school restrictions and notions of good form. He no longer had to apologise for his pursuits or suppress his idiosyncrasies. Though he said at the time that he would not have been surprised if he had got a Second, and a year later lamented that he had not worked harder and got a I.2, he would have lost far more than he would have gained had he done so. Even the clever and intelligent miss much of what is valuable to an undergraduate if they concentrate exclusively on the tripos syllabus; it is not only the old who need time to contemplate and ruminate. Roxburgh still played games as a social exercise, gracefully adorning a tennis court and turning out at soccer for the Scythians, a club which prided itself on never playing a match against any other club. He began to take architectural photographs in earnest and build up the collection that awoke in so many pupils a delight in classical and gothic buildings.[1] It was at this time too that he first wrote articles for the journals and scored a triumph when the editor of The Spectator, St Loe Strachey, having published one, asked if he could visit him at Trinity.[2] The invitation was sent with alacrity, and Strachey, who had expected to meet one of the young Fellows, was a little surprised to find himself dining in Hall at the undergraduates' table. Roxburgh enjoyed expressing his ideas but still more the pleasure of finding the exact words and phrases in which to express them. He particularly relished making verse translations, working up his

[1] When in 1935 he sent to the new incumbent of Hillesden in Buckinghamshire a set of his photographs of the fine perpendicular church there, this gentleman lent them to the Dean of Windsor who in turn showed them to Queen Mary. She was so taken with them that she made them part of her own collection.

[2] 'A Highland Dawning', The Spectator, CVIII, No. 4252 (25 December 1909), pp. 1094-5.

versions with the most exacting care. The following passage, which his friend D. J. Jardine included in the book he was to write about Cyprus, comes from a chorus in the *Bacchae*.

> *Love hath an island,*
> *and I would be there;*
> *Love hath an island,*
> *and nurtureth there*
> *for men the Delights,*
> *the beguilers of care,*
> *Cyprus, Love's island;*
> *and I would be there.*
> *At Paphos she dwelleth,*
> *and wealth cometh there.*
> *Afloat with the kisses*
> *that Ocean doth bear*
> *from the hundred streams*
> *like a shower unfurled*
> *of the Rainless River*
> *born out of the world;*
> *there are the hill-sides*
> *on Earth most fair,*
> *Pierian hill-sides*
> *and melody there,*
> *the voice of the Nine,*
> *is borne on the air*
> *over the hill-sides,*
> *and I would be there —*
> *Olympian hill-sides,*
> *for Heaven is there*
> *with spirits divine*
> *and shining of fire;*
> *and there are the Graces,*
> *and there is Desire.*

The echoes of Shelley and Lionel Johnson faithfully reflect his poetic taste.

As much as anything else he gave his time to discussion. He was an inveterate debater. There was in Trinity at that time a typically ephemeral undergraduate society called the Dabblers which was founded in 1900 with only five members. In June 1909, when it held a dinner, there were twenty-six. Adrian[1] remembered his speeches as 'very good, cheerful and amusing, never pompous and always clear and persuasive'. His old opponent at Charterhouse, W. H. C. Romanis, was another admirer — though his clashes at Trinity with Roxburgh were in the more famous Trinity debating society, the Magpie and Stump, which Roxburgh did not join until 1909.

He made his debut at the Union in October 1908, attacking Hugh Dalton for proposing the nationalisation of land, and a year later attacked Grey's foreign policy. He spoke on the paper in defence of the Liberal government when the House of Lords had thrown out the Budget and was described in the *Granta* (which had at first found his style of speaking ponderous) as 'vastly amusing'. Certainly he enjoyed himself: 'The moderate man,' he was reported as saying, 'wraps himself up in great thick layers of flattering unction.'[2] 'I remember,' he wrote years later, 'proposing Home Rule in the year of grace 1909 or 1910 [it was May 1910] and having a perfectly gorgeous evening.' On that occasion he discovered, in the manner of Union orators, bogies in the cupboards of his political opponents which he proceeded to 'dissect and analyse with logic and wit, and reported that they were harmless'.[2] He declared for example that one must object to the Conservative view of an Irishman as a 'cross between a criminal and a lunatic with violet eyes and a desire to kill landlords'. The greatest orator of that generation of undergraduates, Norman Birkett, the future brilliant advocate and Law Lord, declared that Roxburgh 'was a great favourite at the Union ... urbane, overflowing with knowledge, possessing the most exquisite sense of humour, he delighted the House whenever he spoke.'[3] In those days the two parties in the Union were pretty evenly balanced and understandably just as political feeling in the country ran high so the Union overflowed with excitement. Roxburgh was a strong Liberal, suspicious of the Russian alliance

---

[1] Lord Adrian, O.M., Master of Trinity 1951–65.

[2] The *Granta*, XXIII (1909–10), p. 348.

[3] Percy Cradock, *Recollections of the Cambridge Union 1815–1919* (Cambridge, 1953), p. 101.

('Why ask the Czar to breakfast?') and in favour of Free Trade
and the full Asquith programme. He considered that the Conservatives gave way too readily to the brewers whose influence he
hated. He believed in an aristocracy of taste and talent to lead the
country, but the Fabian variant of leadership was too technocratic
and deviant for him. It is difficult to recapture the mixture of
idealism, self-confidence, ardour and adventure that inspired the
young Liberals of that time. In the nineteen-thirties when the
Liberal party lay in ruins, he reluctantly voted Conservative,
putting it down to 'increasing years and increasing indolence'.
The price one pays for the exhilaration of growing up at a time
of sharp political tension is that later in life no issue ever seems
so vital as those of one's youth. The price is even greater when
one finds one's youthful ideals regarded as irrelevant by the next
generation. Like many other Liberals, such as John Simon, he
moved in later years well to the right.

He was not merely a debater, he was a talker who enjoyed company. Trinity was a sociable college with a multitude of overlapping
sets into which many of the most interesting men of other
colleges drift. The university was then still small enough for
a man of Roxburgh's charm and versatility to know most of
those who found their way to Trinity. One of them, J. C. C.
Davidson[1] of Pembroke, remembered how he 'always had
time to welcome visitors, learning to know and understand
people'. Some of his contemporaries whom he knew well became dons: Adrian, Dennis Robertson[2] who took the Tripos
with him, Jim Butler[3] who was President of the Union, and Frank
Salter[4] another fervent Liberal. With these he kept his friendship
green to the advantage of his future pupils whom he sent in an
ever-increasing stream to Trinity. He did not, however, confine
his circle to scholars, nor did he gravitate to the group of intellectuals and aesthetes who revolved round Rupert Brooke,
discovering Donne and Webster and denouncing Tennyson

[1] Lord Davidson, P.P.S. to Bonar Law and Stanley Baldwin, Chancellor of
the Duchy of Lancaster 1936–7.

[2] Sir Dennis Robertson, Professor of Political Economy, Cambridge
1944.

[3] Sir James Butler, Regius Professor of History, Cambridge 1947.

[4] F. R. Salter, Fellow of Magdalene College, Cambridge 1910.

and Victorianism. As a Union man he found the company of those who knew more about the world than he did particularly agreeable. Cambridge taught him that it was possible to have a society in which the very clever and the very stupid ought to be able to live side by side, in which aesthetes need not fear philistines, and hearties at play became civilised without knowing it.

All this was part of that memorable age of undergraduates who lived in Belloc's phrase for 'laughter and the love of friends'. Cambridge undergraduate existence — at any rate after the nineteen-twenties — was never again so carefree. A man could then always find a niche for himself in the activities of the place. The clever and ambitious could work for the hall-mark of a First but no sort of stigma attached to the average, the lazy or the stupid: their passport to the world could be stamped with a Blue or by making their mark in the Union or in some university club. Those who wished worked hard, others just scraped an Honours degree, many still read for Pass degrees doing the bare minimum as they rode to hounds, played games and made friends. It has been unkindly said that the ancient universities were finishing schools for the governing class. They educated a small élite which dominated the political and professional life of the country, consisting of the sons of the upper and upper-middle classes plus those who had fought their way up the ladder of the State school system and whose parents could scrape together enough money to supplement the scholarships that they won. Some expected to sit in Parliament or in City board rooms. Most expected to enter the professions — to become diplomats, priests, lawyers and doctors, to pass into the Civil Service or govern the colonies, to emerge as dons or schoolmasters. That the majority of this small élite would come from the public schools was at this time accepted as self-evident. This was the pattern of education in which Roxburgh was bred.

One further fact should be recorded. Cambridge rechristened him. The most perceptive sketch of him as an undergraduate was written by Ronald Roxburgh[1] and it is interesting because it contains the first allusion to his manner that made him famous among schoolmasters.

[1] Sir Ronald Roxburgh, Judge of the High Court of Justice 1946–60.

J.F. was among the first to call on me when I went up to Trinity in
the autumn of 1908. Even now I can picture him, framed in a New
Court doorway — his debonair appearance, his gracious smile, and a
touch of the grand manner. He had come so promptly, so he at once
explained to me, out of curiosity to meet another Roxburgh. But we
soon became, and ever remained, staunch friends; and it is small wonder
that from then onwards we were almost everywhere known as 'J.F.'
and 'R.F.', and I was assumed to be his younger brother. Only those
who visited us in our homes knew that in his case the 'F' stood for
Fergusson and in mine for Francis. He was most particular about the
spelling of his second name, and indignant if accused (as he often was)
of pronouncing it with a slightly Scottish accent. He used to argue that
an educated Scot had none. But although little of it had survived
Charterhouse, it would reveal itself attractively in moments of emphasis or emotion to the delight and amusement of his friends. So it did
in the words 'pure Turkish', the tobacco which he used to champion
along with his favourite Lapsang Soochong tea.

The initials stuck. Had he come up ten years earlier his friends
in Victorian fashion would have called him by his surname, had
he come up ten years later by his Christian name. Quite often at
this time public school men began to call each other by nicknames
in order to circumvent formality and found that the nickname
lasted for life, especially when the bearer worked in an institution
such as a ministry or a school. What to-day sounds stilted to many
was then a testimony of affection.

Trinity is the greatest of all Cambridge colleges, the richest, the
largest, the most renowned for its contribution to learning, in
particular to science, combining the power and grandeur of Christ
Church with the scholarly distinction of Balliol. It was always to
hold a lively place in Roxburgh's affections and whenever he
could he steered his pupils to Trinity believing that a university
education gave everyone an extra dimension. It was there that he
acquired his manner and sophistication. He saw Trinity as the
gateway to the glittering world which he enjoyed contemplating
though he was never to enter it. He appreciated it all the more for
at one time he feared he was to be halted at the gateway. During
the end of his time at Charterhouse his father died. Overwork,
campaigning in the Liberal interest during the General Election
of the autumn of 1905 when he was already suffering from diabetes,

weakened him; and when in January 1906 he caught influenza, pneumonia followed and killed him. Broad-shouldered, broad-browed, with fine eyes and a short square beard, he had meant much to his sons. 'Except in the actual school subjects which I was taught by my masters,' J.F. wrote, 'I learned more in boyhood from the conversation of my father and of his brother than from any other source.' Twenty years later, when Roxburgh was to write to one of his Stowe boys whose father likewise had died during his schooldays, he recalled: 'At first one can't realise what has happened, and then it comes to one bit by bit, sometimes in a rush and often at night.'

The blow was financial as well as personal. At first his mother returned to the family house in Edinburgh where her unmarried sister Joanna looked after her widowed father, but she was still only in her early forties and too independent to settle there. For the next four or five years she lived sometimes in lodgings and sometimes in a small furnished house in Heswall. When her husband died Archie was still at Cambridge, J.F. had nearly two more years to go at Charterhouse and Robert's education was all to come; and J.F. had to apply for a subsizarship at Trinity to add to the emoluments of his Exhibition. But the family still went on summer holidays in the Highlands and in 1908 to the Rhône Valley; there never seems to have been any suggestion that the boys would have to forgo their education or chosen careers.

But J.F. remembered it differently. Later in life he was to tell with a sense of offended propriety of the days when his family had been reduced to a 'semi-detached house in Lancashire' adding that his mother 'endured the whole thing with astonishing fortitude'. He had been nicked on a sensitive nerve. He had learnt at Charterhouse to live as an equal with boys who did not live in semi-detached houses and the thought that he might have to forgo a way of life which up till then he had always expected to follow was unendurable. At Trinity his emoluments totalled £115 a year and his allowance from home must have been modest. He was noticeably poorer than those he mixed with, and this at a time when his taste for the lavish and the spacious was developing, and he began to delight in being fastidious and selective. These qualities wither in a lodging-house.

Janet Roxburgh, however, was a capable manager and she was helped by her brother-in-law, Patrick Campbell, a lawyer who had married her elder sister Mary. It was with the Campbell children that the Roxburgh boys often passed their summer holidays at Dulnain Bridge, Invernesshire. The Campbells were devoted to shooting and fishing, the Roxburghs to hobbies and nature study, but both were united by a common interest in photography and Scottish Liberalism. When late in 1910 Janet Roxburgh's father died, her financial situation eased. Although on two occasions she came south and rented an eighteenth-century house on Windmill Hill, Hampstead, the house in Belgrave Crescent became the family's permanent base. There Janet and her sister Joanna were to live for the rest of their days. In later years Janet became an invalid. A bad heart attack in 1928 weakened her health and in the following year she spent a good deal of time in Bournemouth. ('No one could *hope* to go to Bournemouth,' wrote Roxburgh in a letter to one of his Campbell cousins.) During the last nine years of her life she was at times bed-ridden and once or twice in a nursing-home, not dangerously ill but helpless from immobility. In the summer of 1940 she suddenly resolved to visit Bournemouth and her son had to persuade her that as the Germans were planning to invade the south coast of England and air-raids were common the air at Bournemouth would not be as relaxing as in former years. She was nearly eighty when she died in January 1941.

Her sister Joanna had always been an influence in the lives of her nephews. To J.F. she was particularly devoted and, as is sometimes the way when a mother has to bear the full responsibility for growing sons, the sons often found in their Aunt Anna an easier confidante. She who had so much loved and been loved so dearly by her nephews survived all three of them and lived to over ninety, rather blind but still radiating brightness. It was now her great-nephews, Archie's children, who spent their holidays at Dulnain Bridge, and one of them nearly seventy years her junior remembered her as 'the noblest woman I ever met — Victorian through and through; upright and impeccably honest in her ways: tolerant and kindly to everyone, particularly children; and never known to say an unkind word about anyone'.

This, then, was the family circle in which Roxburgh grew up.

It was typical of enlightened Scots middle-class families at the turn of the century. There was much affection and kindness, but also toughness of character and resolution in adversity. They were expansive in their enjoyment of prosperity and of the material comforts that prosperity brought, and more culti-vated in their tastes and respectful of education and learning than their English counterparts. The conversation while the boys' father was alive was of political principles, rather than political gossip about personalities and events in the House, and they learnt to discuss the issues of the day. Such families attributed their rise to their standards of strict honesty, shrewdness, hard work, meticulous care and singleness of purpose while being able to conform to the customs of whatever community they might find themselves in. They learnt to conceal their talents so as not to offend the English. But the truth was that the sons of yet another Scots family were becoming anglicised.

Thus the mould in which Roxburgh's character was cast was composed of three elements. Self-disciplined Scots devotion to principle and to work which he kept below the surface; English upper-class manners which he exaggerated to decorate the surface; and classical learning which taught him to place clarity and precision above all intellectual virtues. The mould was now to receive a blow which showed both its qualities and limitations.

J.F.'s intention of becoming a schoolmaster was well known to his Cambridge friends. Characteristically, however, he found an unconventional way of making himself a better schoolmaster than he would have been had he accepted a post immediately after taking his degree. He decided to spend a year in Paris studying classical literature at the Sorbonne for the degree of *Licence-ès-Lettres*. The standard required was similar to that of an undis-tinguished B.A. degree (just as *agrégation* is a somewhat higher standard than a First Class B.A. degree in England). The *Licence* would take a plodder two or more years while a brilliant *normalien* might take it even before he became a university student as a low hurdle on the way to *agrégation*. The requirements in classics would have been taken by J.F. in his stride. But the candidate for the

Licence was always required to show his paces in French Language
and Literature and it was for this training that J.F. entered for the
exam.[1] He was exceptionally highly placed and in fact was runner-
up for the French Essay. Misled by his florid handwriting the
principal examiner publicly congratulated 'cette Mademoiselle
Rox-bur' on her remarkable achievement. He shared Matthew
Arnold's view of the French. Although he deplored the morals of
his fellow-students and said that English undergraduates would
be superior to them if they could ever be induced to work, he
admired France as an educated nation. By comparison England
was still the land of the philistines. He learnt to appreciate French
lucidity and sense of form, and said that it was at the Sorbonne
that he had been taught that every essay must have a skeleton but
that the bones must never show. He retained lively memories of
many of his teachers there. One of them once lent him money
when he was broke; another, he recalled, with whom he studied
Greek, knew far less of the language than he did; a third was
still corresponding with him as late as 1937 when he sent 'à son
Dear Old Friend un cordial souvenir', and J.F. replied in very
friendly terms.

But Paris meant more to him than the Sorbonne. It was there
that he fell in love. Among his fellow-students was a Russian girl
called Sonia from an aristocratic family who had lost their money.
She was intelligent, full of vitality and as fluent in French as he
was himself. They went on trips together, returning from Ver-
sailles in a surburban train with compartments designed for
twelve and holding thirty. Soon they were deeply in love and
determined to marry. He hid nothing from his family, and his
mother, beside herself with alarm, sent Archie over to remonstrate. They spent a night in argument and Archie returned de-
feated. So long as the pair remained in Paris nothing would
separate them, and when J.F. returned to Scotland he was full of
excitement at the prospect of a formal engagement. The rest of the
story may be told in the words of Ronald Roxburgh who was with
him at Dulnain Bridge . . .

[1] There was also apparently one paper on Shakespeare for which he did no
work at all. He used to tell the story of his discomfiture at his *viva* when asked
where according to date he placed *The Tempest*. 'Le premier', he guessed
wildly. 'Non, monsieur,' came the withering reply, 'le dernier.'

While there, I saw and heard the anguish with which he came to realise the impossibility of further courtship and marriage. There was he in Scotland, on the threshold of a career as a schoolmaster in England, while she was far away in Russia. Neither of them had the means to marry. There followed a painful correspondence, in which she pleaded passionately that marriage was not impracticable and charged him with broken faith. The wound was deep. So far as I know, he never again thought of marriage.

Scots prudence and worldly wisdom had won. But such a judgment is too simple. To-day young public schoolmasters marry without money. Keeping a girl in the station to which she has been accustomed is a phrase from an antediluvian period: we are used nowadays to girls keeping their husbands while they try to qualify for a job. Things were different before 1914. No institution has changed more than the institution of marriage. People then were more sensitive to status and to the need for a particular style considered appropriate to support that status. Novel after novel in Victorian times pictures the dilemma of the young man of promise who fell in love but could not afford to get engaged. If he did marry he and his wife had to live in a style bound by conventions and their margin of manœuvre was in consequence greatly narrowed. That was why the middle classes did not marry young; why J.F.'s father, for example, had waited twenty-five years before he chose a bride. But Roxburgh was facing something more than a decision about middle-class respectability or a choice between marriage and a career. He was having to choose between marriage and a dream about teaching that had formed in his mind. He was having to place side by side the picture of himself married with the image of himself which he had created and was beginning to realise at Trinity. It may be that he should have sacrificed the dream and the image for love but it would have been a real and not an illusory sacrifice. What is certain is that he suffered. He could not deaden his feelings and he was a man who felt deeply. He knew that his family and his friends would all applaud his resolution to put his vocation first and talk of his sense of purpose and unselfishness. But his heart did not join in the applause. Honour meant much to him and he suffered the torments of remorse.

No letters, no tokens, no tangible records remain of his passion.

He expunged it from his life and the story is pieced together from the recollections of friends to whom at different times he told part. Twenty-five years later, so he told one of them, when the emotion had faded and Sonia had become a wistful memory, suddenly the fire would blaze up and he would think of her again with unbearable force. The gods took their revenge. He threw himself into schoolmastering so wholeheartedly that he left himself no time to fall in love again and marry. As the years passed he seemed to envelop himself in a mantle of courtesy, consideration and solicitude for everyone he met and to regard matrimony and all its entanglements with light-hearted mockery. The legend grew that he was a professional bachelor, an elegant misogynist, one of that sizeable band in his generation of English schoolmasters and dons who continued the celibate existence of their youth with scarcely any need to address a word to a woman under fifty and who found their happiness in affectionate relationships with favourite pupils.

There was truth in the legend but it also concealed other truths. 'How wise you are to have married before you were thirty!' he wrote to one of his pupils, who had announced his engagement. 'On that subject you can safely accept the view of a man who tried very hard to do so but didn't succeed. . . .' He had tried hard — in Scotland in the summer of 1915; and there was talk of a romance at Lancing. Unlike many of the professional misogynists with whom he was classed and whose hearts (which their friends assure us are in reality warm) are buried beneath a formidable crust, Roxburgh had a heart that was easily and visibly touched. He lavished affection not only upon a few special pupils but upon dozens in whose problems or lives he became involved. They might be the sisters or mothers of his pupils or someone with whom in the course of his work he had corresponded, had then met and to whom he became devoted. So far from enslaving himself in the routine of schoolmastering to protect himself against the disturbance of love he found in his profession the release to the affectionate side of his nature. It came to mean for him a multitude of friendships, a quite exceptional expenditure of tenderness and care upon men and women, boys and girls, to whom he responded almost before they had expressed their feelings. But though he did not hide his own feelings his friends were always to encounter a final reticence. He could not express love easily in words. Indeed

he may have found that he could tell Sonia in French how much
he loved her whereas he would have been incapable of doing so,
to her or any other, in his own tongue. His fine puritan Scots
heredity became transmuted into Roman *gravitas*. Beneath the
ebullience lay the sense of duty; behind the companionship the
regulation of responsibility. Perhaps because he had so much
affection to give, and because he met with so many demands and
claims, he was never able, after his passion for Sonia, to bestow it
all upon a single person.

Chapter III

Lancing

J.F.'s decision to apply to Lancing for a post seemed strange to his friends. One of them at Pembroke, Dick Harris, probably persuaded him. Harris used to tell the story that when he was fishing a river in Scotland one day in the summer of 1910 he heard the roar of a motorcycle and saw Roxburgh flashing by: later they talked about the future, and Harris, who had already made up his mind to try to join the staff at Lancing, induced J.F. to put in as well. He might also have been influenced by a Trinity friend, Noël Michell, who taught there for a while. There had probably been, as often happens, some work behind the scenes. J.F.'s tutor, St John Parry, had been a member of the Charterhouse staff at one time and knew the headmaster of Lancing, Bowlby,[1] who was a

[1] H. T. Bowlby, Headmaster of Lancing 1909, Canon of Chichester 1925. Bowlby had passed a desolate time at Charterhouse where he made two

Carthusian; and Parry had always encouraged Roxburgh to think of schoolmastering as a career.

His friends found it strange; Lancing did not seem to be the sort of school that J.F. would have chosen. It had been founded in 1848 by Nathaniel Woodard as one of a group of schools that were designed as offshoots of the Oxford Movement.[1] Lancing was not only to teach High Church theology and practice: the school was to stand for a social ideal. For among the founder's most fervently held beliefs was the conviction that through Anglo-Catholic worship lay reconciliation between social classes. Although Woodard envisaged Lancing as the jewel in his crown with a great chapel as the headquarters of his Society of Fellows, the other schools were to be minutely graded according to the class of boy admitted and the fees graded accordingly. Woodard wanted to recapture the educational ideals of the middle ages; he wanted schools in which religion was not merely practised but which were pervaded by the sense of Christ's sacrifice as re-enacted in the Eucharist; and so determined was he to prevent his conception from being secularised that at Lancing a resident Chaplain was established — a kind of Papal legate who was to be a Fellow of the Chapter and therefore independent of the headmaster. The Chaplain was to be officially responsible for the moral welfare of the boys; but since he was a Fellow of the Chapter, he might actually govern the headmaster in matters for which in the eyes of the public the headmaster must seem answerable. When Sanderson was headmaster and Edmund Field chaplain the diarchy worked. But it was by nature unworkable. On Provost Woodard's death in 1892 rows broke out. Neither the new provost nor his Chapter, who refused to modify the arrangement, were as interested in Lancing as they were in the other Woodard schools which seemed to them more closely concerned with the Founder's purpose. Lancing never rose in the public school hierarchy as did other new foundations such as Marlborough or Wellington. It became identified in the public mind with the other Woodard schools, suspected of being socially inferior (Woodard's gloomy emphasis on

friends: Lowes Dickinson, the King's don, and W. A. R. Monro, Rector of Lincoln. They formed a defensive alliance and were known as the 'Three Graces'.

[1] K. E. Kirk, *The Story of the Woodard Schools* (London, 1937).

the middle and lower classes), suspect as to health (typhoid had broken out in the 'eighties) and above all suspect as to religion (it was falsely alleged that Confession was obligatory). By 1902 the numbers had fallen from about two hundred to ninety.

The school was saved by the appointment of a new provost and a new headmaster. Arthur Lyttelton created a School Committee and two Old Boys were added to the Chapter and the Chaplain became non-resident, his duties devolving on to an assistant subordinate to the headmaster. Bernard Tower, the headmaster, a man of ability and charm, was an Old Boy. It was characteristic of his faith that at a time when funds were low and an anonymous donor gave him £10,000 he applied the whole sum to continue the building of the immense Chapel that Woodard and his son had been slowly erecting. Such courage brought its reward: some regarded this act as a symbol, others as a sign of prosperity, and confidence in the school was restored. Although Tower's health broke down after only seven years, there were new buildings, new playing-fields and the school had grown to over two hundred at the time Roxburgh joined the staff. It was a good place for a young man to go. T. W. Cook (who later became a Bishop),[1] Adam Fox[2] and W. H. Ferguson[3] (who later both became headmasters) were on the staff: but there were few senior masters and Bowlby, who had come to be headmaster from a house at Eton, was inclined to give young men their head. He wanted to improve the school's undistinguished academic standing and Roxburgh was one of four men with First Class degrees who came to Lancing that term.

He at once made an unforgettable impression: 'unquestionably the most striking of this striking set of men' in the words of Adam Fox who had relinquished his sixth-form teaching to him. He was tall with keen, bright, friendly eyes, immaculate in appearance and everything about him seemed to flow gracefully. He did not cover up the idiosyncrasies that he had cultivated at Cambridge. He enlarged them. He had the instinct that told him exactly how

[1] T. W. Cook, Suffragan Bishop of Lewes 1926.
[2] A. Fox, Warden of Radley 1918; Fellow of Magdalen, Oxford, 1927-42, Canon of Westminster.
[3] W. H. Ferguson, Warden of St Edward's, Oxford, 1913; Warden of Radley 1925.

far he could go in extravagance. 'At twenty-four,' said Bernard Fixsen, 'he looked to us boys as a mature confident man of the world among inward-looking schoolmasters, a professional in a group that had not yet thrown off amateurism'; and another pupil of a slightly younger generation added, 'The impression that J.F. left with one, and intended to leave, was a mixture of Man of Culture and Man of the World.' His manner towards his colleagues was one of exquisite consideration and courtesy; and his assured flamboyance carried the boys with him — for boys delight in someone who stands out from the staid life that surrounds them at school. Eyebrows at Lancing shot up. His clothes were florid, elegantly cut but of remarkable hue — 'Another new suit, sir?' the boys would ask startled at the latest creation: 'Old as the hills, my dear fellow,' came the reply. It came to be widely believed that his ties were specially made for him from silk squares woven in Spitalfields. His entrances were *dégagés* but exquisitely prepared. The boys brightened considerably in Chapel when J.F. would walk in wearing the startling cap and gown of his *Licenciat ès Lettres*. 'I remember once, as J.F. flowed into Chapel, as usual slightly late and as usual quite unhurried, my neighbour murmured "the Prince of Glory passes on his way" and I intoned "Alleluia".' Perhaps the entrances were a little too well timed. One boy later thought of them as 'a put up job as were his suits of deepest plum or purple, his stoop that seemed to condescend from a superior plane, his high artificial voice and the polysyllables that jetted out of him in all directions.' When he came to Lancing, wrote one of his pupils:

We did not at first know what to make of him. We were not accustomed to anyone quite so gracious, quite so well groomed, quite so stylish. We wondered whether he was, perhaps, a bit bogus. One way and another we gradually reassured ourselves. I remember one raw autumn afternoon when we invited him for a run through the muddy dykes which drain the valley of the Adur and which form a notorious feature of the school's cross-country course. And there was J.F., on time and looking like a god in his spotless Old Carthusian sweater and with his well brushed hair. Off we went, tempering our speed to his maturer pace — over and through a dozen dykes and finishing with a bathe in the Bottomless Pond. J.F. never hesitated — nor indeed did he ever indulge again. But he had started to win our respect as well as our wonder, and that respect grew and became softened into affection as the weeks and months of that first year proceeded.

He seems to have known from the first how to win the affection of boys. Some, of course, disliked him. There were those who feared and resented his sarcasm — and he was too apt as a young man to use this weapon which all schoolmasters should ban. He did not realise that some of the victories that he scored in form were not only cheap but cruel. Others thought him too showy and accused him of courting popularity. He condescended in the grand manner; and it was indeed somewhat ducal to put up notices signed 'Roxburgh' or even 'R'. But from the first his touch was extraordinarily sure. He knew, and his boys knew, exactly how they each stood to the other. 'At all times he belonged to the Cap and Gown Camp and there was never a shadow of doubt about it,' wrote Ivor Cross.[1] 'But he had broken down the fence and under- stood our language. Furthermore he respected our feelings . . .' *Our feelings.* He took account of the fact that boys have feelings, very strong feelings, about matters which are far away from the things that excite adults. And yet coupled with this desire to understand those feelings went the knowledge that however well he knew his pupils he could never be as they. He was not, and never wished to be, a boy among boys. Perhaps his gift lay more than anything else in establishing a master–pupil relationship in which there was friendship without familiarity, and authority with a remarkable concern for the boys as individuals. He astonished his pupils by his generosity. After his first term he 'made a point of being in Cambridge for the January scholarship exams that he might show us round and entertain us during our ordeal'. Or again: 'He was extremely generous — a dinner at Hatchett's followed by Covent Garden to see Max Reinhardt's production of *Oedipus Rex* for six members of his Sixth Form just before the spring term began.' At this time his salary was 200 guineas a year.

He had at once made a name for himself among the Sixth Form by the cascade of his speech. He would stigmatise poor reading as 'a concatenation of discordant vocables', and dub a dreary essay

---

[1] I. M. Cross, Housemaster at Stowe 1923–43, Headmaster of Lapley Grange School 1943–63.

'an amorphous mass of nebulous ineptitude' or 'a cacophonous collocation'. 'The most pejorative expression,' Evelyn Waugh recollected, 'was: "excellent journalism, my dear fellow," by which he meant trite in thought, illiterate, and aiming for effect by smartness and over-statement. He meant the world of the leader-writer, not of the reporter. The lively description of an event always pleased him.' [1] He took endless pains in correcting trans-lations and verses for his classical pupils but he was, in Oxford terms, more a Greats than a Mods man and his pupils who failed to make a mark in the latter often redeemed themselves in the former. It was his habit to set 'paragraphs' rather than essays, his pupils being asked to produce one original idea and to express it as imaginatively and succinctly as possible. As his pupils got used to the flow of raillery and mock indignation they found themselves, in an age not yet dominated by General Certificate examinations, reading books they did not associate with school. If they were wearying of the Romantic poets, J.F. would revive them with Samuel Butler's *Notebooks*, Shaw's plays and the French *Parnassiens*. 'None of this had anything to do with our exams,' wrote one of his pupils. 'In fact French was not officially his subject at all. But this helped to teach us that culture and the enjoyment of ideas were to be part of our lives, not part of our education only. He broadened us out and sophisticated us.' Nor did he keep such excursions for the class-room. 'Some of his finest lessons,' his colleague Griffith Williams[2] recollected, 'were given at the informal causeries of Head's house.'

He was the supreme enemy of that Dullness that Pope so detested. The Sixth Form were made to grope through the Chapel to establish whether a hidden feature was built in the perpendicular or decorated style. His forms chanted poetry aloud together and were taught to declaim it individually. An admission that one had been reading Sapper would be met with a cry of pain and a work on psychical research that had taken his fancy would be pressed into one's hand. He digressed on purpose. 'I have never forgotten his exposition of the Dreyfus case given out of the blue in the middle of a period,' wrote a pupil. 'It took about half an

[1] Evelyn Waugh, *A Little Learning* (London, 1964), pp. 159–60.

[2] Sir Griffith G. Williams, Deputy Secretary Minister of Education 1946–53, *The Times*, 11 May 1954.

hour and has remained in my memory ever since.' He always
appeared fresh on entering the form-room and he could keep his
class bubbling, when they began to get tired or bored. One day a
youth was reciting stanzas from Tennyson's *The Miller's Daughter*
in a voice of gravel tinged with the deepest melancholy: 'And I
would be the girdle About her dainty, dainty waist.' The form
began to titter. 'Go on, my dear fellow, — a very laudable ambition.' Inevitably his attempts to stimulate and strike sparks came
in for comment. In 1915 *Truth* published one of his examination
papers 'set to candidates under fourteen at the last entrance to one
of our public schools [which] seems to show once more the
necessity of examinations for examiners'. The boys had been
asked to compose eight lines of poetry on 'The Song of the Motor
Cycle' and to write an account of the North Sea Fight in which the
Lion and *Tiger* took part in the words (*a*) of the *Daily Mail* reporter,
(*b*) of the Bishop of London in the pulpit. But work with him was
not all high spirits. 'We were not particularly scholarly,' admitted
one of his sixth-formers, 'but some of us at least were infected by
J.F.'s magnificent industry.'

His industry became proverbial. He persuaded the Bursar to
give him a spare 'Pit' (study) where nobody was allowed to visit
him. There he kept 'impossible hours' correcting his Proses and
Unseens and preparing his work for the next day at a five-foot
lectern which he had had constructed for him and which was to
follow him to Stowe.[1] He stood at the lectern so that he should
not fall asleep. In his view the number of activities that a good
schoolmaster should undertake was unlimited. Societies to read
Shakespeare, French and contemporary drama claimed him and
soon after his arrival he was attending debates, still a Radical,
welcoming the Insurance Act and beseeching his audience to
prefer 'justice to jingoism and commonsense before claptrap' in
Ireland. But at a debate on public schools he also insisted in
highly traditional manner that 'keenness on games means keenness on work'. When Bowlby, who was not only headmaster but
nominally a housemaster as well, came in 1913 to choose a deputy,

[1] His colleagues, drifting away from the Common Room at half past nine
to do the same, smiled gloomily when J.F., lamenting the pile of exercise
books that awaited him, continued to entertain the company until past eleven
o'clock.

designated House Tutor, he chose Roxburgh. Two years later J.F. took charge of one of the newer houses which had been created since the numbers in the school were rising to three hundred.

By that time the catastrophe of the First World War had engulfed Lancing. As he was repeatedly rejected as unfit owing to a suspected heart ailment, it was not until 1917 that J.F. was at last accepted for active service. By Christmas 1914 some of the staff were going, and he saw the commanding officer of the Corps, the son of Haig-Brown of Charterhouse, leave for the front where he was killed. Soon he had to bear the casualty lists of his own pupils.[1] Worse still, his younger brother Bob, to whom he was devoted and who was barely nineteen, was blown up when H.M.S. *Indefatigable* was sunk in the battle-cruiser action between Beatty and Hipper at Jutland. The first holiday in that year he was sent to Seaford as a musketry instructor, during the next he learnt signalling and at Christmas he was on a course in Chelsea barracks. He was at last gazetted with Dick Harris in the Signal Corps of the Royal Engineers.

A photograph of him in uniform survives: polished, alert and slightly improbable. He was mentioned in Haig's last despatches for good work during the final advance and recommended for the Military Cross. He was still in Flanders at Christmas 1918 and had time to send to the sister of Eddie Capel Cure, who was one of the boys in his house, this letter:

My dear Cello,
    Thank you awfully for your parcel. It was jolly of you to send me so much for the men. I'm afraid that the puzzles made of little metal wiggles and kinks and scraggles and so on haven't reached the men yet. They have stuck in this Mess of ours, and between tea and dinner tonight the following distinguished people were losing and regaining and relosing their tempers over them:—
1 Colonel, 1 Brigade Major, 1 Staff Captain, 1 Signal Officer. So you see you really *have* been helping to keep the British Army sane. Much need too, on a wet Sunday afternoon in Flanders. I went to

[1] Some verses on his feelings at that time, written by C. L. Graves, appeared in *The Spectator* on 22 July 1916, entitled 'Master and Pupil' and dedicated 'To J.F.R.'

Calais yesterday on a Motor Ambulance to buy turkeys and I
brought back nine huge ones. They were so heavy that we burst
a tyre and reached home at 2 this morning. But they were *lovely*
turkeys. Thank you again for the woggles, Cello. Best of luck and
a happy New Year. If I get out of the Army before next term
begins, I'm going to try and call on you one afternoon.

The war made some returning schoolmasters old and others
young. The old in heart harrowed by the heroism of their comrades were determined to exact sacrifice from the coming generations and make them worthy of the dead. The young, such as
J.F., while never forgetting the sacrifice, were equally determined to put before their pupils the horror and folly of war. But a
sense of proportion and equity was everything to J.F. and when
he returned early in 1919 he continued to serve in the O.T.C. as
second in command not because he greatly enjoyed the work but
because Haig-Brown had convinced him that the Corps did
something for the school as well as the country. His words of
command at all events were legendary. The boys waited expec-
tantly for that mellifluous voice to exhort them to 'unhoik peanuts'
and 'on the word move, moove; mouuuve'.

He had returned to his teaching and to his House, maturer now
at thirty-one, with a wardrobe of fourteen suits (counted by the
boys as they made their appearance) and clouds of brightly
coloured large silk handkerchiefs; brewing at evening parties a
mixture of Taiping and Lapsang Suchong in an enormous teapot
which stood on the floor beside a large tin of assorted biscuits. He
was original as a disciplinarian and sometimes turned a blind eye.
A boy who was returning with a cricket-bag stuffed with bottles
of beer and cider for an end-of-term party had the misfortune to be
offered a lift by J.F. who heaved the bag into the car. He said
nothing as the bottles clinked but when he dropped him handed
him a packet of fifty cigarettes and said: 'Perhaps these will come
in useful.' The discipline at Sanderson's did not compare to that
at Gill's under Dick Harris. Some thought that he left too
much to his Head of House and House Captains and have memories of bullying. But he exercised power over his boys by his
invariable courtesy and consideration. If J.F. was bored by some
of their pursuits, he never showed it. 'I doubt,' said Alan Hilder,
one of Lancing's most famous cricketers, 'if his greatest supporter

could have called J.F. a cricketer, but I only had to go to his room and tell him that there were House Nets for him to turn up and bowl all the afternoon.'

The secret of his courtesy lay in a delicacy of feeling that enabled him to put himself in another person's place. He would journey from Sussex to Yorkshire to advise the parents of a boy not in his house on the merits of various Oxford colleges. He knew how to heal schoolboy agonies. One Friday in Chapel, as the Litany was coming to a close, a boy sprang to his feet, scrambled along the chairs in front of the entire school on their knees, and just made the aisle where he vomited. Then he fled out of Chapel. It was a boy called Rivers-Moore who was in Roxburgh's house, a scholar, small for his age, short-sighted, spotty, devout and, as the son of an East End clergyman, a confessed socialist. Everything about him from his appearance to his politics made him unpopular and he was persecuted. Nobody noticed that J.F. had slipped out of Chapel, but when the boys emerged on their way back to their house he could be seen in the Chapel Quad walking to and fro with his arm round Rivers-Moore. One of those who saw him said: 'It probably never occurred to J.F. that he was being kind: it was his natural reaction. But it made an impression on me. I was one of Rivers-Moore's persecutors . . .'

Among all these activities Roxburgh found time to lecture to the Brighton branch of the Workers' Educational Association. Anyone who has given such lectures knows that it is a most exacting form of teaching: great simplicity of expression must be united to impeccable logic so that the class may be led forward stage by stage, while at the same time the lecturer has to expect far more original and devastating criticism than he would get from his own pupils. Two of the lectures that he gave were published in 1921 under the title of *The Poetic Procession*. It is a short introduction to English poetry and became so popular in the lower forms of a number of schools that it was often reprinted. The theme of the book is that poetry changes with the years. There are many kinds and in the procession each new kind has its own quality. The poet touches our hearts by some simile, some turn of phrase or some word that he uses. The book is an excellent example of the art of talking, but of never talking down, to the reader ('that *is* a new vision — isn't it? — and here is another vision that a poet has taught me to see . . .).[1] Nor was Roxburgh afraid to use epigram ('With Wordsworth it is always Sunday. With Byron it is *never* Sunday.').[2] He was writing before the revolution in poetic taste which the movement in literary criticism of the inter-war years effected and the passages he chose were inspired by the *Golden Treasury*. Over half the book was devoted to the Romantics, the eighteenth century was said to 'lack the essential spirit of poetry' and the procession ended with Rupert Brooke and Masefield. Roxburgh was quite aware of Victorian absurdities: the Sixth chose the poems that they themselves liked and he would comment volubly on their individual taste. But he recognised that his taste was conservative. His most brilliant pupil, Evelyn Waugh, at that time editor of the Lancing College Magazine, had reviewed the book, warning his readers that it was 'not written in that language of J.F. which is quoted wherever Lancing men meet' but rather aims at 'telling simple men the simplest poems he likes very simply'. J.F. at once wrote to express his thanks — accompanied by a specially bound and inscribed copy of the book and a letter of some length, characteristic of the courtesy that he showed to his pupils, in which he said:

> I am glad you made it clear that the book is intended to be simple, for of course it *is*, but I think that whatever my audience had been like, I should have said very much what I said to the 'corduroys' — except on the question of the nature and function of poetry, whereon I should have liked to essay a subtlety or two. The fact is — and you had better know the worst — that I am incurably Victorian about poetry, as I am about most things. I don't understand the Georgians (neo or otherwise) and, as middle age is becoming added to native mediocrity, I find more and more that I don't *want* to understand them either! There are only some fifteen years between you and me, but they are a rather special fifteen years, and I fear I can never really belong to the generation you belong to. I shall have to be satisfied with the past. The future looks as if it would be full of squibs, and I am a man of peace. Hopeless case! you say. Well, I am afraid so, but if you think a rescue is still possible, there is no one to whom I would more gladly owe my salvation. But I am very comfortable now in my groove.

[1] J. F. Roxburgh, *The Poetic Procession* (1921), p. 2.
[2] *ibid.*, p. 27.

It was a good groove for teaching younger boys. In later years it became inadequate for those who were older.

He dedicated *The Poetic Procession* to the head of his house. This was Eddie Capel Cure who had won a scholarship to Lancing the year that J.F. had set the examination paper which *Truth* had condemned. Of all the pupils on whom J.F. lavished special care and affection Capel was his favourite. It was he who most conspicuously combined those qualities that J.F. tried to inculcate: keenness, the most rewarding use of every minute and entire absence of fatuity or purposelessness. It was he to whom J.F. gave a motorcycle, on which to J.F.'s remorse he smashed himself up badly in an accident which ruined his chance of winning a Trinity scholarship and disfigured his remarkable looks. By that time Roxburgh had become a friend of the family, admiring the struggle of the father who was a parson against increasing disability, enchanted by the daughter nicknamed 'Cello' who was ten years old when he first met her, and devoted to the mother to whom he poured out his hopes and fears as they walked round the vicarage garden at Great Houghton and he told her that his birthday would never be complete without a letter from her. Here was a home for the bachelor housemaster where he knew he was welcome. Here was a family that was singularly united and unpretentious. In return he would give charming presents, often disguised, as when he sent a print of Fra Angelico's Annunciation and 'hoped you would not mind having your Christmas card framed'. His pupil brought him the reward that schoolmasters often deserve but rarely get. He modelled his career on that of J.F. and on graduating from Cambridge became a master at Stowe and J.F.'s most valued personal confidant.

It was inevitable that Roxburgh should leave Lancing. He was indeed the outstanding man on the staff, 'one of the predominating influences of Bowlby's Lancing' as his pupil B. W. T. Handford put it in his history of the school.[1] He was Bowlby's intellectual superior in almost every sphere but, although he acted as second master, a post not at that time established, no one could ever say that he usurped a function or pushed himself forward. His colleagues' children were among his strongest supporters. The Bursar's children remembered him walking round their garden one

[1] B. W. T. Handford, *Lancing 1848–1930* (Oxford, 1933), p. 285.

hilarious summer afternoon on a pair of stilts they had acquired. He was the centre among the staff of a genial group consisting of Harris, Whitworth and Brent Smith whose gales of laughter in the Dining Hall startled some of the boys into believing that their masters lived lives of their own.[1] He was marked out to be a head-master but Roxburgh possibly sensed that he was a little too young and unconventional for an age when Norwood, Vaughan, Malim and Spenser Leeson were to be among the leading appointments made.

And then a curious opportunity arose. The public schools were among the many commodities that boomed in the immediate post-war years. In addition to their regular clients were many who had held a commission or made money in industry during the war and who now wanted to enhance their social position or obtain a good education for their sons by sending them to a public school. The schools were overwhelmed with applications and prep school headmasters were faced with frustrated parents. One of them, E. H. Montauban, who owned a prep school in Hampstead and was a prominent member of the Association of Preparatory Schools, formed a group of prep school headmasters to agitate for the foundation of a new great public school, which should be open to fresh ideas but otherwise in the familiar pattern.[2] Just at this time Stowe House came into the market. The first and second Dukes of Buckingham had squandered the family fortune; the third Duke had died without a male heir; and Stowe had descended to his daughter, who retained among all his titles only that of the barony of Kinloss. So long as her elder son, the Master of Kinloss, lived she struggled to maintain the great house and its park; but when he was killed in the war Lady Kinloss decided to sell Stowe. Montauban obtained from the purchaser the offer of the bare mansion itself and of 280 acres of grounds as a gift for

---

[1] In later years the group were scattered. Nonetheless from 1926, when Harris took over his brother's preparatory school at Worthing, until the Second World War, these four, with E. B. Gordon (who had left Lancing as a boy in 1912 and returned to it as a master three years later), gathered spontaneously every January for a hilarious evening in London, booking always a private dining-room at Jules: 'the chatter and gaiety – "the foolish old forgivable talk" made it all an occasion not to be missed.'

[2] For an account of the foundation of Stowe see R. P. Croom-Johnson, *The Origin of Stowe School* (Ipswich, 1953).

the new school on condition that he could obtain financial backing. Having enlisted the support of Cyril Norwood,[1] at that time Master of Marlborough, and of a number of prospective parents, he tried to raise part of the money by offering nomination rights to prep schools in return for gifts of certain sums — a scheme which he hoped would guarantee him good boys but which might equally have embarrassed Stowe's headmaster. But he could not raise the money in time, and as the summer of 1922 passed it looked as if his plan was doomed. For there was opposition as well as enthusiasm: the immediate post-war boom had collapsed and the deflation of the inter-war years was beginning. The Times crabbed the idea in a leader from the start, and the retired headmaster of Eton, Edward Lyttelton, followed its line in urging that, as the present demand for public school places was probably only temporary, it would be better for the existing schools to expand.[2] Just when all seemed lost, another much stronger committee with its own educational plans and financial support came forward. Its president was Lord Gisborough, its members included Field-Marshall Sir William Robertson, Dr David, a former headmaster of Rugby and then Bishop of Liverpool, and Dr E. A. Burroughs, subsequently Bishop of Ripon. The Secretary was the Reverend P. E. Warrington. They offered to buy Stowe and appointed a Council for the new school which Montauban was invited to join.

Roxburgh had taken an interest in the news that another public school was to be founded. His friend the Bishop of Oxford tried to dissuade him from applying for the headmastership using much the same arguments as had appeared in The Times, but it so happened that one day Roxburgh was lunching with the literary editor of The Spectator, Amabel Williams-Ellis,[3] to discuss some reviews of classical books. Her husband,[4] who had already been

[1] Sir Cyril Norwood, Headmaster of Bristol Grammar School 1906–12, Master of Marlborough 1916–25, Headmaster of Harrow 1926–34, President of St John's College, Oxford 1934–46, Chairman of the Allied Schools 1934–1954.

[2] The Times, 17 January and 29 April 1922.

[3] Amabel Williams-Ellis, daughter of St Loe Strachey, editor of The Spectator, and sister of John Strachey, M.P.

[4] Clough Williams-Ellis, architect and designer of Portmeirion, North Wales.

appointed architect-in-general at Stowe, was attracted by Rox-burgh's personality, and urged him to persevere. There were originally nine candidates: four were short-listed and these together with one new candidate appeared for the final interviews on 2 December 1922. The Council was divided, but he won a clear majority and was called back to be congratulated. 'When we told him,' wrote Montauban, 'he said nothing. He simply sat there. His face didn't move. There was only a tightening in his throat — just going in and out — but you could tell by that how deeply he felt the tremendous responsibility he had undertaken.' That evening he sat down at the Athenaeum and wrote:

My dear Mrs Capel,
    I am writing to you first and Eddie second (I wired to my Mother). The news I have to give you is this: To-day, after one of the most trying days I ever remember, I have been appointed Headmaster of Stowe . . . the new school they are opening in that splendid old house.
    What an adventure for a young man! — but what a responsibility and what a labour! And of course it means leaving Lancing — and that is going to be the biggest wrench I have ever had.
    To-night my feelings are mixed and I am absolutely exhausted also. So forgive the shortcomings of this letter. May I still have your love and friendship — and those of all of you. My love to you both.
                                        Yours ever with affection

Bowlby was kind enough to release him at the end of the term; and in April next year, a month before Stowe opened, past and present members of his house gave him, in traditional style, a dinner at the Trocadero, the menu featuring Poulet Polysyllabique and Puits d'Amour Crystalline. It was indeed a wrench to leave Lancing. Whatever touched him touched him deeply, and he could not bear to revisit the place. Not until thirty years after he left did he return. He wrote to a friend: 'I went to see Lancing again. I was lucky in my weather and came away loving the place, if possible, more than ever.' There he thought of what Lancing had done for him. A month before he died he wrote, 'I learned more at Lancing than I have ever learned since I left it — and infinitely more than I ever taught there.' It had taught him a secret about the spirit of schools. At Lancing the immense Chapel and its great High Altar dominated school life. As we shall see later, the religious tradition of the school was alien to Roxburgh: but he recognised that this was the soil in which whatever existed of culture at Lancing was nourished. Through the Chapel boys might be touched not only with Christianity but with emotions that led them to poetry, to history, to legend and myth, to intellectual propositions and architectural proportions. The Chapel turned its back on material considerations, and its very size was a lofty dismissal of utilitarian calculation. Writing an encomium on Bowlby, Roxburgh praised 'his ability to see how the school's future could be made continuous with its past'. Stowe had no past but it had inherited a past in its eighteenth-century mansion and park; and from Lancing Roxburgh learnt how to make use of this asset and infuse its spirit into the culture of the new school.

Chapter IV

The first years at Stowe

Among all the ideas that Roxburgh developed at Stowe none was nearer to his heart than his desire to awaken in boys a feeling for poetry, architecture and nature, and to give them freedom in their daily lives. It was an astonishing accident that the place in which he was to create his school should embody in its ambience and in its history beauty and liberty.

Stowe stands in the most sublime setting of any school in England. The Temple family employed the architects and landscape gardeners of the eighteenth century to rebuild the house and surround it with elegiac scenery. On either side of the North Front sweep elegant colonnades as you approach the tall portico which Vanbrugh built. From the portico you pass through a simple square entrance hall into a great oval saloon with white marble floor and pink marble pillars carrying a classical frieze of three hundred figures which move in procession above the cornice. You then walk out on to the noble Corinthian loggia of the South Front, thirty-one steps above ground level, and gaze over the park, heavy with vast and noble trees, as it stretches into the distance across a lake and onwards to the summit of a long slope where there stands a vast triumphal arch. Robert Adam made the design, later modified, for the South Front which houses the enormous state rooms; Soane built the Gothic library; Kent, Valdré and Borra were among the artists who embellished the interior. But the setting is more remarkable than the house. Throughout the grounds are scattered *temples d'amour*. For eighty years artists and amateur architects were to build them, pull them down or improve them until Stowe was unrivalled in the number that adorn the domain. It was here that the revolution of landscape gardening began when Bridgeman surrounded the park with a ha-ha, it was here that Capability Brown began his career as an under-gardener. The avenues and the western part of the park consist of great vistas which lead up to a column or a rotundo or pavilions. The eastern side is a contrast. It is the creation of Kent who 'leaped the fence', as Horace Walpole wrote, 'and saw that all Nature was a garden'. Massing trees and shrubs in one place to form a dark and melancholy backcloth, shaping them in another to form a touching retreat, or parting them to frame a distant view, Kent placed his temples and alcoves with such variety that you are for ever coming upon some fresh sight. It may be a Palladian bridge, or a towering monument or a grotto or an arch or a tiny fountain. Sometimes it is a long vista that stretches from a classical portico past a Gothic confection to a ruined façade; or a great valley, flanked with beeches, hollowed out and leading to a Roman temple perched on a rise above it. The meandering streams flow into a lake that in turn cascades over a rococo waterfall into eleven acres of placid water.

Stowe was the headquarters of the Whig faction called the Grenville cousinhood. Lord Cobham, under whose instructions the building and park first took shape, and who had been one of Marlborough's generals, went into opposition against Walpole, and when the Pelhams came in returned to power with 'Cobham's Cubs'. Among them were his heir Richard Grenville, Earl Temple, to whom his titles passed; his nephew George Grenville, later

Prime Minister; and the husband of his niece, the great William Pitt, Earl of Chatham. But Stowe was not only a hive of politics: it was an arbour for poets. Cobham's ease of manner and largesse attracted Pope, Vanbrugh, Congreve, Thomson, Chesterfield and his own nephew George, Lord Lyttelton, many of whom, enraptured by the beauty of the place, left verses or inscriptions on the temples which conjure up eighteenth-century ghosts. They also embody Whig principles. On the east wing of the South Front recline the figures of Peace and Plenty, and on the west wing those of Religion and Liberty. Not far away among the trees lie hidden Kent's Elysian Fields. There to Cobham's instructions he erected a Temple of Ancient Virtue with niches for the busts of Homer, Epaminondas, Lycurgus and Socrates; and adjoining — as Horace Walpole observed 'His Lordship being then in opposition to the Court' — a Temple of Modern Virtue was built as a ruin. Both buildings symbolically looked across a lake to the Temple of British Worthies. Here are commemorated in a semi-circular row of busts and inscriptions the heroes of the Whig interpretation of history. 'No priest appears among them, and a line referring to priests is left out of the quotation from Vergil. Lord Cobham was not fond of the predominantly Tory Church,' notes Laurence Whistler.[1] Shakespeare and Milton are balanced by Gresham and Raleigh; John Hampden 'begun a noble Opposition to an arbitrary Court in Defence of the Liberties of his Country'; Queen Elizabeth 'took off the Yoke of Ecclesiastical Tyranny'; King Alfred 'protected Learning, established Juries, crushed Corruption, guarded Liberty and was the Founder of the English Constitution'. There is Bacon 'rejecting vain Speculation' and Newton 'whom the God of Nature made to comprehend his Works'. Above all there is Locke 'who best of all Philosophers, understood the Powers of the human Mind, the Nature, End and Bounds of Civil Government; and with equal Courage and Sagacity, refuted the slavish systems of usurped Authority over the Rights, the Consciences or the Reason of Mankind'. The spirit of the English Enlightenment hovers over the place.

Roxburgh immediately sensed what the grandeur of Stowe and its history could mean to the school. He named the houses in the school after Whig lords who had built or been connected with the

[1] Laurence Whistler, *Stowe, A Guide to the Gardens* (London, 1956), p. 21.

place. He was indeed a Whig at heart. He believed in the existence of a ruling oligarchy and venerated the country's institutions though he was willing to see them reformed. He believed that a democracy must inevitably be ruled by the select few and that the public schools 'must keep up the tradition of conduct, bearing and speech which marks off the well-bred Englishman from others. The first justification of an Aristocracy is that it shall give leadership and service. But the second is that it shall maintain a standard of culture and refinement to which other classes can look — and eventually rise.' 'We should all like', he continued in another context, 'to see the English Nation a single Nation. But it does not do any good to pretend that it is a single nation if it isn't. We have got to face the fact that the division into classes does exist. What is more, we do not want to obliterate the division and make the Nation one Nation by any process which involves levelling down. We do not want to secure a universal standard by securing a universally low standard.'

The education that the élite were to receive at Stowe would be distinguished in two ways. In the peroration to the first public speech he made as headmaster, before the school had even opened, he said: 'There is one more thing that we can teach boys at Stowe — or one more thing we can let them learn. You will know what I mean if you have ever looked up one of our long green valleys at the great south front of Stowe in the light of a spring day. . . . Every boy who goes out from Stowe will know beauty when he sees it all the rest of his life.'[1] Every boy was also to enjoy liberty. For although Roxburgh claimed that 'we have attempted to do nothing revolutionary . . . we have simply attempted to modernise and liberalise and humanise the boarding-school methods', he advocated the spread of freedom in the schools with a vigour and sincerity that shocked traditionalists among the headmasters. He would have drunk with enthusiasm the old Whig toast: 'Civil and religious liberty all over the World.' Religion, as we shall see, mattered much to him; but it was not to be imposed on the boys and certainly not in a bigoted form. Most boys enjoy games but the incompetent should be released from playing them as soon as possible. He demanded good manners and defended the social conventions as the means of rubbing off

[1] Croom-Johnson, *op. cit.*, p. 27.

sharp social corners; but his aim was to teach boys to consider other people's feelings and he would have no boy-made rules — 'the piling up of prohibitions about waistcoat buttons, hands in pockets, methods of carrying books'.[1] Locke was the first philosopher to argue that the end of government was to make men happy. Roxburgh tried to organise his school on similar principles. He thought of men as creatures with fears and affections, with reticences and exuberance, who needed care but above all sympathy.[2] He was later to tell a Jesuit Father from Stonyhurst that he had started Stowe with two ideas, freedom from fagging and freedom from beating; but that he lacked the courage to abolish both for fear that the school would be labelled a freak. He wanted boys to be interested in what they were taught. 'The centre of every boy's education is (or ought to be) the work he does on a subject that appeals to him': but it must be one that 'provokes more mental activity than is required for mastering it'.[3] From the beginning of a boy's career he wanted him to have not only choice but also periods in school in which, freed from routine subjects, he could learn about the arts.

The headmaster of a new school starts with immense advantages. If he is never to be free from financial worry, he can at any rate exercise a personal control that a headmaster appointed from outside to an existing institution cannot hope to achieve. Roxburgh implemented his plans by retaining in his own hands powers that had fallen into the hands of housemasters in other public schools and by ensuring that a boy had mentors other than those that existed in his house. In this he was helped by the environment. The first four houses had to be carved out of the mansion itself and their boundaries often overlapped; the next two were attached to the main building though self-contained; only two were free-standing. The boys assembled before meals in the great Saloon and ate them together in the State dining-rooms. They were treated from their arrival as members of the school

[1] J. F. Roxburgh, *Eleutheros* (London, 1930), p. 46.

[2] He started a Zoo in the early years at Stowe because he believed that some boys needed a pet as an object for their natural affections: but it did not last long as the rate at which the rats multiplied presented a problem and other animals, including a bear, were uncivil enough to decline domestication.

[3] *ibid.*, p. 66.

rather than of the house. Roxburgh himself dealt with all entries; every boy could call on him before supper for advice or to discuss his grievances or worries; initially he looked after boys' future careers and until his retirement dealt personally with entry to Oxford and Cambridge. As a result there was a court of appeal from the housemaster. He also created among the staff forces to counter-balance him. He employed devices to make form masters more important and in the Upper School created Tutors who gave individual tutorials as well as classes and often established close personal relationships with their pupils. The Sixth Form were to have as many privileges as the prefects and were exempt from the need to play any games; and all boys were to have one afternoon a week free to pursue their own hobbies. Whenever a master or a boy showed an interest in some topic Roxburgh encouraged him to develop it. Individuality was the prize.

It is important not to claim too much originality for these ideas. In the experimental schools there was more freedom and often contempt for the social conventions which Roxburgh delighted to preserve. He added practically nothing to educational theory and introduced hardly any new ideas into the curriculum. Yet within the public school framework he contributed at that time something precious. His speciality was the treatment of boys, and his passion for bringing out in each his unique quality, even if it meant sacrificing the corporate side of the school, took many years to be tolerated let alone accepted. Only a year or so before the Second World War Peter Ustinov's end-of-term report at Westminster could read: 'He shows great originality, which must be curbed at all cost . . .'[1]

Some of Roxburgh's ideas are to be found in the small book he contributed to Kegan Paul's widely read 'To-day and Tomorrow' series. The title is significant. *Eleutheros* was the word that Aristotle used to distinguish a free man from a slave. 'The slave's job in life was just to work; the free man's job was to be the best possible kind of man'; and Roxburgh bases his book on Aristotle's dictum: 'there is a form of education which should be given to our sons not because it is useful and not because it is necessary, but because it befits a free man and because it is noble'. The book is cast in the form of a Platonic dialogue. Dr Archdale (the name as

[1] *Sunday Times*, 29 December 1963.

a disguise for Roxburgh was so transparent as to be diaphanous) is talking in the club with Burgess, an enlightened business man. They are joined by Colonel Callaghan, a parent of the old guard who does not care what his son is taught so long as he learns to serve the community, and by M. D'Orsay, a French diplomat, who puts exquisitely polite but searching questions. Why is it, D'Orsay asks, that the English persist in deprecating the intellect when their experts at international conferences are the ablest and their scholars the equal of any? ('In your profession, Colonel, I know it is different. People tell me that clever men are discouraged there, and I can well believe it, for I have read books by some of your Generals.')[1] The answer, Burgess says, is simple. Education in the academic sense seems to Englishmen not to be concerned with reality and as a result public schoolboys learn nothing and emerge with good clothes, good manners and a totally empty head. The rest of the book defends the schools against these charges. Dr Archdale exerts his charm to disarm his reader — and also to evade some awkward issues. 'I believe all the things I said [in my speech] about the Public Schools,' he declares, 'but I did not say all the things I believed.'[2] For Dr Archdale knows in his heart that all is not well with the schools. He can turn aside the complaint that they do not make the boys conversationally fluent in modern languages because a school is far better employed in laying a grammatical foundation and teaching foreign literature and history. He finds it simple to confute his old school friend's naïve faith in the utility of certain subjects: a schoolmaster must teach the boy not the job. But he admits that, while the scholarly boy is as well taught as anywhere, the majority of the boys do not work hard enough and are bored by their work; and he adds that if the schools do not raise their standards they will deserve to be taken over by the State.

In 1923 Roxburgh was a new kind of personality among public school headmasters. Headmasters were then pontifical, towering, be-gowned figures, who protested their other-worldliness, composed hymns, were still often in Holy Orders and on their way to a bishopric or deanery. Or they were excellent linguistic scholars who could write witty parodies and were noted for their brisk discipline and powers of organisation. They did not willingly

[1] Roxburgh, *op. cit.*, p. 22.   [2] *ibid.*, p. 9.

admit that anything was wrong with the schools other than what was already being beneficially changed. Roxburgh struck a different note. He told the public schools that the average boy was learning too little and idling too much; that they neglected the visual arts and literature; and that the aesthete and the athlete should be taught to respect each other. He was also ostentatiously welcoming to those parents whom he regarded as having a right to consult the headmaster about their sons' progress. He was too cautious and adroit to make a great issue of such matters — in every pronouncement he proclaimed his belief in the public school system. He knew that the last way to influence the Establishment is to print manifestoes and statements of general principle. Unlike Coade of Bryanston or Kurt Hahn of Gordonstoun, he had no explicit educational philosophy. To follow his career, therefore, is not to study the translation of such an educational philosophy into action. It is to watch a matchless showman creating a school through the exercise of his personality, which was strung to its highest pitch in the art of teaching and influencing boys.

Ancient foundations shun publicity: the new must court it. From the day that he was appointed Roxburgh knew that he not only had to organise the undertaking but to project Stowe before the public eye. The school had to commend itself to parents and prep school headmasters before it could possibly establish a reputation. There was only one person who could do this and that was himself, and for the first year he dictated forty letters a day and wrote another dozen in his own hand. He had got a prospectus out a fortnight after his appointment; established an office at 74 Eccleston Square; and persuaded the Council, on 21 December 1922, to lay plans to open two houses at Stowe in the following spring. He was clever in knowing how to strike the right note in his first public appearances. At a dinner in March he informed the headmasters of Charterhouse and Westminster who were present that 'their schools would never beat Stowe at football — unless they changed over to rugger', and declared that the school was 'not going to be a little Charterhouse or a little Lancing: it was going to be a little Stowe and very shortly it was going to be

a big Stowe'.[1] He spoke again six weeks later at the Mansion
House in aid of an unsuccessful attempt to raise an endowment.
Soon Imperial statesmen attending a conference in London were
planting oaks in the grounds, the first of a stream of visits by
public figures which culminated in 1927 with that of Queen Mary
to lay the foundation stone of the Chapel. Roxburgh was a master
of discreet publicity. He used many arts in order to impress: he
took care to furnish sumptuously both his own study and the
Gothic Library where parents were to wait for him. He saw to it,
for instance, that the flowers in the garden outside his study
window were in full bloom on the day that the school opened.
Many hours were devoted to showing prospective parents and
visitors the beauties of Stowe. 'As we walked through the spacious
corridors,' recalled his old friend R. F. Roxburgh, 'J.F. would
turn on all the lights to point out to me their magnificence, while
the Bursar following closely behind us, turned them off. This
procedure, J.F. commented, illumined their respective functions.'

During the first months of 1923 Roxburgh continued to work
indefatigably. At a Council meeting in mid-January grants were
allocated for certain purposes: £2,000 for teaching staff, £200 for a
Dame and a sum for Roxburgh himself — though he was puzzled
to find himself still paying out sums from his own personal funds
at the end of the month. A Bursar was appointed in February; the
Chaplaincy was considered in March, though no appointment was
made until a month or so after the school had opened. There were
several speculative ideas in the air then that did not materialise.
One was that the Great Central Railway would build a branch line
from Buckingham to the school: to the relief of the railway chiefs
who, forty years later, closed the desolate station of Buckingham
this did not materialise. Another, mooted by L. S. Amery at the
Mansion House dinner, was that Stowe should become an Empire
school, and scholarships endowed to enable boys to proceed from
Stowe to Empire universities — but the funds were never forth-
coming. Before the school had opened Roxburgh had five hundred entries covering every term but two up to 1934; and he
stressed at that dinner that his educational policy 'would be
guided by two convictions — the one that respect for the individual was the first duty of the teacher; and the other, that it was

[1] Croom-Johnson, *op. cit.*, p. 26.

not what one did to a boy that counted, but what he could do for himself'.

The school opened on 11 May 1923 with ten assistant masters and ninety-nine boys. The boys were photographed by the press shaking hands with their headmaster whom *The Queen* described as 'the Rev. J. F. Roxburgh' — an indication of what a head-master was still expected to be. He did not resemble a clergyman as he stood there slim and smiling, with irreproachably creased trousers, light grey trilby hat, black shoes and spats. He had chosen for the school a comfortable but *comme il faut* uniform remote from the funeral-black suits and grotesque hats of the older schools. The boys wore grey suits on week-days and blue on Sundays and from the first he insisted that tidiness could go with comfort as a part of good manners. The fashionable, cheerful and scrupulously polite figure, devoid of pomposity, was to appear to new boys as quite unlike the conventional picture of an elderly unapproachable headmaster who in those days was a reality.

In the afternoon of my first day, a cold January day, I was standing in the North Hall, doing nothing, when a man walking through saw me, stopped, put both hands on my shoulders, and said, 'Good after-noon! What's your name?' I said, 'Dulley.' I didn't call him 'Sir' because, while he was obviously important, he didn't seem to be one of the masters. He replied, 'Ah, yes, *David* Dulley,' in a rich, pleased, businesslike voice that suggested that I was the most distinguished member of a distinguished family, and that now I had arrived the school could really get going. Of course this was the standard greeting to new boys but our conversation left a glow which warmed not only the rest of that cold afternoon but in a sense the whole of my life at Stowe.

It was a standard greeting and it was all the more remarkable for that. As generation of boys succeeded generation he knew their Christian names and seemed to find an opportunity of greeting them casually during their first few days in the school. One of the early Stoics within a day of arrival was addressed by his Christian name and J.F. asked after his father who had been ill; another, scuttling downstairs in his first fortnight, cannoned into his headmaster and heard him say: 'Dangerous fellah, Jock'; another who had met him at his prep school for ten minutes the term before he entered Stowe encountered him in the darkest part of the passage outside the headmaster's study and was greeted, 'Hullo, Michael — it *is* Michael, isn't it?' J.F. would even be able to perform this feat when he visited prep schools and was introduced, for instance, to 'young Bruce a future Stoic'. 'Commonly known as Nigs,' he replied. Perhaps understandably some critics regarded this as a knack, a slick piece of public relations work, but his boys did not so regard it. They were convinced that it was the visible sign of a personal interest in each of them. 'I remember when I had been at Stowe for only a few days I happened to meet J.F. somewhere about the school,' one of them recalled. 'He addressed me not merely by my Christian name but by the diminutive form of it which was always used at home. There was not the slightest hesitation in his doing this. He already *knew who I was* . . .' Boys who had been taught to regard themselves as anonymous objects, boys from severe Victorian prep schools, boys in their first days of bewilderment and apprehension at school, were greeted by their first names and diminutives; and years later, after they had left, that prodigious memory would still produce their Christian names without hesitation. What was more he knew their birthdays and wished them many happy returns. It did not matter whether or not they were important; a small boy would be stopped and congratulated and sent away beaming. 'My dear Douglas,' he said to one on his fourteenth birthday, 'many happy returns of the day! — you don't look a day older.' He was of course proud of this feat and referred to it as a trick, but he was able to perform it only because he knew the history of each individual and because it was sustained by a genuine emotion — pity for the desolation of small new boys who are landed in a strange unheeding place.

This intimate knowledge and treatment of boys by a headmaster was something new, and when it continued for generation after generation it became unique. To compare their headmaster's knowledge of boys, as Stoics did, with that of other headmasters was hardly fair as in this respect a man who starts a school has a clear advantage; but the comparison was made and Stowe soon gained the reputation of being a school where the headmaster knew all the boys. No headmaster of a leading school at that time pretended to such knowledge: they delegated the task to housemasters. His tone of voice was also new. To-day we are accustomed to far greater equality of treatment between age-groups, and a headmaster may well address a thirteen-year-old by his first name. It was not so then. Roxburgh treated his senior boys with great solicitude. He at once instituted Prefects' dinners, to which a number were invited each time, held at his own table with admirable glass and silver. Wine was always served and followed by a cigarette. ('He gave me,' a prefect of a later generation recalls, 'my first glass of port and my last Egyptian cigarette.') Over the coffee, when all prefects assembled, school affairs were discussed; but at dinner 'J.F. would pick up a glass and say, "This is rather pleasant, I think; I had this set made for me in Venice. Have you ever seen glass blown?" Nobody had, of course; so he would then give us a lecture on the blowing of glass, leading it on to stained glass, and tell us about Chartres cathedral.' He treated all boys as adults and, determined that the junior forms should appreciate that they were no longer prep schoolboys, would seek their help in translating from Latin or French into English receiving, as one of them put it, 'their inaccurate if well meant suggestions with the courteous consideration he would have given to one from an Oxford don'. He was anxious to bring some dignity into school relationships. He always spoke of 'members of the school' and never referred to them as boys: it was a hint that differences between masters and their pupils should be minimised. He also tried to convey to boys that each had his own dignity and that they ought so to regard each other. 'It was clear from the earliest days at Stowe,' wrote a notable footballer, 'that it was no odder to write poetry or paint pictures than to box or play rugger.'

Giving boys leisure was an essential part of his plan to help them grow up.[1] Not only did he start fencing, golf and tennis for boys who were no good at team games, he refused to lay down bounds so that they were free to roam beyond the grounds to the

[1] He gave great offence in the 'thirties when as guest of honour on Speech Day at a famous girls' school he deplored the way in which adolescents were regimented from sunrise to bed-time and were unable to amuse themselves at anything which did not fall within the school programme. There was a roar of applause from the girls, scant clapping from the platform and the headmistress's face was a study in fury and indignation. The headmistress, a dedicated and capable soul, who kept her school alive during the war when it was requisitioned for military purposes, was typical of the generation in that profession who were outraged by Roxburgh's methods.

Ridings or to ride for miles on bicycles. He saw to it that there were times when nothing was planned. Schoolmasters frequently find that it is difficult to educate for use of leisure without removing it in the process: some boys will be bored from idleness and through boredom get into trouble. That was a risk Roxburgh was prepared to take. An Old Stoic schoolmaster after long service in three public schools commented that 'not one of my headmasters had begun to understand what education meant in the sense that J.F. interpreted and implemented the process', and that two of them 'regarded leisure as a dangerous waste of time from which boys must be safeguarded'. Similarly he kept fagging (which he attempted to disguise by terming it 'officing') under control 'enough', as he put it to the headmaster of Canford, a sister school founded within four days of Stowe, 'to keep things tidy in the boy's own quarters . . . Too much personal service, though good for the boy who gives it, is sometimes bad for the boy who receives it.' Although he wrote that he was revolted by the notion that a small boy might be beaten for an alleged deficiency in personal service, and although fagging was always to be light in comparison with other schools, he wrongly allowed it to be extended later. Gradually school rules were evolved, and when later they came to be tabulated and published Roxburgh wrote in a characteristic preface that 'they all deal with things which in themselves do not matter much, because things which matter cannot be dealt with by rules'. He added that 'good order, though easily secured by force, is better when it results naturally from the good sense and good feeling of everybody'. He varied his methods of securing order and respect to the age of the boy concerned: and he sharply distinguished between enjoying a liberty and taking it. One boy, who caught his headmaster vaulting over his garden wall, exclaimed, 'You must have got that Kruschen feeling.' J.F. looked at him quizzically. 'Meet me in my study in five minutes.' He arrived. 'Down that,' said Roxburgh — and handed him a glass of Kruschen salts.

The first term was a family party. Stowe was hardly more than a glorified prep school: five senior boys (four from Lancing) had been hand-picked to start the school but most of the ninety-nine were barely fourteen or under, and although some were to win scholarships and first classes at the university, others had scraped

Common Entrance or failed it elsewhere. 'I doubt,' one of the first members of the staff wrote cheerfully, 'if any public school has ever contained a Form of less promising mental equipment than the first form III at Stowe.' The geography syllabus had to be scrapped as being too hard. As J.F. put it in answer to an enquiry — with an economy of explanation characteristic of headmasters — the standard of entry was to be the Common Entrance 'possibly with a small modification which will assist me in my endeavour to secure boys from good homes and good schools, rather than clever ones at the start'.

He wanted boys from good families very badly indeed. So did every public school. The reputation of a public school depended not on its academic record or its exploits at games or its antiquity, or on the distinction of its alumni. Although all these carried some weight, it was ranked primarily by the class of boys that it attracted, and in the nineteen-twenties class was still measured by Edwardian standards. Every school wanted to attract the sons of the aristocracy and gentry, of regular army officers, the upper clergy, lawyers, diplomats and the older professions and of well connected City bankers and company directors, because, so ran the theory, these boys coming from homes where there was a tradition of upper-class behaviour would act as a regulator towards those who came from the shiftless cocktail belt of the Home Counties or those whose parents were on the way up. Roxburgh had an exact estimate of the importance that his countrymen attached to rank and breeding. To watch him with a countess was a' marvel: there was no hint of obsequiousness but he somehow managed to convey that, while to talk on terms other than those of equality would be odious, there was a subtle difference between her and the humanity round and about. The County do not normally have much in common with schoolmasters but J.F. was welcomed at the houses of the leading families around Buckingham and in the holidays liked to dine out. He declined, however, to assist the mayoress in the slicing of an ox or to propose the toast of Fox Hunting at a local farmers' dinner — though he saw to it that the Grafton began again to meet at Stowe. He had no difficulty, of course, in persuading liberal-minded parents who were looking for something different from the old public school régime, and part of his success was due to the fact that his friends backed him and sent him their sons; but he knew that if Stowe was not to be just another school, it was imperative to win the reputation of one that educated some upper-class boys.

He wanted clever boys too. Any school in the front rank had to gain a number of open awards at Oxford and Cambridge. If Stowe did not soon do so it would be treated as a dumping ground by the prep schools for amiable but thick-skulled boys, and the scholars would continue to be the preserve of schools such as Rugby and Shrewsbury. He made quick progress: the first Stowe entrance scholars who were later to gain University awards came in 1925. All his early addresses and pronouncements to the school emphasised the need for work and for modesty. The character of the school, its loveliness, its history, he would say, were all inherited wealth, not earned; they could not take credit even for their youth. It might seem pardonable now to do less than one might at work or games; but if they thought of the welfare of the place and not of themselves there would never be a time when it was more important to set standards. He was always anxious to raise the quality of the entries but from the start there was no doubt that he would get an adequate number. Before the first term was out he could announce sixty applications for entry in a single week and before the school had been in existence a year there were more than a thousand names on the books. These numbers gave him more than elbow room to pick and choose. In 1926 on Speech Day he announced with satisfaction that sixty boys had been ploughed that term in Common Entrance, which he hoped would kill 'the popular belief that any boy could get into Stowe'.

He had not only to charm parents: he had also to persuade staff to join him — staff who would reflect the tone of the school and translate his ideals into action; and perhaps among all his early successes none was so subtle as the variety of talent that he induced to work with him. His first four housemasters were all different. Ivor Cross, who had been under him at Lancing before the war, was a Liberal in politics and a supporter of the League of Nations, which boys were then apt to regard as vaguely anti-patriotic; he taught not only modern history but politics and government. Ernest Earle had been headmaster of the prep school Bilton Grange and there had experience of teaching small boys. He resembled a Victorian squarson, for though in Orders he liked to hunt and would hack round the park with boys on half-holidays. His kindliness and sense of the comical reassured parents and pleased boys who exploited it. The next two house-masters were Ian Clarke, a rugger Blue who came of a Scots academic family and had been three times wounded in the war, an all-round schoolmaster with natural authority, common sense and dependability; and Major Richard Haworth, a regular soldier with the D.S.O., then a senior instructor at Sandhurst. Haworth was a gentleman of the old school and the reverse of a martinet — his house was not noted for meticulous discipline; but his courtesy and friendliness, though of another vintage from those of J.F., inspired a remarkable personal loyalty and he attracted to his house the kind of boy who was going into the army or to farm an estate. Three of the first masters were later to enter the Board of Education: Philip Browne, a man of first-class intellect and a gifted musician; Francis Arnold, who taught English and soon took on a house; and Douglas Simmonds, classical scholar and boxing Blue.

As the first generation of boys grew up Roxburgh began to organise his Upper School. He divided it into Sides in which boys, once past the School Certificate stage (i.e. roughly equivalent to the present O Levels), would specialise in the normal university scholarship subjects; but he split the Natural Sciences into two because he wanted to emphasise biology and provide courses for incipient doctors to pass the first and second parts of the First M.B. The essence of these 'sides' was that a boy remained under the tutelage of one man for the rest of his school career and was given a tutorial each week in addition to classes. He was also given a number of periods of unsupervised work in his own study on the principle that the pupil's only lasting knowledge is what he learns for himself and in the hope that on going up to the university he would already be accustomed to study on his own. Such periods, which were additional to prep, might amount to as much as one or two fifths of the total number of periods. The only form in the Upper School with any existence was the small Sixth Form which met on Sunday evenings in Roxburgh's study: the Middle and Lower Sixth and the Upper Fifths never met and were merely groupings according to age and status. There were no marks or form order in the Upper School. Little, if anything, in this was wholly new but the sum total went well beyond what was usual in schools at the time. The plan was characteristic of Roxburgh's trust in a boy's natural goodwill and sense of responsibility, provided that his Tutor worked to win an equal trust and respect from him. Not only did it give the clever boy freedom to work for the university scholarships: the average boy also had time to cultivate his mind, read some literature and become acquainted with the arts and politics. Roxburgh understood that the two freedoms were inter-related. The schools most successful, he noted, 'in turning out boys with active minds . . . are just the schools which have the highest standards academically'. Even so, 'the real test of a school's efficiency is not the number of scholarships it gains but the training it gives the ordinary boy': the average boy needs the stimulus of the scholarly boy and also 'as much association as possible with high-minded and highly educated adults'.

Could he find such adults to be Tutors? He certainly found some. Among the scientists he interviewed was a thickset, serious intellectual who ignored most of his questions and gave the wrong answers to the others. Roxburgh appointed him: he seemed to him to have intellectual energy. This was Hugh Heckstall-Smith whose recreation was Socratic discussion and who troubled housemasters when his circle continued to grope towards unsettling and awkward conclusions long after they were meant to be in bed. In those days the gramophone companies were in the early stages of recording the repertoire of classical music, and on Tuesday evenings Heckstall-Smith would hold gramophone recitals of symphonies and concertos. In the long summer term he would play through *The Ring* reading extracts from Shaw's *The Perfect Wagnerite*.[1] Roxburgh needed men who would give intellectual life to the place; and he was perhaps luckier than he knew in having a scientist as his leading intellectual. Heckstall-Smith's lectures on atomic structure fascinated even the innumerate and the state of his room introduced boys to the idea that the life of the intellect could not be circumscribed by tidiness and convention. Books sat in piles on the floor, symphonic themes were chalked above the fireplace, and at one stage a boat was built in it. J.F. once surveyed the carnage awe-struck. 'What superb disarray!' he murmured, and

[1] His book *Doubtful Schoolmaster* (London, 1963) contains a picture of Stowe in its early days.

recoiled. The tutor of the history side was a contrast. Martin Mac-Laughlin was a prima donna given to dramatising issues, a stimulator who kept the temperature high in his forcing house. He grasped what Roxburgh had in mind from the start and Roxburgh, who was bold to pick him, nursed him sympathetically: he ran the Debating Society, founded the Twelve Club, doyen among school intellectual societies, and made Stowe into the best school for fencing in the country by persuading boys who did not shine at team games to take up this elegant exercise. English was at first organised on a different footing. The English tutor might have one or two pupils attached to him but he was universal Tutor to the Upper School; and Charles Spencer, who was teaching the subject throughout the school, aimed to carry this out by setting and personally dissecting two major essays for every Upper School boy each term. This heroic undertaking foundered as the number in the Upper School passed the hundred mark, but Spencer's delight in paradox jabbed into activity minds which otherwise might not have stirred. He was to produce the most spectacular of all Stowe's open air productions when in 1931 he staged *Comus* in front of the Temple of British Worthies, the audience seated on the far side of the lake, the orchestra moored on punts. To prepare the school he requested that every form in the school should be taken through the masque; he viva-ed them all personally; declared himself appalled at their lack of comprehension of the nature of poetry; set them tasks and examined them all. The task he set consisted of being able to supply the missing word in any line of the text. He would quote: 'Thus I hurl My —— Spells into the —— ayr, Of power to —— the eye with —— illusion'; the form were expected to supply the highly poetic words, *dazling*, *spungy*, *cheat*, *blear*. After several whirlwind visitations by Spencer one aspect of the nature of poetry dawned upon them; the school hummed to the sound of boys testing each other's memory; and the method became a recognised way of learning the Shakespeare play or the Chaucer text for the School Certificate. This was the kind of teaching that Roxburgh encouraged whatever havoc it played with the timetable.

There never was a system which more patently revealed the defects of its merits. It had an interesting advantage from the point of view of the teaching profession: it made tutoring an alternative

career to housemastering and catered for the fact that there exist
two types of masters of high excellence, which in some other
schools had been denied either to the exclusion of the intellectual
schoolmaster or by appointing to houses men who were more
suitable as sixth-form masters. But at the same time conflicts were
bound to arise between tutors and housemasters both of whom
had responsibility for the same boys. Where personal knowledge
and contact were thought so important there could be no clear-
cut division between the tutor's guidance of the boy's mind and
the housemaster's guidance of his moral development. Roxburgh's scheme depended on tutors and pupils combining tolerance and liveliness with his own Scots sense of purpose and
industry. Others found it hard to develop his complementary
virtues. Sometimes housemasters and tutors supplemented each
other admirably; at other times the imagination of an unconventional tutor collided with the conscience of a dutiful housemaster.
Then, again, as the numbers of the Upper School rose to exceed
200 at the beginning of the school year, the tutor was overwhelmed by his task. He could not give individual attention to so
many pupils and the non-academic boy suffered. In most houses
studies were shared and for such a boy a study period was apt to
denote a place rather than an activity. It is notoriously hard to
provide for the non-academic boy whose programme cannot be
extended to subjects he cannot master, and he is therefore likely to
have more time in which to do less. But in favourable conditions
the scheme worked well at least up to and into the Second World
War period: it served the needs of the 'twenties and 'thirties
before Advanced Level passes became an invariable condition
of university entry.

If it was the tutors' job to watch the progress of their Upper
School charges, Roxburgh himself kept a check on the younger
boys. He would 'read over' the form order of the Lower School
every week and of the Middle School every fortnight. He stood in
the centre of the Marble Saloon, by this time known as Assembly,
the form master beside him, the boys ranged along the southern
wall, each boy coming forward to stand in line as his name was
read out, while J.F. praised good work, pointed out weak subjects and urged those at the bottom to improve their performance.
It was another way of getting to know and keeping watch over

every individual. The Stowe end-of-term reports also reflected his purpose. Consisting of a series of slips of paper (one for each subject) within a folder, they were a good deal more substantial than had been usual at most schools and came to be widely copied. Some of the housemasters followed Roxburgh's practice at Lancing and wrote personal letters to parents; Roxburgh himself went through all the slips before adding his own report, which was never soapy and often told parents unwelcome truths in a kindly way.

At the end of the first term Warrington had written: 'It is an outstanding achievement on your part and I congratulate you and thank you for what you have done for Stowe.' In September 1923, 208 boys arrived for what Roxburgh called the Last First Term; from then on his powers of organisation and improvisation were to be tested. The school was expanding at a sensational rate. The numbers rose in the second year to 342, in the third year to 420 and to just under 500 by 1930. A sanatorium, new class-rooms and dormitories were begun; the two new houses in the central block were opened; and a year later the foundations of a seventh house, which was to be free-standing, were laid. A gymnasium, which as the numbers grew was used temporarily as a Chapel, came into use, and a large area on the outskirts of the park at the end of the Grecian Valley was scheduled to be levelled for playing fields. It was characteristic of Roxburgh's flair for the up-to-date to realise that games of individual skill were going to become as important as team games. He encouraged the laying-out of a golf course and tennis courts. There were inevitable delays, but, apart from some financial anxieties and an occasional protest over some item from the Governors, Roxburgh's requests were met. In November 1924 a loan had to be raised from the Norwich Union which was opposed by one of the bishops on the Council and by Arthur Burroughs, but Warrington negotiated the matter successfully. The whole expensive capital equipment of a modern school was in fact being provided at break-neck speed. It was not as if the historic house had been lavishly equipped. The sales of 1834 and 1848 by the first two Dukes of Buckingham had stripped Stowe of its treasures, the sale of 1921 stripped it of its essentials.

There was but one fitted bathroom; there was also a gloomy tank that had once been the Duke's swimming bath; and no adequate water supply existed. The modernisation and restoration of the mansion came first; the new buildings second; the conversion of other buildings such as the Gothic Temple into the armoury for the O.T.C. was a parallel priority; and accommodation of every variety was needed — some of it was improvised, like the railway carriage that J.F. himself bought for the wireless club. The masters endured discomfort for years: indeed two masters of the original company preferred to take sleeping bags and, with a hurricane lamp to guide them, seek the shelter of the more isolated temples.[1] Not until 1930 was it possible for bachelor masters in the Power House Yard rooms to get a hot bath at bed-time or in the morning; and it says a great deal for their loyalty and Roxburgh's magnetism that many of them stayed. Stowe was soon faced with a staffing problem: there was no accommodation at the school for married men. Masters who abandoned celibacy had no alternative but to leave because marriage debarred promotion to a House, and in consequence some of the best departed. After the school had been running for two years only one man in a staff of thirty was married and even by 1937 two-thirds of the staff were still bachelors. Not that J.F. complained. Bachelors are bound to give more in time and energy to a school than men with families; the average age of the staff remained low and so hence did the bill for salaries; and he had no time to entertain wives still less any desire to be entangled in their problems. He had enough domestic troubles on his hands as it was. It was long before a bursar could be found adequate to the post. The first, as if in acknowledgment that the task was herculean, gave up after a short trial and joined a religious community. Roxburgh brightened when one of the applicants for the post was said to be an Old Shrewsbury boy; but it turned out that although the description was accurate he was not an Old Salopian. Neither Roxburgh nor Warrington approved of the man who was appointed and who was soon being attacked by Warrington for 'low habits' and 'pub-trotting'. Nor could he get a competent lady to supervise the domestic staff. In 1929 he was offering a payment of £100 from his own stipend supplementary

[1] P. A. Browne, 'Random Recollections of the First Term', *The Stoic*, No. 46, July 1938, p. 195.

to such a woman's salary and saying, 'the right sort of woman would save me so much friction and trouble that she would be worth quite a lot of money to me by merely keeping domestic problems away from me!'

The school's health caused him concern. During the first winter an influenza epidemic had brought a disproportionate number of cases of pneumonia. Pneumonia appeared later on several occasions when, for instance, there was an epidemic of measles. In 1927 there were fifteen cases. The new sanatorium was badly ventilated, inefficiently heated and, in a crisis, too small. A Ministry of Health official visited the school and improvements were made, not least in replanning the disgraceful quarters of the resident waiters and maids. But there was more than a suspicion that some of the outbreaks were due to over-crowding. The Governors were in a dilemma. In order to raise loans to provide for the capital cost of the vast building operations they had to raise the income of the current account. This could be done only by raising fees or by increasing numbers. Fees were as high as a new school could charge, but increased numbers meant more buildings. Yet if the school did not grow quickly it would lose whatever chance it had of being ranked among the leading schools. Prudence suggested that the build-up should be slow, sedate and phased; but Roxburgh's common sense told him that much of the capital equipment, such as a sanatorium or a gymnasium, would be required whatever the size of the school and that the cost would not be materially decreased by building them to suit a school of 200 as opposed to a school of 500. He was confident from the entry list that the indebtedness which the school was incurring was not in itself serious. He also had confidence in Warrington's apparent ability to obtain capital loans to finance the rapid expansion. Nor, although Warrington was continually sniping on small points of expenditure, did he dissent from Roxburgh's views; and Roxburgh wrote to him, 'You are such a magician in these matters that I do not worry perhaps as much as I should when you tell me things are temporarily difficult.'

During the first decade, as we shall see, Roxburgh became ever more worried about the government and finances of the school. But among his consolations was the support that Stowe received from his friends. One of them paid for three squash courts, another parent contributed to the cost of the gymnasium; gifts and small endowments for prizes were showered on the school. The pace had been set in 1924 by a signal example of Etonian generosity. The Governors had been unable to find funds to buy the Grand Avenue, which runs the two miles from the Lodge gates on the outskirts of Buckingham to the Corinthian Arch, and in order to save it from speculative builders, the school architect, Clough Williams-Ellis, in a singularly imaginative action, had temporarily bought it. Then an anonymous Etonian wrote privately to the Vice-Provost asking if Eton could not help this new school at the other end of Buckinghamshire and enclosed a cheque: whereupon the Vice-Provost, Hugh Macnaghten, appealed through *The Times* to Old Etonians and their kinsmen for funds to present the Avenue to Stowe; Queen Mary and Prince Henry contributed; Prince Arthur of Connaught presented it, unveiling an inscription of exquisite Latinity by Macnaghten recording the gift. 'Eton has taken us on trust,' said Roxburgh, 'and that means more to us than it is at all easy to say'; and he gently added a little polish to the simple letter of thanks that the Head of the School wrote to *The Times*. But the boldest enterprise was yet to come. On the school's first Speech Day in 1925 (when Lord Lincolnshire was to describe Stowe as 'the best two-year-old in the country') Roxburgh had announced that a Chapel Building Fund had been opened by a parent's gift of fifty guineas, and a year later another parent offered £5,000 on condition that the Chapel was in use in three years. A committee consisting of Roxburgh, three Governors and three parents made plans and in the end appointed Sir Robert Lorimer, architect of the Scottish National Memorial Chapel in Edinburgh, who already had a son at Stowe. In its finished form the Chapel was in keeping with the style of the ancient buildings. It incorporated columns from the Temple of Concord in the grounds and the cedar woodwork with which Lord Cobham had embellished his private chapel in the main building.[1] Boys, parents, governors, staff, old boys, friends all gave something, but the eventual cost exceeded by over a third the

[1] The woodwork had been bought by Cobham on the demolition of a seventeenth-century Stowe house in Cornwall. Singularly enough the sober edifice of Vanbrugh's Temple of Bacchus had to be demolished to build the Chapel.

original large-minded estimate and came to well over £60,000 — far more than had been subscribed. The school's indebtedness had been severely increased: but Roxburgh was still confident that his vision in planning a rich and spacious Chapel would be justified by future events. The profits on current account and the size of the entry list suggested that Stowe was entitled to plan in terms of such magnificence. He was involved in every detail of the planning — the wrought-iron screen, the cartouches and armorials on the stalls, the design of the alms dish. He had to obtain donors for the stalls and consult their wishes over their armorials ('I would rather have a little correspondence beforehand than much indignation afterwards'). He also wrote to ask Prince George to be present and to read the Lesson when the Chapel was opened on 11 July 1929. When all was over Lorimer wrote to thank and congratulate him, adding a curious sentence: 'I heard several of your Governors inveighing against your lovely flowers on the Communion Table — I could only say to myself, poor blighters!'

Why should some Governors blame Roxburgh for putting flowers on the Communion Table? And why did Lorimer not call it an altar? Why did Roxburgh write to Lorimer, 'I do hope you won't use the phrase "the design as approved by you" in any communication with the Governors. I have no right to approve anything, and the Governors do not fail to remind me of the fact at intervals. Will you remember to tell M. Williams that Haloes are considered Papistical? If they are to be shown at all they will have to be very faintly indicated, and little should be seen of them in the preliminary drawing.' Why indeed did Lord Davidson, the former Archbishop of Canterbury, decline the invitation to dedicate the Chapel? These and more critical matters will become clearer when we examine what was to be Roxburgh's greatest burden — a burden all the more galling since it should have been his greatest support — his first governing body.

Chapter V

Roxburgh and Warrington

The chairman of the first Council to govern Stowe was Lord Gisborough. But Gisborough was a figurehead — his talents did not permit him to be anything else. The prime mover was the Reverend Percy Warrington, vicar of Monkton Combe near Bath, whom journalists were later to call 'the financier in the surplice'. Stowe was not the first school he had bought. In 1922 he met Mr (later Sir) John Bayley[1] and purchased from him a school in Wellington, Shropshire, which he renamed Wrekin College. Wrekin College Company immediately entered upon a contract to purchase Stowe House with Wrekin College as guarantor and security. No sooner was this done than the Company bought Canford, Lord Wimborne's home in Dorset, Wrekin and Stowe

---

[1] Sir John Bayley, Headmaster of Wellington (later Wrekin) College 1880–1920, Vice-President of British and Foreign Schools Society.

now guaranteeing the new foundation. Fourteen schools, or properties which were turned into schools, were eventually brought into the group: each school guaranteed the others and was itself guaranteed by each of them in regard to mortgages, debentures and bank securities. Warrington bought them for a purpose. He was the mainspring of an Evangelical group known as the Martyrs Memorial and Church of England Trust whose purpose was to buy up advowsons and to take over or found schools in order to propagate Protestant principles and combat the spread of Anglo-Catholicism.

The Evangelical party in the Church of England (as distinct from the Evangelical movement) long before the beginning of this century was notorious for its virulence and bigotry. The greatest of all Victorian Evangelical laymen, the great Tory reformer, Lord Shaftesbury, had said 'I have received from the hands of the [Evangelical] party treatment that I have not received from any other. High Churchmen, Roman Catholics, even infidels have been friendly to me; my only enemies have been the Evangelicals.' [1] They had not changed with the years. In mitigation it can be said that they had had to watch the introduction into the service of the Church of ceremonies and rituals which were certainly not in normal usage when Victoria came to the throne. They were baffled in their efforts to stop the innovations. If they prosecuted ritualistic priests they incurred contempt as persecutors; and even when they won, the ecclesiastical courts grew less rather than more willing to act. There were, however, still quite a number of elderly lay-men in the Church who were willing to contribute to the battle against 'lace and smells' (vestments and incense), and Warrington had appreciable financial as well as moral support, though totally inadequate for the final scope of his enterprise. He was also secre-tive to the point of duplicity. Roxburgh had not been informed, when he applied for the headmastership, of the religious bias of the Council. Had he been, he might, as a master at the best known of the Woodard foundations, have hesitated even though he was not in sympathy with its Anglo-Catholicism. For the first two years when Montauban and Field-Marshal Sir William Robertson were members this was not much in evidence, but as the schools in the

[1] G. W. E. Russell, *A Short History of the Evangelical Movement* (London, 1915), p. 124.

group multiplied the Council which dealt with them all came more and more to be dominated by militant Protestants. In the very first term there had been correspondence in the Press which disturbed Roxburgh and in 1924 he was compelled by the Council to refuse the offer of a Cross for what is indubitably called in the Book of Common Prayer the Lord's Table. The Council clearly had reserved the right to have a hand in the appointment of the chaplain, but it was another matter when they demanded one master's resignation on the grounds that he was a Roman Catholic and questioned the religious status of another; it was also embarrassing when the sister in charge of the sanatorium was alleged to be extravagant and met the objection by protesting that it was not her expenditure but her possession of a crucifix that was in dispute. The activities of the Protestant Trusts did not go unnoticed outside Stowe. In the months after the Chapel was opened a Brighton clergyman drew attention to them in *The Church Times*: Warrington countered in *The Record*, an Evangelical organ with a long history of intemperate partisanship, with allegations of Anglo-Catholic plots relative to the chaplaincies of schools. A quarrel of astonishing venom then arose in the ecclesiastical press — one of Warrington's letters ran to seven columns — the name of Stowe was often mentioned and Warrington was styled its Founder.

For these and other reasons Roxburgh in 1929 was contemplating resignation. He was saved from it by his friends. Cyril Norwood advised him on his rights as a headmaster; and Cosmo Lang, Archbishop of Canterbury, who had confirmed him when he was at Lancing, had as a former Scots Presbyterian himself some fellow feeling for Roxburgh's spiritual position and gave his ecclesiastical support. So did his friends among the Governors: Burroughs, the sweet-tempered, moderate Evangelical Bishop of Ripon; and Pickard-Cambridge who had inspected the school on two occasions and was the only Governor expert in educational matters.[1] The Archbishop and Norwood advised him to submit a memorandum to the Council which, while declaring that the

---

[1] Dr A. W. Pickard-Cambridge, Fellow of Balliol 1897–1929, Vice-Chancellor Sheffield University 1930–8, Chairman of the Stowe Governors 1934–50. He conducted inspections at Roxburgh's request on behalf of the Oxford and Cambridge Schools Examination Board.

Protestant nature of the school was not in question, expressed the view that Stowe could never stand in the front rank of the Public Schools if the impression were given that its foundation was 'primarily a move in a party contest' made by 'a militant section of a particular Church party'. After some drafting and counter-drafting Roxburgh won the day and was authorised to send a letter 'to parents and others as may seem (to the Headmaster) necessary' which made it clear that the purpose of the school was 'to produce men who shall be Christian in character and in faith, and not to propagate party views or to change the type of Christian belief in which any boy may have been brought up at home'.

He was revolted to the depths of his being by the whole affair. It was contrary to all that he believed was the essence of Christianity. Nor could he endure to associate with men who were such malevolent fanatics. 'I do not think,' he wrote to Pickard-Cambridge, 'that I can go on indefinitely serving under men whose bigotry and virulence make me ashamed whenever I come in contact with it.' 'All my instincts,' he told his old Cambridge tutor, then Vice-Master of Trinity, 'prompt me to cut adrift from people whose behaviour makes me ashamed, but if I withdraw from here after a quarrel with the Governors on such a subject the Housemasters will follow me (at least they vow they will) . . .' and that, he felt, would be unfair to parents and prospective parents. What depressed him was that the Council meetings had been marked on several occasions by squalid scenes between its members and denunciations of other clergy. In 1931 the abscess began to swell again. A group of parents revived the old request for a cross on the altar, canvassed their fellow-parents and reported to the Governors that out of 500 parents 400 were in favour. After two years of petitioning and wrangling in which Roxburgh was inevitably involved, the Governors adopted the compromise which he had often suggested, of placing a Crusader's sword behind the altar with the hilt showing above it. Compromises are unheroic, but by this time Roxburgh confessed in private that he was sick of the affair and wanted a cross because its absence marked Stowe down as a partisan school. Not until many years later were a cross and candlesticks placed in the Chapel.

But the religious question, wearing though it was, was intermittent. A much more exhausting problem was always with him: Warrington. Warrington was small and sleek with minute eyes that looked humourlessly out from behind gold-rimmed spectacles. He had boundless energy, iron determination and ran almost single-handed the network of schools which he brought one by one into his Trust. The Governors of a public school are responsible for authorising all major expenditure and for exercising general financial control; they may delegate to the Chairman, or to a Secretary working in conjunction with the Chairman, power to authorise routine expenditure and to take certain decisions in their name. But the powers that Warrington exercised were quite exceptional. Roxburgh found in the days immediately after his appointment, for instance, that side by side with his own letters a stream of orders and instructions was issuing from Warrington's parsonage at Monkton Combe, often causing confusion — at one moment it looked as if not only Clough Williams-Ellis but a rival firm of architects would provide plans for the kitchens. Letters from Warrington continued to pour in and it was obvious that he regarded himself as having the right to probe and control every detail of the school's administration. Clearly in the founding of three schools, Wrekin, Stowe and Canford, within a few months of each other a co-ordinator of exceptional acumen and drive was needed; but the tone of some of Warrington's communications was curious and although Roxburgh took no offence at their peremptory note, he soon realised that he was dealing with a man who regarded himself as the founder of the schools and expected his word to be law; and Roxburgh had to explain tactfully that some matters were the province of the headmaster alone.

There were further grounds for uneasiness. The Governors had promised him on appointment in December a sum in lieu of salary, but two months later he was still paying all expenses from his own pocket. When, in February, a polite request elicited only £59, he contemplated, but did not take, the drastic step of withdrawal. He used to say that, whenever he did so again, reason came to his aid and asked: 'What do you propose to do if you do *not* go on with the task you have undertaken?' From then on he operated as headmaster in conditions of financial uncertainty that were often humiliating: what is more he suffered in isolation and silence since loyalty to his Governors and concern for the reputation of the school forbad him to consult friends. A fortnight after the school opened Warrington had written: 'Don't worry about finance, that is quite all right.' Before two years were past Roxburgh was paying out of his own pocket part of the fees in one or two cases of need and providing equipment for the Fencing Club. He did not claim his car allowance, in order to rent and hence ultimately save for the school the approach to the North Front known as the Straight Course. Later Haworth had to pledge his own money to enable the cadet corps to remain in existence. Warrington's resourcefulness was worse than his parsimony. Roxburgh had to oppose suggestions that new parents should pay a year's fees in advance and that the fees of the boys in the new boarding house should be raised. The terms of the loan from the Norwich Union, which was secured on the masters' lives, were reasonable from the point of view of the insurance company but spelled as much future trouble for Stowe as they gave immediate advantage. So at the end of the second year Roxburgh felt bound to suggest that his own salary should be reduced. Hitherto this had consisted of a basic sum augmented by a capitation fee in order that the headmaster should participate in the school's success. His salary in the end was fixed at £2,500 — a substantial reduction on what he could have claimed — and he was still forced to draw upon it for school expenditure.

In one respect Warrington and Roxburgh thought alike. They thought big and planned for the distant future. 'We are building for posterity,' Warrington wrote to him in 1924, 'and I do not care for the policy of saving one or two thousand now.' But Roxburgh could not help noticing that Warrington did not seem to have the judgment to pursue this policy disinterestedly. He oscillated between sanctioning major schemes and making allegations of extravagance. The Dame was extravagant, the matrons were extravagant, the architect was a demon of improvident prodigality. He would admit that a bursar was inefficient but would then back him against the matrons. 'Economy is not the only thing to be considered,' he would write, and then quibble about the doctor's salary and question Roxburgh's urgent recommendations to disinfect certain quarters at a time when the health of the school was at issue. Roxburgh found that he was for ever being urged to take more boys than he could reasonably accommodate; and when he obtained promises that new buildings should be erected as a condition of the increase in numbers, the promises were not honoured. They were not honoured because Warrington was finding increasing difficulty in raising money and the rise in fee income was naturally insufficient to pay at once the capital cost of new buildings. In 1930, 155 vacancies had been promised for the following autumn whereas only sixty boys were due to leave before then. Warrington promised that a new house would be built, went back on his promise and then wildly suggested the use of Vancouver Lodge (a large master's house some distance from the school), the raising of a partition across the gymnasium to form a house-room, and a double-shift supper in the masters' dining-room, the boys eating first, the masters afterwards.

Roxburgh could expect no help from his Chairman. In the school's first term Gisborough had presided when Sir Owen Seaman had presented a thousand-year-old Samurai sword on behalf of the Agenda Club. The ceremony was held in the school library in the presence of the Governors and the boys, the masters being seated in the gallery which at that time was not known to be unsafe. Gisborough opened the proceedings with a vaguely improper story, paid a tribute to a master for his altruism in joining the staff (he later had to leave for being unable to keep order) and rose to his climax: 'I now have the greatest pleasure in introducing to you, Sir . . . Sir . . .' and had to turn to J.F. to ask Seaman's name. Other speeches by Gisborough on Speech Days were riotously embarrassing and put Roxburgh on the rack. Gisborough would add his own feeble imprecations to Warrington's stream of orders, counter-orders and complaints. They were not only degradingly petty, they invaded spheres that were the concern of the headmaster and his staff alone. The Governors pressed upon the school a school song written by the Bishop of Ripon, wrangled over the tune and required the boys to sing them the final version.[1]

---

[1] After a tactful interval the song was interred and never heard again as being contrary to J.F.'s notion that Stowe should dispense with the paraphernalia of the Old School tradition. There was no school 'language' and any attempt to foist 'traditions' upon a school that prided itself on being free from them was met with satire and contempt. Roxburgh did, however, pun deplorably in Latin on the school's name. The school motto was *Persto et*

They then forbad Roxburgh on temperance grounds to serve a stirrup-cup to the Grafton when it met on the North Front. When the Governors met at Stowe they would commandeer the head-master's dining-room for lunch where they would unpack their London hampers but never invite him to join them. Warrington met Roxburgh's concern for the school's health by requiring the boys to gargle daily and declared that throat troubles were due to excessive eating of sweets. In November 1927 he sensibly ordered bars to be placed across the windows of certain dormitories. The two housemasters concerned politely protested to the headmaster at being neither consulted nor informed. Roxburgh, who knew nothing of the matter, asked Warrington for enlightenment. Warrington complained of gross impertinence and demanded an apology. Roxburgh replied that the housemasters could not be blamed and that if blame fell on anyone it must be on himself, but Warrington had the last word: 'I repeat that no housemaster at any of the schools may with impunity presume to call any action of mine into question.' This outburst reminded Roxburgh of Warrington's indignation some time before when he claimed to have discovered compromising *graffiti* scribbled by boys upon a wall: examination revealed the record of a child's weight and height and a date: *dix-huit août 1893* — a relic of the childhood of the Duchesse de Guise who was brought up at Stowe during the exile of the Comte de Paris who died there in the following year. The courtesy and firmness with which Roxburgh answered the stream of letters was exemplary. He was tactful and conciliatory, but he never failed to defend his staff against Warrington's accusations and he would not toady to him when Warrington caustically detailed the failings of his fellow Governors.

The association between two such different men could not last. Roxburgh's mind was liberal, elastic and generous; Warrington's was taut, humourless and entirely unscrupulous. Warrington had opposed Roxburgh's appointment and when the final vote between him and another candidate took place Warrington as Sec-

---

Praesto (I stand fast and I stand first); roll call was termed Stance at which each boy as his name was called answered *Sto*; and as an expression of Roman virtue which he admired (as distinct from the Greek philosophy) he ordained that members of the school were to be called Stoics.

retary counted the votes and announced that the vote had gone against Roxburgh by five votes to seven. Field-Marshal Sir William Robertson gently pointed out that there were only eight Governors present. Warrington then admitted that he had added the votes of the four absentee members of the Governing body alleging that they had asked him, or given him leave, to do so. Gisborough declared this proceeding to be invalid and Roxburgh was appointed. To do Warrington justice, it should be said that he realised Roxburgh's worth from the start and did not intrigue against him: his letter of congratulation after the first term was warm and his sympathy when Roxburgh's mother suffered a series of heart attacks was decently expressed. It is also true that he was less bigoted than some of the Protestant fanatics on the Council and sometimes would intercede for Roxburgh's point of view: as well he might for his contempt for them knew no bounds and he regarded them as his creatures. He spoke not only of them but of all his colleagues in scathing terms, referring to the Bishop of Ripon as 'that conceited little prelate'. His conduct on the occasion of Roxburgh's appointment showed that he was prepared to treat them as so many proxy votes which he could use to achieve his will. He saw to it that on the central body set up to allocate resources between the schools there were few to contradict him.

By 1931 Roxburgh was again on the edge of resignation. 'I will go on trying a little longer, but I cannot go on indefinitely,' he wrote. A new row had blown up, Roxburgh pointing out that the appearance and even the cleanliness of the school buildings were not being maintained, Warrington responding that what was needed was not paint but soap and water vigorously applied by the matrons on their knees. But beyond such pettiness everything came back in Roxburgh's mind to finance. He felt that he must give his parents value for money and that it was unwise to instigate 'a régime of economy without efficiency . . . in a school which was among the four or five most expensive in the country'. He was distressed that his staff were so ill-paid. There had been some slight improvement on the initial basic salary of £200 for assistant masters and £80 for matrons a year (housemasters and tutors receiving a supplementary payment) and he had screwed a pension scheme out of the Governors. He also knew that a new house must be built for boys already accepted and he now acknowledged that accommodation must be provided so that housemasters could marry. Yet he was being told that this kind of capital expenditure could not be authorised. It was all the more puzzling because Roxburgh knew that Stowe had been making a handsome profit on current account for years. Warrington himself claimed that in 1932 it exceeded £35,000. With such profits debts could have been amortised rapidly. Four years earlier one or two Stowe parents had privately discussed with Roxburgh the possibility of Stowe being adopted and financed by a well-known City Corporation. In 1930 Roxburgh informed Warrington that there was a wish to explore this possibility in greater detail. Warrington did not demur; but the scheme never had a chance of success. Warrington and his colleagues would never have allowed Stowe, their most successful money-spinner, to be released from its cross-guarantees, and no financier in his senses would have assumed responsibility for the whole group. For the finances of the schools were in a state of almost inextricable confusion.

In later years when the history of Warrington's dealings was being pieced together the full scope of his undertaking came to light, although areas remained where the details were still obscure. If he was not as blindly bigoted as some of his intimate colleagues, he floated on the same clouds of delusion and fantasy as they did. They saw themselves as the spearhead of the Protestant defence against the insidious wiles of Rome and the even more treacherous machinations of the Anglo-Catholics. They would smite these Jebusites, they would unmask the dastardly conspiracy to pervert the youth of England, they would guard every entrance to their schools to prevent a Jesuit infiltration or a Puseyite insinuating himself into the confidence of their headmasters. The air they breathed was full of conspiracies and plots: they wrote letters to each other denouncing spies, pronouncing anathema and announcing the Day of Judgment to be at hand for their opponents. Warrington was also drunk with power. He boasted that he had bought Canford and Westonbirt without any resolution being passed by any council or company, and justified his conduct by saying that none of his colleagues would have had the nerve to do it. He bought school after school — one of them in Kenya — raising money initially by mortgaging each property, then by obtaining second mortgages and increasing the bank overdraft, and in the end, as matters grew more difficult, by private borrowing and bills of exchange. Some of the schools were at once a success; others faded at the time of the economic insecurity that led to the formation of the National government in 1931; a few were failures from the start and never paid their way. Some were large country houses which he converted into schools without estimating the capital cost of such an enterprise; but even when he had learnt something about the cost of equipping and maintaining a school he did not pause to weigh his liabilities, take stock of the situation and reconstruct his affairs.

It would be wrong to picture Warrington as a man of vision at work in the world of education, a narrow but sincere enthusiast who overreached himself through financial inexperience and was caught in the credit squeeze of the Depression. Even at the end when he was trying to get three months' extension of credit on some bills, he never contemplated the reduction of his liabilities. He continued to increase them. For he could not see his activities in business terms. To him they were the operations of a mighty Protestant vanguard, himself the general, and each purchase the establishment of a redoubt on which he planted the banner of anti-Popery. Nor did he view his activities with the sense of responsibility of an honourable man. He had no thought for the schools as entities in themselves entitled to equitable treatment and fair dealing. One of his campaigns was the purchase of advowsons so that he could control the presentations to livings and instal in these parishes clergymen of his own persuasion. By the end he had bought three hundred advowsons to whose purchase the schools had contributed £17,000: the schools as such had no interest or prospective advantage in acquiring such property, and to buy these advowsons was a misuse of their funds. In the early nineteen-thirties his interest turned from schools to seminaries. The schools paid £18,000 towards one institution in Oxford and the funds of Stowe in particular were used to support a theological college in which he had developed an interest. Yet at this time the writing was already on the wall.

In April 1931 Warrington wrote to Roxburgh that he 'had been victimised by Share Pushers', and Roxburgh was appalled to hear that the Public Prosecutor had been brought in. The main anxiety

seems to have been whether Warrington would be forced to produce documents and appear in court as a witness, and Roxburgh
did much to rescue him from the awkwardness of the situation.
Warrington's methods of raising money and allocating it became
ever more precarious and shady until in 1932 the largest creditor of
the group of schools, the Legal and General Assurance Society,
refused further loans unless they obtained representation on the
Council. Warrington and his associates had no choice but to accept
and William Workman and Edward Wykes joined the board. And
now Warrington's creatures began to snarl at his heels and plotted
to oust both him and Roxburgh whom they accused of filling
Stowe with Anglo-Catholics. The air was thick with acrimonious
recrimination, the prelude to disaster. At last the day came in 1933
when Roxburgh was informed that the bank would no longer
honour the weekly cheques for wages and provisions.

Stowe was saved from closure by the Legal and General. They
took over the first mortgages from the Norwich Union and
assumed financial responsibility for the schools. In September 1933
they demanded Warrington's resignation. They demanded the
resignation of the Governors of all the schools, retaining only
those in whom they had confidence. Then they re-organised. That
Christmas they asked a young chartered accountant, Kenneth
Adams,[1] to disentangle Warrington's web, a task which taxed
even his patience and ingenuity as the accounts for the previous
two years hardly existed and the ramifications of his dealings were
both dubious and bizarre. He had to bring unpalatable news to all
the schools (some of which were disposed of) and to work out the
details of the reorganisation. Each school was to have its separate
governing body. There was to be a central committee under Sir
Cyril Norwood's chairmanship on which each school and the
Legal and General were represented: it was to link the management of the various schools, allocate resources and ensure that
each school from then on was treated equitably. A subsidiary
company, the Allied Schools, was also set up to administer the
group. The Stowe governing body was entirely reconstituted.
Gisborough remained on as chairman for one year and was then
succeeded by Pickard-Cambridge, and among those appointed

[1] K. H. Adams, General Manager of the Allied Schools, Governor of
Stowe, Hon. Treasurer of the Governing Bodies Association.

were parents who were friends of Roxburgh's, John Buchanan[1] and James Webster;[2] while Workman and Wykes began years of able advocacy on behalf of the schools with the Legal and General. The Martyrs Memorial Trust retained only two places on the Stowe governing body. From then on Stowe was over the years to receive as much support from the other schools as it gave to them. The immediate, no less than the long term, future was assured. The Legal and General acted in the best traditions of the City Livery Companies such as the Grocers' and Merchant Taylors' which govern colleges and schools. Unperturbed by the sizable financial burden they had assumed, they proceeded to increase it. No impediment was put in the way of building the eighth house; new class-rooms were put up in a style that harmonised with the old buildings; accommodation for married masters began to be built near the school; conversions and maintenance were sanctioned on a generous scale; and they charged a modest rate of interest on the outstanding loans. From that time on religious bigotry on the governing body vanished, and the school's finances were built on rock instead of on sand.

When the crash came, Roxburgh had little understanding of the nature of Warrington's operations. He wrote to Mrs Radice expressing the hope that 'poor Warrington might be kept out of the courts' and that 'some means will be found of paying the little man the tribute he deserves'. In the years that followed Warrington bombarded Roxburgh with hysterical letters full of accusations. In 1936 he received one of twenty-four pages denouncing him as an insidious cultivator of Roman and Anglo-Catholics but telling him: 'I have never forgotten your great kindness and sympathy with me when I was cruelly tricked by Share Pushers.' Now Warrington was contending that his secretary had forged his signature, now he inveighed against mysterious enemies who poisoned his food, now he turned to rend two of his former colleagues whom he dubbed the Serpent of Stowe and the Adder of Felixstowe. He became ever more violent and demented. In 1939 he sent Wykes a denunciation in seventy-six foolscap pages and declared that 'nothing less than the closing of Stowe will

[1] J. N. Buchanan, Chairman of Minerals Separation 1943–64.
[2] J. A. Webster, D.S.O., Private Secretary to the Right Hon. Winston Churchill at the Board of Trade and the Ministry of Munitions.

satisfy me': a year later injunctions were brought to prevent him slandering two Governors who represented the Legal and General and Roxburgh himself. Roxburgh replied to his letters, when driven to do so, that he had only one wish, namely to keep clear of all these matters. During these years he came to realise that Warrington had run his empire single-handed, duping those ~~Governors who were too feeble to comprehend his activities and~~ deceiving those who were upright and could have called him to account. His wild letters proved that his ability to deceive himself was immeasurable. He had in fact transformed the Schools Trust into a concern which lent financial support to any institution that Warrington wished to capture or which he believed would further the cause of extreme Protestantism.

Roxburgh now had to face the fact that the profits that Stowe had made owing to his genius and organising power had vanished like sand in the sea. Year in year out there was the fear that bankruptcy proceedings or other processes against Warrington would bring the whole matter into the open and shake confidence in the school. But he never became vindictive. He would not stoop to join the chorus of denigration, still less add his voice to Warrington's former associates, one of whom wrote to ask if 'you would kindly help me bear this burden for the sake of Him for Whom we labour and suffer'. Years later when it was customary to curse Warrington's name, J.F., who had suffered in the blasting of his hopes more than anyone, summed up magnanimously. He remembered Warrington's demonic energy, his refusal ever to take a holiday — 'It is true,' he wrote, 'that he did his best to prevent my appointment at Stowe . . . and that he was an intolerable Governor to work under; it is true that . . . in 1933 he went near to ruining the place. Yet I can never forget that without his original efforts Stowe could not have opened at all. Then again the disgust and indignation which Warrington more or less continuously provoked are very different from the contempt and loathing which I came to feel for the mean and treacherous men who profited by all his villainies and would never have had the courage to commit one of them.' It was characteristic of Roxburgh to make such distinctions.

Chapter VI

The Years of Achievement

The financial crisis and the continual domestic friction, which a
succession of bursars did nothing to allay, strained Roxburgh's
stamina. He was to suffer a further anxiety. In the autumn of
1932 a serious case of poliomyelitis occurred at Stowe; and
when a second case (though it proved much lighter) developed,
Roxburgh sent the school home for three weeks. There was
an outburst in the Press at his decision. As no further cases developed his action could not be faulted and had he not so acted
many parents would on their own initiative have removed
their sons. The criticisms caught him on the raw. He had
always carried his burdens lightly and the school did not know
what to make of it when on occasions he would stop in the
middle of morning prayers in Assembly, put on his mortar
board and walk out. One of his ex-prefects sitting next to

him at a dinner in later days asked what had occurred. He replied:

Towards the end of a term I often used to find myself getting very tired. Sometimes I got to the point where I felt I could not, in this instance if you like, go on reading prayers. I had a sort of blackout and I had to stop. Believe me, it was very embarrassing. I found there was only one thing for it: to go off and talk to someone to whom I could pour out my thoughts, and almost at once I felt quite all right again, free in fact. Responsibility, my dear fellow, can be very wearing, as I expect one day you yourself will find.

His doctors told him to cut down on outside engagements and restore his digestion and his nerves.

The outside engagements had multiplied. He was by now a public figure and had hit the headlines in 1930 by a speech to the Parents' Association in which he had said, 'The English are a lazy people . . . who use their brains only under provocation . . . Our secondary education,' he had continued, 'fails to turn out men who are intellectually alive because it does not honestly value intellect . . .' and he entreated the public schools to change and to ensure that they made a contribution to the intellectual as well as the moral life of the nation. The next year in the *Daily Telegraph* he was advocating the teaching of economics which if 'they do not reveal the foundations of the universe, do reveal the foundations of civilisation'. He was pressed to do a multitude of excellent but time-consuming jobs such as sitting on the Admiralty selection board for Dartmouth,[1] and in 1936 a feeler was put out to see if he would become Director of Talks at the B.B.C. His success and his judicious publicity for Stowe had made him a subject of conversation — and with admiration went suspicion, distrust and detraction.

There may also have been some jealousy as the first results of his methods began to be visible. The decade of the 'thirties at Stowe were the years of achievement. The halcyon days of the early terms were past and with them some of the things that J.F. valued most. He was never again to mix with such freedom

---

[1] As usual he stood out as the member of the Board who was remembered by the diminutive candidates because he helped them. Lord Mottistone's son remembered: 'He made me laugh and then all the others laughed too.

among his boys nor was his staff to have the same feeling of working almost as partners in a new and speculative experiment. But Stowe had become a school which not only had a future but a past. Good schoolmasters are said not to measure their finest work in terms of worldly success; but they would have to be singularly unworldly if they did not rejoice when their former pupils distinguish themselves. Of the earliest vintage John Boyd-Carpenter,[1] the future Cabinet Minister, and Toby O'Brien, boys in whom J.F. had taken an especial interest, were both Presidents of the Oxford Union. Bernard Gadney captained England at rugger, and golf succeeded fencing as the game that people associated with Stowe, especially when P. B. Lucas[2] and John Langley were both in the Walker Cup team, the latter while still a boy at the school. The eight awards gained in 1929 at Oxford and Cambridge proved not to be a freak but only slightly higher than average, and Stoics began to gain Firsts. The variety of achievement was a tribute to Roxburgh's ideals. David Niven became a film star. There was a stage designer and composer, an Olympic runner, an Oxford Chancellor's medallist; and Stoics began to appear as poets, novelists and journalists. On one level the Sword of Honour was won at Sandhurst, and on another John Cornford died fighting in the International Brigade during the Spanish Civil War.

The tyranny of athleticism had been one of Roxburgh's targets and he did not want games to absorb the school's emotional life. The part that organised games played in a boy's life depended a good deal on his housemaster and on the prefects and monitors in his house, but they dominated the lives of the physically inept and the eccentric less than at most other schools at that time partly because there were fewer rituals connected with competition in games between houses so that the temperature was not being artificially heightened. But Roxburgh did not intend in this sphere, or in any other, to be revolutionary. Athletic grace and vigour pleased his eye. He used to watch school matches, affably perambulating round the ground, walking stick in hand and hat on head, applauding a piece of play but leaving expert analysis to others.

[1] The Right Hon. John Boyd-Carpenter, Conservative M.P. for Kingston 1945; Minister in Conservative administrations since 1951.

[2] P. B. Lucas, D.S.O., D.F.C., Conservative M.P. for Brentford 1950-9.

He kept his ears open for news of a fine performance in any team, so that a bowler with a good analysis in a match or a forward who had played a blinder would receive that evening one of his characteristic notes in his own hand. At the same time he insisted that the rights of other individuals should also be considered. Although he himself set the example of watching matches, boys were not compelled to watch them as they were elsewhere. This moderate attitude to team games produced, as might have been predicted, moderate results. At rugger Stowe won the majority of their school matches though they could rarely beat the incomparable sides produced yearly by Oundle; and cricket was not played in a spirit likely to produce a deathly hush in the Close to-night — there was more of the air of genial Saturday exercise about it.

Despite low salaries and meagre living quarters, Roxburgh had also succeeded in attracting a staff with a variety of talents and he now saw them maturing. Among them were three who were to become over the years his principal lieutenants. On coming down from Cambridge Eddie Capel Cure rejoined Roxburgh, took over a house in his twenties and was as remarkable in dealing with clever boys as with athletes whom he could usually defeat in any game. In Patrick Hunter J.F. found someone fastidious enough for his taste to take on the classical side; later as Senior Tutor he was to become principal adviser on the curriculum. The third was 'Fritz' Clifford who made Roxburgh's ideal of service to the community his own special concern. He kept the Stowe Club for working-class boys before the eyes of the school and after long service as tutor and housemaster Roxburgh chose him after the war to be Second Master. J.F. was remote from what a games player expected a headmaster to be, but he had a knack of persuading some excellent men to join him. He won Humphrey Playford, a famous rowing Blue, by showing, in contrast to other headmasters who were after him, no interest whatever in his rowing; and at one time, to succeed Ian Clarke as master in charge of rugger, he had three internationals.[1]

One of his successes in the nineteen-thirties was the emergence

[1] John Tallent, centre three-quarter for England; David Ian Brown, full-back for Scotland; Donald Crichton-Miller, wing forward for Scotland, and later Headmaster of Taunton 1936–45, Headmaster of Fettes 1948–58, Headmaster of Stowe 1958–63.

of an Upper School Geography Side that offered a broadly based
course including some economics. It could be taken by a boy who
might later read Geography at the university, but it also provided
the kind of education that Roxburgh had always thought was
lacking in the public schools for those who were not academically distinguished. Such a boy might leave a year early through
frustration if he was made to study one of the traditional university entrance subjects. It was a variation on the old Modern Side
of Victorian public schools. There the difficulty had always been
to provide a course which held boys' interest by appealing to
different abilities while at the same time remaining academically
respectable and stretching the mind. Harold Kinvig, who was
tutor of this Side, surprised some sceptics by showing that
geography was not just a subject which every gentleman instinctively knows but has forgotten.

In those days the public schools regarded the arts as perilous
activities. Acting led to swollen heads — or worse; modern painting and sculpture were good for a guffaw or obloquy; only music
was respectable, and this in some cases was exactly what it was.
Although many schools possessed excellent music masters and
performed Handel oratorios with spirit, composers later than
Debussy were rarely heard. Roxburgh had no ear for music. No,
he would not, he told a mother, listen to an early opus by her
aspiring son. 'I only sometimes go to concerts at Stowe as a
matter of duty and only last term I narrowly escaped hearing the
Rio Grande performed twice in the same evening. I hardly know
when I shall have courage to go to a Stowe concert again.' But he
had seen to it that there was a music master who within a year or
two of the first performance of Constant Lambert's setting of
Sacheverell Sitwell's poem conducted the school choral society
and orchestra in a concert that included this work. Leslie Huggins
was not only courageous in his choice of music: he assisted Roxburgh in one of his characteristic enterprises. J.F. considered the
syntax and sentiment of most hymns deplorable. He therefore
compiled a special book, *Cantata Stoica* (used in addition to the
normal hymn-book), which consisted of great religious poetry
which could be sung arranged chronologically. Huggins set many
of these poems to music. There were hymns sung in Latin such as
Abelard's *O quanta qualia*, or Aquinas' *Lauda Sion*, or *Tantum ergo*

sacramentum which he himself translated; there were poems by Nicolai, Herbert, Crashaw, Quarles, Fletcher, Addison, Shelley and Chesterton. The book was a subtle educational bait. As boys sat vacantly waiting in Chapel for the service to begin, a handful would open *Cantata Stoica* to relieve the tedium. They learnt the names of new poets and an idea of when they lived. They might discover for themselves how seventeenth-century diction differed from late Victorian; and with four metrical versions of the twenty-third psalm put side by side they could make comparisons between different kinds of religious sensibility. They also discovered for the first time how powerfully religious emotion could be expressed. The book was in a sense the product of the first sermon that Roxburgh ever delivered at Stowe on the theme 'The apprehension of beauty is one of the directest routes to God'. Another skilled appointment in 1934 was that of a Canadian, Robin Watt, as art master, which coincided with the opening of the new art school. He and his wife made it into a centre that touched dozens of activities, where more and more boys spent their spare time painting and potting, or designing scenery and costumes for the succession of plays that now began to be produced. Here again Roxburgh chose a man rather than took a lead himself. He had in fact been more at home with Watt's predecessor who taught boys in the approved public school manner to draw classical pediments and capitals and keep a good sketch book; but he recognised that here was the kind of teaching that he was seeking and all too rarely finding.

The ethos of the intellectuals whom Roxburgh appointed to the staff was also beginning to change. By the early 'thirties Heckstall-Smith, MacLaughlin, Spencer and Hankinson (the first head of the medical Side) had all left — Heckstall-Smith to a headmastership, the rest to other jobs. But some of their successors had this in common with them — they were not in the ordinary run of schoolmasters. They made variations on the dark suit or grey flannel trousers and tweed coat which were then almost a uniform with public schoolmasters by wearing green ties or polo-necked sweaters which contrasted agreeably with the Savile Row air of their headmaster. They brought variety to the teaching as well: one would teach Shakespeare and German simultaneously through the Tieck-Schlegel translation; another (who became an excellent historian) was an assiduous reader of Claud Cockburn's *The Week*, and enlivened Present Day periods by retailing the scandals of the Third Republic and analysing the rise of Hitler; a third, dressed as if in rivalry to J.F., started pioneer courses in economics; and William McElwee, who began to publish his own historical work, was already introducing his pupils to Namier, under whom he had done research. McElwee, outstanding for his success as history tutor, created with his wife at Vancouver Lodge a circle in which not only his history specialists but other boys of different talents met. There was in general considerably more freedom for masters to take boys on expeditions and treat school rules flexibly than was usual at most schools. The most devastating impact was made by T. H. White[1] who established an English Side and introduced the work of I. A. Richards and Cambridge literary criticism into the Upper School. This was at once serious and iconoclastic, and his clever pupils began to argue about 'the meaning of meaning' and to construe Eliot or Auden as if they were classical specialists spotting a hendiadys or hysteron-proteron; boys were encouraged to approach the Romantics sceptically and to admire the Metaphysical poets and Gerard Manley Hopkins. To read D. H. Lawrence, whom White regarded as the best antidote to brittle cleverness, was obligatory; and unintellectual boys were puzzled to find Stella Gibbons' satire *Cold Comfort Farm* a set book. He published a pamphlet on bad writing and taught boys to use their imagination and employ metaphor and simile instead of fussing whether a sentence ended with a preposition. Slim, wasp-waisted, with red moustache, his enemy was the bogus. He loathed snob culture which flourished (as it always does) among clever boys, and in pitying tones he would ridicule them in the hope of inducing them to make their own response to poetry instead of framing epigrams, cribbing Aldous Huxley, and avoiding the unpleasant truth that they were emotionally bankrupt. He took pleasure in shocking: produced a pacifist play and published novels under a pseudonym whose mild improprieties brought a

[1] T. H. White, author of *The Sword in the Stone* (London and New York, 1934); *The Once and Future King* (London and New York, 1958), etc. He published three volumes of fiction while at Stowe, and *England Have My Bones* (London, 1936) describes the surrounding country and its pursuits.

protest from a parent — a situation which J.F. handled with tactful calm drawing very proper distinctions. But he was less interested in his clever pupils than in the boys who went fishing, shooting, hawking and flying with him — for White had declared war both on dandyism and English open road heartiness. He was then in the midst of living out a fantasy to resurrect Renaissance man who should be equally skilled in paunching a hare in the morning, stretching a canvas in the afternoon, landing an aircraft in the evening and writing poetry at night. On a Saturday morning his gown and grey flannel trousers concealed breeches and hunting tops and as the bell rang for the end of his period he would dive for his old Bentley and hurtle to the meet. Heckstall-Smith gave the impression that he was indifferent to most things that were not part of the search for truth: White that he hadn't much time for truth because he was doubtful if it existed, but that it was of the utmost importance to experience things and define your emotions accurately. Intellectual vitality was apt to take priority over intellectual discipline. Roxburgh granted his staff the same freedom in their sphere as he granted the boys in theirs. Both at times abused it, but he continued to believe that on balance the school gained. Masters of this kind, however, created a certain tension in the common room; tension brings protests to the headmaster at satirical words and accusations of disloyalty; and as J.F. grew more tired he was more ready to prefer solidity with peace to cleverness with dissension.

Most of these masters conveyed a culture quite alien to that which Roxburgh felt at home in. They were of the 'twenties and found their models in the artistic and social revolution of the times. Roxburgh was pleased that they should invite Walter de la Mare or Edith Sitwell to Stowe but he bewailed, not at all convincingly, his inability to comprehend Picasso, Valéry, Yeats or Joyce. His taste in literature was in fact extraordinarily circumscribed. It would have been miraculous had he welcomed Eliot and the post-Symbolists or sympathised with the experimental novel. But he drew an astonished 'Oh, Sir!' from Frank Tuohy in the 'forties when he told him that Hardy should not have given up writing good novels to write bad poetry; and his comments to John Cornford on D. H. Lawrence were philistine. An Old Stoic who sent him his first two novels received kindly and painstaking letters, but J.F. begged him 'to find rather nicer people to write about — people who were a little more normal and reminded one more of one's own self and one's friends'. That literature communicated experience, and that experience can be raw was not an idea that he took to kindly. His taste had been fashioned by the classics: he wanted experience to be distilled into pellucid drops, he wanted art to be chiselled and worked over and framed in familiar forms such as the alexandrine or the hexameter. There was a touch in him of the Victorian delight in craftsmanship: the worth of a poem or picture could be judged by the amount of work that had visibly been expended on it. He often made the classroom read Gautier on Art:

> Oui, l'oeuvre sort plus belle
> D'une forme au travail
> Rebelle,
> Vers, marbre, onyx, émail.

Poetry for him was the assonance or dissonance of words, the counter-play of rhythm and metre. He would hold up for admiration the skill with which Keats incorporated 'perilous' into an anapaest in his line 'Of perilous seas, in faery lands forlorn'. He would chant languorously:

> Mon enfant, ma sœur,
> Songe à la douceur
> D'aller là-bas vivre ensemble...
> Là tout n'est qu'ordre et beauté
> Luxe, calme et volupté.

He did not, however, press the form to read Baudelaire's more disturbing poems. His criteria enabled him to enjoy equally Racine, Hugo and Leconte de Lisle, Milton and Tennyson; but the reconciliation of classical and romantic poetry once accomplished, anything that could not be docketed easily under these headings was dismissed. It was because this approach to poetry, which concentrated on 'beauty', excluded so much, particularly literature written after 1910, that the revolution in criticism began; and the emphasis on art as emotional experience and the analysis and judgment of the quality of that experience through different techniques such as the study of texture is so well established that one is in danger of forgetting the value in Roxburgh's approach. That it was valuable will be evident when we read recollections of his power as a teacher.

But in the nineteen-thirties his intellectual vision was beginning to grow dim. He was losing his magic for the clever Sixth Former. In that decade politics, the revolution in art and pyschoanalysis were the particular topics that intelligent boys returned to time and again. Roxburgh's interest in politics had waned and in modern art was stunted. He continued to be absorbed by psychology but while he would not discourage the discussion of Freud it was clear that he did not see how seminal Freud's theories were in other intellectual fields; he did not pursue them because he found them unattractive. Some boys in the Sixth Form wanted to know, not whether he found them attractive but whether he believed them to be true. He showed no sign of having read Jung: Adler he dismissed. It is a miracle when schoolmasters find time to keep acquainted with what has appeared in their own teaching subjects, let alone with the culture of their times. In the past Roxburgh had done so by reading late into the night, but now under the burden of the Warrington affair he began to suffer from insomnia. His reading became therapeutic and Capel Cure used to supply him with piles of detective stories as a night-time sedative. He was beginning also to suffer from an occupational disease of headmasters. Headmasters are often inhibited from asking disturbing questions or throwing back shocking answers. As a sixth-form master at Lancing Roxburgh would ask boys what if anything they imagined survived after death.[1] In a headmaster's heart, however, there is usually a flutter that some boy will misunderstand and misquote him, and the school, which is identified with his name, will suffer. So caution, pedantry, softsoap, and platitude seep upwards. The awkward question is evaded by a worldly retort: or the sting is removed and the questioner made smaller by placing the question in its intellectual context and therefore suggesting that it has been put and dealt with many times before. Moreover when men become absorbed in administration and practise the art of getting other adults to

[2] Evelyn Waugh, *op. cit.*, p. 157.

work together by compromise, they lose their appetite for discussing abstract principles — and such discussion becomes much harder at the schoolboy level where even if callow and priggish it can be intensely serious. In the 'thirties J.F. began to find his Sixth Form Sunday evenings something of a strain. He was often too tired for Socratic discussion at which he never excelled: he preferred lively, entertaining talk and this did not flow if the numbers were small and too many prefects among the Sixth Form were absent on house duties. Sometimes he would engineer an occasion. One of his Sixth Formers remembered the night when J.F. turned the conversation to the contrast between the ancient Romans and Italian taxi-drivers.

The contrast was, he said, that the Romans revered above all the quality of *gravitas*, whereas the taxi-driver had many endearing qualities, but *gravitas* — no. Somebody suggested that we had no proof that the Romans possessed *gravitas* — we had only their word for it. This was the cue, and J.F. launched into a brilliant exposition of the theory that it was because they themselves were so conspicuously lacking in *gravitas* that they admired it so much in the few individuals who possessed it. It was a real *tour de force*, illustrated by quotations from obscure classical authors which were verified on the spot.

He was too self-critical a man not to notice his limitations. He may even have told himself when he went to Stowe that the time would come when he would be unable to do for the Sixth Form what he had done at Lancing. Headmasters inevitably teach less than other masters on the grounds that they are submerged beneath administrative chores, and when they teach they usually confine themselves to some sixth-form periods and a few others with selected forms. When J.F. wrote to one of his Lancing boys who had become a schoolmaster asking him to commiserate because at Stowe he was now no longer a teacher but a hotel keeper, it might be supposed that he too had set himself an easy teaching schedule. The very reverse was the case. He regularly taught nineteen hours a week, a régime that other headmasters thought suicidal. Once a week he taught each one of the seventeen forms in the Middle and Lower School and managed to spare an hour for the Classical and another for the Modern Language specialists in the Upper School. This was one of the ways which helped him to remember by name every boy in the school and to treat him as an individual. It was certainly the way which many Stoics best remember him. Picture him then striding into form, a suitcase swinging by his side and slammed on to the desk out of which come copies of Horace's Odes which he flings round the form. He then pulls out a voluminous coloured silk handkerchief, waves it twice across his face, sniffs and starts with the accustomed 'Well, Gentlemen . . .' He at once begins to quote:

O fons Bandusiae, splendidior vitro,
dulci digne mero non sine floribus,
cras donaberis haedo . . .

A pained look. 'Gentlemen, I can't do it, I can't do it. Horace is untranslatable. Crump . . . let us hear the views of the imperturbable Crump . . . a better epithet than "splendid". "Brilliant"? — oh, my dear fellow, let it be "exquisite", "exquisite". Who can attempt the next passage?' — and he goes round the form — 'enlighten . . . illuminate . . . clarify . . . elucidate . . . expound . . . unravel . . . expatiate . . . enucleate!' He himself puts forward four alternative translations, declares them all totally inadequate and returns again to the delicacy of the poet's perceptions. Then he puts a boy on to construe and when he begins to grope, J.F. again goes round the form. 'You're dying to help him out, Ritchie . . . as you were about to say, Fyfe . . . the words are trembling on your lips, Colt . . . get it off your chest, Galitzine . . . impatience is choking you, Brown . . . I didn't quite catch it, Buchanan . . . a brilliant paraphrase, Black . . .' until having himself finally unravelled the passage he turns on the translator, 'Go on, go on, my dear fellow, for heaven's sake.' However good a young scholar's attempt at translation might be J.F. gave him the impression that the perfect comprehension and translation of the passage lay just beyond.

Among the classical specialists he got such scholars and he liked to stretch them. To anyone who translated a Latin word by using the English equivalent he would say, 'You can't translate from one language to another by a series of puns.' Whatever the form he kept up their appetite by varying the diet. Sometimes they found that the book thrown at them was, say, Bernard Hart's

Psychology of Insanity, which stimulated a discussion on the unconscious (called by J.F. the subliminal self): this led in turn to the *Golden Bough* and the Priest of Diana at Nemi, thence to Greek and Latin religion, and it might end with J.F. intoning the passage from the Aeneid when Dido turns silently away from Aeneas in the mists of Hades and the dead stretch out their arms to Charon's boat and the far bank with pitiable longing. He delighted in poetry as incantation. All his forms, high and low, were made to chant Racine or his favourite *Parnassiens*, he himself leading the form and giving expression to a particularly delicate passage. He would coo with La Fontaine's doves or spit at Catullus' mistress. His delectable choice of words, his eloquence, the splendour of his voice as it poured out torrents of Latin or French poetry, his knowledge, which to schoolboys seemed encyclopaedic, and his ability to instil at any rate for his own period a desire to match his own high standards, were unforgettable. By now he had learned to chasten without scorn. He would put a boy, hopelessly stumped, out of his misery by bellowing at him with great good humour 'You execrable moribundity', or address another 'Oh rustic and disillusioned Ness!' as if to say, 'Why don't you let me help you educate yourself?'

A fellow schoolmaster might sourly have observed that such teaching was self-indulgent. It is selfish to leave others to drive syntax and grammar and accuracy into boys' heads and pleasant to allot oneself the task of implanting interests and stimulating enthusiasms. But a headmaster has the joy of being able to do what he will in form and is entitled to use his talents to their best advantage. The multitude of reminiscences of his teaching are the justification of his efforts. He did instruct on occasion. The classical and modern language specialists were compelled to unravel passages; or he would go through a prize essay with the winner dissecting, though always encouraging, until the boy scarcely knew how he had won the prize; or he would pause on an unfamiliar word in a poem such as *fanon* so that the French for a cow's dewlap became imprinted for eternity on the mind. So did his rebukes. 'Unresp*i*ted, unpitied, unreprieved,' a luckless fellow declaimed one day. 'Unresp*i*ted, unresp*i*ted, you miserable youth: un*res*pited. How can you murder Milton's rhythm in this boorish way?' If a book slid on to the floor, 'Drop it on the floor, drop it on the floor and now stamp on it!' A cough brought an ominous frown. Someone would always be despatched if a workman burst into song in the vicinity; and once the sound of bagpipes brought an expression of anguish to his face.

The humbler forms could be bewildered. 'J.F.'s periods were thought to be a bore; chiefly I suppose,' wrote a former inmate of one of those forms, 'because we were so dim-witted and couldn't keep up with his line of reasoning.' And yet he nearly always left in the lower forms something at the conscious level, at the very least the love of a particular poem. 'I find my fondest memory is of him taking us in English and going through *The Ancient Mariner*' is a familiar comment. Or another: 'Architecture — King's Chapel — Wordsworth, he did not teach us to learn it, he taught us to love it, and I for one have never forgotten.' With responsive forms his enjoyment was so great that it was bound to be infectious. 'What one chiefly remembers,' said Roland Oliver, a pupil of the late 'thirties, 'was the excitement of that wonderful period once a week when, whether it was Gothic architecture, or Vergil, or Racine, one could be absolutely certain that there would be no boredom for forty minutes. There one was faced with the alertness of a lion-tamer, the polish of a great actor and the tremendous communication of energy which is insepar-able from great teaching.' He was determined that every boy should be roused, if it were in his powers to do so, to catch in his first years in the school a glimpse of the world of the intellect and the imagination. Perhaps his most original contributions were his periods on architecture because appreciation in the Fine Arts was then so dismally neglected in the curriculum of the schools. He was able too in these periods to relate Stowe architecture to Italian and French models and thus what was learnt in the class-room spilled over into everyday life in the buildings and grounds. And his teaching had another quality. 'He was putting on an act,' noted David Dulley. 'He did not have the usual adult prejudice against showing-off. He did it himself, and he encouraged us to do it. He was a great releaser of people's inhibitions, and altogether a life-giving kind of man.'

Roxburgh was always teaching in many places other than in the class-room. He was himself a fine reader and he made it his per-

sonal responsibility to practise Sixth Form and prefects before
they read their first lesson in Chapel.

He would sit [recollected P. B. Lucas] in the very back row of the
Chapel. The victim would walk up the aisle to the lectern and allow a
short interval. After you had been reading for one or two minutes, he
would roar, 'When are you going to start?' You would start again,
until 'Stop, my dear fellow, stop,' J.F. would cry, 'I cannot-hear-one-
word-you-are-saying. You cannot-read-like-that. No one will hear you.
Start again, pronounce each *vow-el* and take it much more slowly. You
are not scoring a try for the school now.' There were not less than four,
but not I think more than seven, critically sarcastic interruptions before
the performance reached the minimum standard which J.F. felt he
could tolerate in one of his prefects. It was all rather testing. But as we
parted company there was the customary reassuring hand laid on the
shoulder. 'My dear fellow, you need not worry. You read very clearly.
It will be much easier when the Chapel is full and you have forgotten
all about me.' One wondered what he really thought. Two days later,
when the ordeal was over and disaster had not overtaken one, there
came one of those thoughtful and endearing little congratulatory notes
written in his own familiar and distinctive hand.

Something more than a note might well arrive. He loved to
give presents to reward those who loved art or learning. Knowing
that his parents were in India, J.F. asked a boy how he proposed
to spend his summer holidays. Bicycling across Holland to Germany to improve his German. Did he know Dutch? No. That was
unfortunate — he had far better accept a return ticket to Salzburg
and Vienna where he could listen to music. 'This was the most
wonderful, the most educative and the most formative holiday
of my life. It was to that journey that I owed my music scholarship
at Cambridge.' Or, meeting another whom he remembered to
have missed some of his periods on architecture through illness.
'My poor fellow — I'll send you a brief book on the subject.'
A sumptuous illustrated tome arrived. One cloudless summer's
afternoon a boy who detested games was reading in his study
which he shared with two others: alone at last in the deserted
school, he looked up to see that J.F., his head and shoulders lean-
ing through the window, had materialised and had scraped his
feet on the gravel to attract his attention. 'I was going to be quite
angry with you for being indoors on such an afternoon,' J.F.

said gravely, 'but I have changed my mind.' He then de-materialised. A fortnight later a parcel arrived for the boy: it was the magnificent Florence Press two-volume edition of Keats' poems that he had borrowed from the School Library and had been reading that afternoon.

There are other occasions which headmasters use to teach boys wisdom. One of them now forms part of the educational rituals of the nation — the annual ceremony of Speech Day. Every year headmasters deliver an address. They spend many hours in composing and polishing these speeches to ensure that what they say will be good, wise and memorable. The boys hardly ever remember a word. Explicit moralising is the least effective way to influence and yet it is so near to the heart of many dedicated teachers that they cannot resist. J.F. was no exception. But because he gave special attention to the minutest details of *how* he framed what he had to say and because he was a connoisseur of bores, his Speech Day addresses were entertaining and brief. Some of them were delivered at other schools and he used the occasion for repeating the themes of *Eleutheros*. He warned the boys at Framlingham that 'vague thoughts, wild thoughts, and thoughts based on emotion constitute a breach of duty in an educated man'. This was characteristic of his *gravitas* and respect for reason and also of his fear of emotion running out of control and hence into channels which one could not predict would be profitable. There was in him a Scots distrust of waste and of the incalculable. But in this particular case the warning referred, not to the excesses of Bohemia, but to the political temper of Nazism. An older theme to which he returned was that 'there ought to be no such thing as a school in which a clever boy feels himself to be an alien'.

Headmasters also have another duty that obliges them from time to time to address the school. They are ultimately responsible for discipline. They are supposed to know how to control and influence boys and rebuke them for neglecting their duties; make them ashamed if they have betrayed their trust; punish them for every variety of schoolboy crime; introduce them to high standards and induce them to live up to them; show them another world, the world of learning, and encourage them to enter it. It is very wearing. Wearing because boys know that many of the prohibitions that they endure are artificial and trivial; and at an age when in many respects they are adults, and invariably feel adult, they are stopped from doing normal things that adults do and they are allowed to do at home. Adolescents are by definition immature; but they are highly sophisticated and brutally direct in their judgments. Sometimes they ignore the school norms of behaviour because their home life conspicuously deviates from them; more often because the values and prohibitions at school as interpreted by schoolmasters who appear to them to live strait-laced lives seem dim, dreary and dingy; perennially because high spirits, or cruelty, or malevolence, or calculated revenge, or a sense of the comical and inappropriate, or an outburst of boredom, or venom against authority induces them to revolt. Great head-masters infuse their addresses to the school with their own memorable personalities: that is why their wrath or disdain appears to their one-time pupils through the mists of time to have been Homeric or Aristotelian in its splendour or magnanimity. Unfortunately there are also times when it appears Pecksniffian. To discriminate between what is wrong and what is foolish, or between vice and misdemeanour, is difficult, and to avoid stifling spontaneity in moral treatment is exhausting. The most successful disciplinarians manage to restrain schoolboy crime because they are recognised to be fair, flexible and imaginative. Faced by them a boy feels he would rather not break a law and may eventually prefer to keep it. Whatever the régime, crime continues, and the stricter the régime the deeper it is driven underground.

Roxburgh's régime certainly had principles but depended ultimately on his personality. It started from the premise: 'Liberty itself is the best teacher . . . if we learn from our liberty it will be a blessing to us; if not, it will be a curse.' There were to be as few rules as possible but they must be kept. It is an error to picture Roxburgh as a latitudinarian. He was strict to the point of pedantry about *small* rules, and hoped that by being so he would deter those who were tempted to break important ones. A head of house who kept a library book out longer than the prescribed time was told to 'return the book and remember that you are part and parcel of authority and should wield it accordingly'. Unpunctuality, inattention to detail, slovenly dress always brought reproof. But it was a special kind of reproof. 'My dear Dudley, how very nice of you to turn up,' was his way of greeting the Prefect of Chapel who was entering Chapel simultaneously with J.F., having been delayed by his parents' car getting a puncture. 'My dear Krabbé, do you see that someone has been trying to forge your signature on your desk?' 'I see a large portion of naked Croker; pull up your socks, my dear fellow, pull them up.' 'Are you coming to get your hair cut?' — he would remark but he did not ask a boy when he was going to get it cut, still less order him to do so. Even when the reproof was grave, it would end by Roxburgh putting the incident in proportion. One boy who was to have been head of the school was demoted for bad behaviour by J.F. in a bleak interview.

Gradually he became more expansive. He began making clear to me the distinction between the seriousness of a particular action in one context and its comparative innocuousness in another. A code of behaviour was relative: certain things were perfectly permissible for a man as a private individual but ceased to be so for him when he held a post of responsibility . . . I came away aware perhaps for the first time in my life that although school affairs mattered they were, in the context of life as a whole, not so vastly important as all that.

His secret was not to rely on emotional appeals, or moral uplift or on man to man pleas for discipline and decency. He never appealed to 'the honour of the school'. 'I think now,' wrote Wayland Young, 'that if I respect Stowe as I knew it, it is mainly because it — or at least J.F. — never demanded my respect.' Perceiving that many of the things that schoolboys are forbidden to do are in themselves trivial, he tried to make boys feel that it was childish or absurd or inelegant or unsophisticated to behave in such a way; he played on their vanity, preferring to let them acquire a sense of responsibility rather than issuing a series of prohibitions. If he had to allude to the fact that on the last day of the previous term some boys had spent the afternoon cutting down a tree on neighbouring property, he would stress the impoliteness of their trespass and express his astonishment that anyone after being educated at Stowe could be so bereft of re-

sources as to indulge in such a fatiguing pursuit. He would truth-
fully say that the grounds were so large that he was helpless
to prevent smoking: the boys rather liked this candour. Or he
would say: 'Gentlemen, I know as well as you do that nothing I
can say can stop you smoking the most *enormous* cigars behind
every bush during *every* break, but . . .' Inveterate smokers went
on as before knowing that if they were caught he would punish
them, but some responded. 'He won his point and I never smoked
and looked down on those who did as boorish and immature.'
He used the same technique in checking bad language, persuading
people that 'sanguinary' uttered in his all too imitable drawl was
the more positive adjective, and that the word that he pronounced
'buggah' was surely 'an inelegant disyllable' which since it was
'not very euphonious' might be dropped.

It was all the more startling, therefore, when he was incensed.
Bad behaviour and hooliganism angered him. A Stoic had once
taken a pot shot at the clock as the special train steamed through
Padbury: J.F. sailed into Assembly really roused and the school
cowered. Wanton damage always enraged him and the defacing
of the balustrade of the Palladian Bridge made him so angry that
he broke his own rule of not inflicting collective punishment and
cancelled a half-holiday. But he normally relied on his well-tried
methods. The stone pillars of the South Front were being chipped
by boys and Roxburgh talked at length of the history of the
façade and how Temple had first rejected Borra's proposals and
commissioned Adam, and later had accepted Borra's modification
of the Adam design. Then he turned on the school and said: 'And
you young gentlemen are lounging on the portico watching some
sporting contest, and slowly demolishing this stately pile by per-
forating these pillars with the points of your plebeian umbrellas.'
The school laughed and the pillars were spared. He often had to
deliver warnings in respect of the long-suffering but outspoken
farmer whose land marched with that of Stowe. This he did by
uttering simple sentences lethargically so as to make a trivial
matter stick in the mind. The farmer had noticed, he once said,

some boys who he thinks most likely came from this school — and I
think his assumption is probably correct — climbing over the fence
into the field on the north side of the Corinthian Arch, where there is
a bull running free. He wishes me to tell you that the bull is liable to

attack anyone entering the field, but that there is no danger of your getting hurt if you remember *this*. The bull has a ring in its nose, and from the ring hangs a chain, and all you have to do if the bull molests you is to take the chain in your hand, and you will be able to lead the bull without any danger to yourself. That's the farmer's advice. My advice is that you keep out.

Even when he had good news he would convey the value that he attached to it. Giving permission to visit the newly-opened Silverstone motor-racing circuit he added: 'Should any of you wish to witness the spectacle of a Siamese prince circulating at *incredible* velocity you may do so.'

He was indulgent towards certain kinds of crime. To possess firearms was forbidden but a good deal of poaching went on in the grounds. He once met a boy returning before breakfast, barrel down trouser-leg, butt under coat and smallpiece concealed beneath hat: 'Don't bother to take it off, my dear fellow.' He had a good nose for what was going on. 'By the way,' he said on the last night of term to two boys who were leaving and had come to say goodbye, 'how much have you both made shooting and selling rabbits this year? I think it would be a kindness to tell your housemaster that you've been doing it as he knows nothing about it.' He was careful also to make a distinction between harmful breaches of discipline and those that required some daring. Four boys had climbed an interior ladder of the main building at Stowe to reach a part of the roof that was out of bounds. One of the Matrons caught them, justly rejected their plea that they were surveying for the Corps, and reported them to the Headmaster. Roxburgh received them with 'Gentlemen, please show me how you managed to get on to the roof'.

We took him along and showed him, whereupon he insisted on climbing up the rickety ladder. When we arrived on the roof, he started pointing out the many landmarks which could be seen for miles around, and in conclusion said that if at any time we wanted to come up on the roof again we had only to ask him. Of course we never did. Indeed, can there be a better way of stopping a boy from doing anything than to tell him he can do it?

He gave traditional punishments for traditional offences. He sacked some (though not all — he made distinctions) for sexual offences and beat those discovered drinking and smoking. Here was a personal problem that he failed to resolve: did he really dislike inflicting corporal punishment? He certainly said he detested it. 'The whole thing is utterly foul,' he told a friend, partly perhaps because he recognised the sexual implications of the act, more probably because he felt that violence destroyed the relationship that he wanted to establish with every boy. He would try to re-establish that as soon as possible. He flogged one boy severely for doing a brisk and profitable trade in exam papers but there and then settled him down with books on architecture.

He taught me in that half hour more about the Greek orders of architecture than I ever learned at any other time. As I was leaving to go to supper he gave me a chit excusing me my prep for that evening. I think he minded very much having to beat me, or anyone else for that matter, and went to such pains to make it clear that his duty as a disciplinarian had nothing to do with his feelings as a man towards his boys.

But it was a weakness that he never thought through his attitude to punishment. It was inadequate to tell himself that if he expected housemasters and prefects to beat boys, he must do it himself for graver offences. He visited Kurt Hahn but did not like the honour system that prevailed at Gordonstoun nor that at Gresham's, Holt. But other schools were experimenting with new methods of keeping order and his lack of interest in educational theory and his too ready belief that to try new methods would be *outré* stopped him thinking what could be tried as a substitute.

How far his methods succeeded must depend on one's definition of the aims of education. They would have been regarded as too traditional by the experimentalists and certainly Roxburgh had no theory of discipline: he played it by ear. On the other hand, the guardians of tradition referred to Stowe as a juvenile university full of idle, charming boys who were not tough enough — although, as an army officer noted, they seemed to adapt themselves at Sandhurst to the chasing and shouting of an officer cadet's life rather better than those from some military schools because they had more self-confidence and knew that the noise was part of an elaborate game and of no importance. Some of Roxburgh's housemasters complained that their task was made more difficult because other masters debased J.F.'s manner and relaxed discipline to such a degree that boys oscillated between one standard of conduct outside the house and another within. Some of those who coached games complained that all-conquering teams were trained in sterner stables than those that he managed. Discipline was always a contentious issue between him and members of his staff. But Roxburgh never wavered. If a farmer's implements had been misused amends must be made, but the whole countryside would not be put out of bounds: if someone had 'propelled a pedagogue's velocipede' into a lake apologies and restitution must follow, but mass punishment would not be exacted. He continued to appeal to reason and not to retribution and to relax the tension of discipline wherever he could.

On one occasion he found it less difficult to ease the school's tension than his own. In 1933 on Empire Day, acting in the spirit of the Oxford Union motion of refusing to fight for King or Country, two harmless individuals who had become pacifists decided (when very few people were about) to burn a Union Jack in Assembly. Reprisals followed, and about two hundred boys assisted in throwing one of the incendiaries into a pond. The morning papers, according to their political outlook, printed headlines such as 'Our Comrades at Stowe' or 'Public School Spirit not yet Dead'. The publicity was all the more unwelcome because only a week or so later the Prince of Wales was due to visit Stowe in celebration of the school's tenth anniversary. Everyone waited to hear J.F. address the school. Some moralists hoped for a patriotic condemnation of a despicable act: other moralists hoped for a denunciation of mob rule. They were disappointed. All that he did was to murmur that water was known to be an antidote to fire and that reprisals must cease. The school relaxed. But Roxburgh did not. He had fears that the Royal visit might be cancelled or that comment would be passed if it were not. The Prince came, he made his speech, he duly asked that an extra week's holiday might be granted. Afterwards the prefects were to entertain him to tea. One of them noted:

J.F., having made the introductions, turned to H.R.H. and said, 'And now, Sir, I expect you would like to be left on your own with the prefects.' 'What, headmaster,' retorted H.R.H., 'leave me alone to be pushed into that pond?' Before J.F. could leave the room, the Prince had added to us in an aside: 'Incidentally, that is why I gave you fellows that extra week's holiday. My mother said to me that, if I didn't, you would push me into Cobham Pond too.' Roxburgh threw back his head and gave vent to a somewhat artificial guffaw. His relief seemed to be intense.

Chapter VII

War

During the nineteen-thirties Roxburgh put the finishing touches to his scheme of education. He was troubled with one problem which he can hardly be blamed for failing to resolve as it still plagues English education. That was the problem of early specialisation.

The English educational system is wonderfully haphazard. Neither Whitehall nor the local authorities can easily dictate to the schools and even the examining boards set up by the universities to conduct the Certificate examinations are under only nominal university control. Officially standards in the schools are maintained by periodic visits of H.M.'s Inspectorate who write discreet reports on the state of the schools for the benefit of their governing bodies but do not intervene unless provoked by iniquitous conditions. Examinations can be modified with far greater ease than the Baccalauréat or Abitur in France or Germany. Nevertheless the school curriculum is in fact dictated by university requirements. Before the Second World War the educational standards and curriculum of the major public schools were in effect laid down by Oxford and Cambridge for those were the two universities which their boys wished to go to. The standard of the scholarship exams, organised and marked by the *Colleges* in subjects in which boys specialised in the Upper School was high: the standard of the entrance exam set and marked by the *University* (Responsions and the Previous or, colloquially, Smalls and Littlego) was out of mercy low. It was low because it was designed to test only the ability to read for a *pass* degree. Individual colleges might hold their own entrance exams to see if a boy was fitted to read for honours, but the sole public examination which was then virtually obligatory at school was the exam that exempted boys from Smalls and Littlego and enabled them to matriculate at Oxford and Cambridge. This was the School Certificate (roughly equivalent to the later G.C.E. O Level) as set by the examining boards of the ancient universities which exempted candidates if they had obtained credits in five subjects and passes in requisite subjects such as Latin. Once a boy had leapt the School Certificate hurdle he was free to specialise. The college scholarship exams by including translation or general papers ensured that he had to go on studying some ancillary subjects: but from then on a mathematician need do no history, nor an historian mathematics — and neither need ever have done any science, for a bare pass in elementary mathematics exempted candidates from any test of scientific knowledge. It was partly due to these circumstances that the well known English system of early specialisation came into being.

By the nineteen-fifties this system had introduced some strange distortions into secondary education. The School Certificate was set at too low a level for university entrance. Although the standard demanded to pass Smalls and Littlego had hardly changed for years, the standard of work in the schools had been slowly rising and it would have been possible twenty years earlier, when the pass man at Oxford and Cambridge although still vociferously visible was beginning to disappear, to have insisted on a higher standard of general education as a condition of entry to the ancient universities. Oxford and Cambridge missed that chance. To have taken it in the 'thirties would have been difficult because during the slump they were anxious about being able to replace pass men by honours men capable of paying their high fees for tuition and lodging at a time when State grants to needy undergraduates were only just beginning to be offered. But they missed the chance largely because there was no single university officer or responsibly-minded body whose duty it was to watch the relations of the ancient universities with the schools and study their effect upon them. Nor were the civic universities greatly different. There the faculties filled the role of the colleges and set faculty requirements for entrance. But as the requirements were designed to test the ability of the student to study the faculty specialism, they too were unconcerned with raising the standard of *general* education. As a result English boys began to be urged at the age of thirteen to decide whether they would opt for science and mathematics or for the humanities and after the age of fifteen and a half the abler boys would virtually abandon the study of one or the other. It was a system alien to that of France, Germany or America. Its merits were undeniable: so are the lamentable consequences. The severer the competition for university places became, the more time science specialists spent upon their scientific and mathematical subjects and the more deplorably innumerate arts specialists became. The application of science and technology to industry was hampered and the development of the social sciences and their application to administration hamstrung.

Why then in the inter-war years did Roxburgh and other headmasters welcome such a system? The answer is that it gave them freedom to teach boys of widely differing ability according to their aptitudes. In a public school, as distinct from a grammar school, the clever and the dense grow up side by side. The very dense were told to shoot at an attainable — though for most an inappropriate — target in the School Certificate. The average and less skilled boys got a general education for three years and their interest was revived by being allowed to specialise for their last two. If they were unable to endure the rigours of grammatical or mathematical exactitude they could read history or join the Geography and Economics side which Roxburgh had instituted.

The able boy who passed his School Certificate two years after arrival, at fifteen and a half, was granted a boon beyond price: he had two to three years uninterrupted work for his scholarship exam and learnt to study a subject in depth. Thus the system gave great play to the principle which governed Roxburgh's whole attitude to education: teach boys to enjoy their work. Boys work best at subjects which they enjoy and they cannot enjoy those for which they have no ability. General education is necessary: a minimal standard in all subjects must be reached. But in language and mathematics, so the argument ran, boys will reach their level and no amount of coaching will get them over it: trigonometry and the calculus, Tacitus and Ste-Beuve, will always be incomprehensible to some, and if they are forced to defeat them with smothered curses it will be by cramming and not through education. Roxburgh did not want his boys to be held back indefinitely from doing well in subjects near to their heart for inability to tackle one that they could not master. He accepted the need for this to happen at School Certificate level. (A boy who failed for instance in elementary mathematics or language had to sit the whole examination again.) But what always concerned him was the needs of the individual boy: Roxburgh determined to give him the freedom within an overall system to do well whatever he was capable of doing.

But what was to be done with the boy who was so precocious and had been so well taught at his prep school that he could matriculate in the School Certificate after one year's work? Although the Upper School Sides all studied English[1] and some learnt French and Latin, so that there was no question of boys studying in only one field, it was unwise to compel a boy to choose his main subject at so early a stage in his career. In 1932 Roxburgh therefore instituted an Upper School Form called the Twenty for these young scholars who were to continue general studies for a year before specialisation. The scheme did not succeed: partly because the boys could not see how these studies were geared to the work that they would do in the Upper School and partly because they considered that they were being held back and therefore rested tranquilly on their oars for a year. By 1934

[1] After the inspection of the school in 1936 by the Board of Education they also all studied Divinity.

this form had become part of the Middle School and the scholars were taking two years over the School Certificate.

Once again an educational experiment was broken on the wheel of the examination system. A public examination induces boys to work but at the same time strangles the initiative of teachers. The public examination in mathematics after the School Certificate was inappropriate for a boy who was incapable of thinking like a mathematician but capable of benefiting from being taught statistics in a lively way; similarly a science specialist could not get a Higher Certificate in German without rendering every phrase in a short passage of unseen translation with exact felicity when what was appropriate was to test whether he could jumble out the general sense of a long passage with a dictionary. Examinations fall too easily into the hands of pedants. They refuse to recognise that ability to think rigorously will be tested adequately in the subject in which a boy specialises and that there is no need to apply the same disciplinary standards when examining him in ancillary subjects. But the donnish mind finds such reasoning indecent. To treat an ancillary subject so light-heartedly would be to call in question its respectability and, worse still, one's own respectability as an expert in it. The academic profession is devoted to respectability.

In another of his educational ideals Roxburgh succeeded. This had been to teach English as a subject throughout the school and to give it precedence. Naturally English was taught at other public schools but in those days it tended to be a spare time subject usually taught by classics masters over-concerned with grammar and insensitive to literature. There was a curious theory that a boy learnt English through Latin translation and that while he should be introduced to selected passages from authors such as Shakespeare, Milton and the Romantic poets, English literature was a subsidiary cultural activity. Roxburgh made it central. He admitted, what few then were willing to admit, that Latin at School Certificate level did not introduce anyone to the delicacy of the language or to its literature and that as many boys abandoned it after this stage it was only practical to make English the main stream of the school's culture. Every master, he urged, whether or not he taught the subject was to regard himself as the custodian of the English language. He looked for masters who had taken a degree in English at the universities — a comparatively newly instituted degree which many headmasters despised. He wanted forms to write essays but he also wanted them to attempt compositions designed to stimulate their imagination; and in this Roxburgh was in advance of his time.

He was, however, by no means in advance of his time in regard to science. He would have been astonished by the idea that it formed part of our culture. To his mind just as the school should have good workshops for boys who liked to use lathes and make things with their hands so there should be labs for boys with scientific aptitude. In the top forms of the Lower School every boy was taught science but in the Middle School only three periods of physics were compulsory in the Removes (or pre-School Certificate year) and in the Fifth from which a boy took the School Certificate he might drop science entirely. What was worse, it was in the Middle School that the able boys who got entrance scholarships or passed Common Entrance creditably were placed on entry and therefore the ablest were required only to take these token periods which paid lip-service to the notion that every boy should do some science. Anyone who wanted to do more had specifically to opt for specialisation in science in preference to Greek or German. Of course in practice boys with mathematical ability chose to do science, but the fact remained that it was possible for the cleverer boys in the school to have done virtually none. Such a situation was not unusual in public schools at that time; and no criticism was made of it when the school was inspected. Roxburgh was characteristic of the arts man of his time in regarding science as a technique. His early advocacy of biology was induced by his belief that this was a sensible way to teach sex. No doubt he betrayed his inner feelings when he said after the war to a physics master who had over-run his time in the form room in which J.F. was to teach: 'Well, my dear fellow, if you have finished showing your pupils how to blow the world to eternity I would like to show mine how we might put it together again.' Nor did he have a positive view on the merits of the Higher Certificate — the forerunner of G.C.E. Advanced Level. He left his tutors to decide whether or not they entered their pupils for it. He had no faith in exams for their own sake and was ready to listen to those who praised his Upper School system as giving

tutors freedom to educate in the wide sense and to avoid cramming. But the evergreen school problem remained: namely that
many boys work harder and train their minds better if they have a
goal in sight, the goal being provided by the exams. These problems became ever more complex, and in March 1933 Roxburgh
appointed Patrick Hunter to a new post of Senior Tutor, his
function being to co-ordinate the Upper School and to be the
headmaster's lieutenant in the organisation of school work and
internal examinations.

In 1936 Stowe was inspected for the first time by the Board of
Education. On these occasions Inspectors sidle into form rooms
to listen to the lessons and the boys play up splendidly by releasing
their favourite butts from ragging and appearing to hang on every
word with rapt attention. The Inspectors are seldom deceived; but
their report does not take the form of a catalogue of criticisms
and concentrates rather on making suggestions for improvement.
Roxburgh could be justly satisfied with the excellent Certificate
results in the Middle School because he had insisted on considerable time being spent on matters which were unrelated to exams.
In the Lower School there were weekly periods of nature study,
musical appreciation, current affairs and in either fine art or car-
pentry. Boys were also taught how to strip a car or play in a brass
band. Much time was spent in modern language periods in working at the pronunciation of French and German, and Roxburgh
characteristically put the boys' interests before those of the school
by encouraging a considerable number in their last year to leave
in December or in April so that they could go abroad and learn
languages. Science was weak, and the labs inadequate; and when
the standard in mathematics was good it was very good and when
it was poor it was horrid. The outstanding achievement was in the
teaching of the History specialists, the general teaching of English
and the work in the art school. But the Inspectors noted that the
turnover in staff was far too high, and too little attention had been
paid to the masters' needs and living conditions. They suggested
that a development plan for the school buildings should be drawn
up. Roxburgh had seen to it that as the school grew the great park
and its vistas remained unspoilt; but at the same time the new
buildings straggled in ribbon development west of the house and
the opportunity to mass them in courts in that area had been

missed. Landscape gardening is one of England's few original contributions to the arts and Stowe the greatest example of this art; the development of the school had proceeded so fast that the chance to exploit the art had been missed.

Roxburgh had set out to raise the standard of work in the public schools. By giving greater freedom of choice and by trying to get his staff to make class-room teaching more enjoyable, he raised the *quality* of the work; and the freedom that he cherished gave many boys the chance to blossom who would not have done so in a sterner climate. He succeeded in developing a liveliness of mind in boys who would have withered in a traditional public school but who got university awards in History or English, because their imaginations had been stimulated and ambition to work aroused. But whether the general level of achievement was higher is more doubtful. Although he had hoped to get his share of clever boys from the prep schools, he got fewer of those paragons than Stowe's academic record might have suggested. Such boys are especially valuable because their natural ability, well trained in their prep schools, enables them to perform the mental gymnastics of mathematics or linguistics with enviable ease and by so doing set standards which lift their more moderate contemporaries up to their level. There was something in the atmosphere of Roxburgh's Stowe that militated against exacting from boys the highest standards of industriousness. His encouragement of cultural activities in and out of school benefited many of them and made some intellectually more lively but it did not enable them to go through a textbook quickly or pay attention to accuracy and detail; and the mastery of techniques is an essential part of education.

The appointment of Hunter as Senior Tutor was Roxburgh's first essay in delegation. He did not delegate much else. He continued to preside over numerous school activities. When a Film Society started by showing Pabst's *Kameradschaft* he was there to speak on the nature of the cinema and to express his belief that if a new art was to be born there had to be an audience intelligent enough to welcome its new discoveries. The number of his engagements continued to mount however hard he tried to cut them down. He refused visits to Canada and the United States, but there were a mass of invitations, such as preaching at prep schools, the occasional broadcast or lecture, local obligations and Old Stoic functions which he believed he ought to accept for the good of Stowe. Three Old Stoic dinners a year in London and at Oxford and Cambridge were a burden even though his listeners were delighted to hear the familiar voice expressing pleasure that there were so many Old Stoics 'some in the Arm-ah, some in the Nav-ah and some propping up the pound in the Cit-ah'.

It was in the late thirties that he began ominously to limit his holidays. In the early years he had taken regular holidays, a few days at Christmas and a solid break either at Easter or in the summer. He used at least once a year to visit his mother in Scotland; made trips to France frequently; and in 1931 went to Munich and Vienna. In 1925 Sir Henry Lunn revived the Hellenic cruises and the next year J.F. went on a cruise though he refused to lecture. 'The squalor of a small boat', he said in a letter to a friend, 'is one of the things I find most hard to put up with.' But when conditions had improved he went again, contributing an article in 1929 to the proceedings of the Hellenic Travellers Club; and in 1930 he lectured at Melos on the famous Venus in the Louvre, basing his text on the researches by a French Academician, Jean Aicard, which he had studied when he was a student in Paris. He loved Greece and the Hellenic tours brought this alleged misogynist a friend. On the cruise in 1926 he met Miss Muriel Currey, a woman of intelligence, courage and humour with a knowledge of international affairs. Because she accepted him as a pleasant companion and knew nothing of his reputation he relaxed in her company. They both enjoyed taking pictures and were amused by the same incidents: the discovery that the daughter of a public figure across the table, whom they had been discussing with some freedom, was deaf and a skilled lip-reader gave them a certain scope for inventiveness. She indulged his foibles. They had arranged on a subsequent cruise to meet at Marseilles where she found that Roxburgh, having lost his luggage, was embarrassed by the colour of the new raw leather suitcase that he had had to buy. So at Volo she bought him a tin of brown boot-polish to disguise it, using beautiful Mediterranean gestures, while he lurked in the background pretending to disown her: immediately she had bought it the shopkeeper engaged them both in fluent American. At Delphi after a long day's sightseeing they sat together on a

hillside in silence while he, occasionally looking up to gaze at that
spectacular landscape, worked out the next term's timetable.
Unfortunately he began to find on these cruises that too many
people knew him, or knew of him, and he could not get the
privacy he needed in this form of holiday. He got away for long
periods from Stowe on fewer and fewer occasions and his holidays
became confined to family visits in Scotland and a brief excursion
or two to France.

To the anxiety of the Warrington business was now added the
possibility of war. During the early nineteen-thirties when paci-
fism was at its height and when opinion had turned bitterly
against the policies of those who were held responsible for the
appalling losses in the 1914–18 war, Roxburgh's Armistice Day
sermons were memorable for their sanity. In 1934 he said:

You may reasonably wonder why you are asked by members of a
generation to which you do not belong to honour the memory of men
whom you never saw. The War in which these men fell began before
you were born and ended when the oldest among you were two years
old. And not one of the men who fell in it was a Stoic.

Yet there are reasons why you may properly be asked to join in our
Commemoration ceremony. In losing the men who fell in the War the
Country lost the men who should have been leading and controlling it
now. They would have been just in the prime of life — of the age to be
heads of Businesses and Government Departments and Schools and
Regiments, to be doing much of our writing and inventing and to be
leading our thinking. But they are not here to do all that. And as they
are not here we have to look to men who were not killed in the War —
which means in practice to men who are too old or too young or of
inferior quality. For remember that it is the best who were killed. War
results in the survival of the unfittest, for, although often enough brave
men and ordinary men and cowards are all killed like cattle together,
most often it is the bold and enterprising who risk and lose their lives.
Therefore, though you cannot mourn for the individuals who fell in
the War, you may rightly feel a sense of your own loss in that the
flower of the generation ahead of yours was cut off between 1914 and
1918. You are growing up as a result into a world which has been
managed for sixteen years by men less good than the best.

There is another reason for your presence to-day. The last War was
ours. The next, if there is one, will be yours. Now if the men of our
generation in all the countries in Europe had known what war was

really like, there would have been no war in 1914. We therefore think it fair to you and to your children to pass on to you, before we disappear and leave the world in your hands, not indeed a knowledge of what the last war was (because no words could make you realise that) nor a knowledge of what the next war may be (because we can only guess at the horrors of that) but something of the sorrow which we feel for the loss of our beloved contemporaries, our brothers and our friends, some consciousness of the fact that war seems not only public disaster but also private grief and private desolation.

Do not let us talk politics this morning. But on one thing surely there can be no disagreement — the conviction that 1914 must not be repeated. Let us resolve then that whatever we can do to prevent its repetition shall be done. One thing I would ask of you. Do not believe what it is now fashionable to say — that your countrymen were not heroic in 1914. 'There is no particular virtue in getting killed' is the sort of comment that one hears. I cannot describe the indignation which that kind of statement arouses in anyone who has seen brave men throw away their lives or endure unimaginable misery with a smile. No — do not believe that your countrymen were not heroic in 1914. But neither must you believe that war is in itself a heroic thing, whatever poets and historians say. It is the supreme folly of civilisation and the deepest shame of Christianity. If war ennobles a few individuals, it degrades whole nations. It cannot begin without hatred and it cannot continue without lies. To look at the old newspapers of England and Germany in the War years is to gain a new conception of the blindness and folly of the human race. To read the sermons and prayers of the clergy in both countries is to gain a new conception of the weakness and venality of our religion. Let us resolve then that, so far as we can affect the issue, our Church shall in future raise its voice not in prayer for victory but in condemnation of war, and that our Country shall work throughout the world for justice, truth and the rule of law.

His interest in politics was by now detached. He could criticise the National government for 'action . . . inadequate in relation to the Unemployment Benefit and Devastated Areas' but he followed their lead in foreign policy. In some respects he went rather further. Muriel Currey as a lone woman journalist had covered part of the campaign in Abyssinia in 1935 and was there again in 1938. She was a staunch admirer of Italian aims and methods. Roxburgh followed her in regarding Mussolini's conquest of that country as a legitimate piece of colonising and was taken in by the dictator's claim to be bringing the virtues of Roman order to a benighted area. 'I firmly believe in the substitution of order for chaos,' he wrote to her, and three months later added, 'I am afraid you will find that you and I and Bernard Shaw are the only three people in England who do not want to boil Mussolini in oil.' He dismissed the Spanish Civil War with the phrase 'a plague on both your houses'. He had begun to change his ground about the League of Nations and in 1938 complained to Lord Allen of Hurt-wood that there were those who 'will have the Old League or nothing. The world has changed but the League must not change. They would rather it disappeared than that it secured survival by adaptation to its new environment.' These were private expressions of opinion: in public he seldom permitted himself political views. But like the vast majority of his country-men he favoured appeasement and approved Neville Chamber-lain's policy of peace and orderliness at almost any cost. Munich saw him cracking a bottle of champagne with Haworth, Clarke, Capel Cure and Hunter in joy at deliverance. It was understand-able enough. His horror of seeing the slaughter of the First World War repeated was heightened by his knowledge that the first fifteen years of Stoics would by their very youth be among the first to be killed. And then the school of his creation had reached a new height of achievement and renown. The Duke of Gloucester had visited Stowe on the school's fifteenth birthday. There had been a record number of entrance awards to Oxford and Cam-bridge; exceptional exhibitions in the Art School; a Summer Exeat bringing blissful relief to staff and boys had been estab-lished; the first XV had won all its school matches; and Roxburgh himself was fifty years old. But in the autumn of next year the war began.

Reflecting on those times John Boyd-Carpenter, who in June 1939 had become the first Old Stoic to sit on Stowe's governing body, wrote:

He took the war very hardly . . . He felt it would destroy his work. The Stowe casualty list, which was of course particularly heavy, showed that this fear was not unreal. But both before and during that war his emotional horror of it was extreme. It took the spirit out of him; and coming on top of his immense exertions he never really recovered from it.

There had been for some years signs of the toll that those exertions had taken. Sometimes petulance, sometimes an ever increasing determination to do more, sometimes an odd outburst in form as when one day after the Warrington crisis for some unfathomable reason he anathematised the Welsh, saw a boy by the name of Llewellyn sitting in front of him, apologised elaborately saying that he hoped he had not minded, and had then been struck dumb when the boy with some courage said that he minded exceedingly. Whenever incidents of this kind occurred and he was conscious of having been unjust or in the wrong, he suffered far more remorse than those he offended could have guessed, and would not sleep for nights. A feeler had been put out to see if he would contemplate accepting the headmastership of Cheltenham, but though he consulted the Chairman of the Governors as a matter of form he had no doubt what his answer should be. Now he had to brace himself for a fresh effort. For what? Writing in *The Stoic* he answered that question:

> . . . The old conditions will not return. Darkness has come down upon the road before us — the road which was once illuminated with so clear and cheerful a light. . . . We worked in a world that seemed progressive and secure; we planned for a future that was to be full of new achievement and was already full of hope. We dreamed of the service that we could render to an England steadily advancing towards justice and happiness. Our dreams are dead. . . . When one dream dies another may be born — and one dreamer may dream them both. We have a new dream now. It is a dream of a changed England and a changed Stowe, and in the new dream as in the old the School is seen to be serving the Country to the best of its power. What form that service can take we do not yet fully know. But when we see more clearly what the Country requires of us we shall be ready and able to provide it. We were not founded to face a future of upheaval and impoverishment. But we shall face it if need be, and we hope that we shall face it not ignobly.

Work and organisation were his relief. When war broke out a nucleus of masters and matrons returned to receive any boys whose parents wished them out of town and a start was made on black-ing-out the school's thousand windows. The army immediately claimed two masters, Huggins and Hamer, as Territorial Army Officers. Death claimed another — Ian Clarke, who died during the first month of the war, a man who, Roxburgh wrote in gratitude, 'by doing what he did became one of the creators of Stowe and by being what he was helped to give it some of the qualities of which it is most proud'. On 12 April 1940 in a broadcast he said that on the surface the life of most public schools had been surprisingly little altered by the war: digging for victory and Savings Certificates were the most visible signs; only for the senior boys had there been a major change which had brought them a new maturity. The fall of France made that broadcast out of date. All the masters who remained were thereafter at full stretch, with training or practice in Home Guard, fire-fighting, farming and night-watching. Clifford, who had become head of the Corps in 1934, and Haworth as an ex-regular officer, had particularly exacting responsibilities. German planes used Stowe and its lakes as a landmark, but only two sticks of bombs were dropped during the war and only one did any damage by breaking some windows.

In some respects Stowe was fortunate. It was not requisitioned and the only accommodation that had to be vacated was some class-rooms, and then only for four terms, to house an R.A.O.C. unit who were amiable and helpful guests. Although masters began to melt away and in the end more than twenty left, their departure was gradual. Roxburgh had the good fortune to find some excellent replacements. Two or three who came remained after the war as valuable members of the staff; and the excellence of three women teachers was something that Roxburgh had not expected to acknowledge. He was most fortunate, as he had been in the past, in his new English staff. John Davenport brought back some of White's knowledge of the personalities and intellectual tendencies in modern literature. Wilson Knight was a Shakespearian scholar with an international reputation as a critic. Roy Meldrum, known better in the world as a famous Cambridge rowing coach, was the most diverse of the three: painter, farmer, historical novelist, W.E.A. lecturer, writer of works on teaching English and Latin verse, he exemplified J.F.'s dictum 'A form in which a master's voice is always heard is a form where no one is being educated.' Meldrum's silence produced excellent Sixth Form discussion though it was less successful with duller forms. Curiously enough he and J.F. made little of each other.

But in other respects the school was not so lucky. Inevitably some of the replacements were in their sixties, and in one case even older, and had had no experience of teaching boys. This was common to all schools but Stowe's distance from any large railway station or town made the recruitment of staff more difficult. The recruitment of boys also suffered. Stowe had always relied on the motor car. Parents would arrive, be captivated by its beauty and Roxburgh would do the rest. Petrol rationing made the place almost inaccessible. By the summer of 1943 the numbers had fallen by 100. In the previous year Roxburgh had been compelled to ask his teaching staff to accept a twenty per cent salary cut — he himself proposed to the Governors that his own salary should be substantially reduced — and the Legal and General for their part waived all interest on outstanding mortgages for four years. Numbers rose appreciably in late 1944 but Roxburgh feared 'with some sacrifice of quality'.

Part of the fall in numbers was due to Roxburgh's own conscientiousness to his boys. Although he was critical in the first year of the war when some boys left early to go up to the university before being called up, he was soon encouraging them to do so, believing as he did that the university strengthened the judgment of those who would have to run the country after the war if they survived. In a letter to an Old Stoic dated December 1943 J.F. wrote, 'the age level of the school is lower than it has ever been and the age level of the teaching staff is higher than it has ever been. Major Haworth and I think ourselves pretty ancient but we are mere boys compared with some of our wartime colleagues . . . the Head Prefect took office one week after becoming seventeen; and nearly half the First XV were under sixteen and a half.' He was unhappy that the school had become distorted, the boys too young, the masters too old. Like so many in reserved occupations he felt uneasy if he caught himself relaxing. Not that there was much chance: his relaxations had now been reduced to gardening, and practically the only time he left Stowe was when he drove over to Great Brickhill, twenty miles from Stowe, where with thoughts of his eventual retirement he had bought some land just before the war and leased two cottages. In April 1941 he had 'a fortnight's strenuous gardening . . . I am becoming quite an authority on the cultivation of onions and potatoes.' His other relaxation — driving his car exceedingly fast and dangerously — was now curtailed.

The war was harder to bear psychologically for those who were in a reserved occupation or too old to be active in it. He much approved of a letter that Lord Kennet[1] wrote to his son warning him that those not in the war were too apt to fuss and advising him to attend as little as possible to the war news from day to day. Unfortunately this was not possible for Roxburgh. He had made a resolution at the beginning of the war to 'keep in touch with all the Old Stoics who take part in it', and on top of his work he spent untold hours in the writing of personal letters to congratulate, condole or fortify those of whose honours, losses and misfortunes he came to hear. This exchange of letters threw a stupendous burden upon him; but it did a great deal for the community of Stoics. The effect on those taken prisoner was, as one unfortunate put it, electrifying. 'The first ray of light and my first letter was from J.F. Two pages of interest, comment, good cheer with an offer to send me any books I might want.' His famous memory for names and faces was at work overtime. Old Stoic officers were greeted by name and wished many happy returns to the astonishment of their brother officers; and he would make them stay for beer and sandwiches or for a weekend in his apartments if they could spare the time.

The Stowe losses broke him. Every schoolmaster suffered in seeing the names of boys whom he had cared for recorded as dead or missing, but for Roxburgh it was perhaps specially hard to bear. 'We were all in a very personal sense his family,' one of them said. 'He never talked to me about the Stowe losses,' Christopher Barlow noted, 'even when I spent the whole Easter holidays with him collating much of the information for the Memorial Book. But there were certain names that he could pronounce only with difficulty . . .' In 1943 Peter Choyce found him 'older and tired and dreadfully distressed by the heavy casualty lists of that time

---

[1] Edward Hilton Young, Lord Kennet, Minister of Health 1931-35, Liberal M.P. for Norwich and later Conservative M.P. for Sevenoaks; served on the *Vindictive* at Zeebrugge.

and by the large number of Old Stoics whose names had appeared therein. He seemed in no way consoled by the number of familiar names which also appeared in lists of decorations for gallantry.' That year Jock Anderson won the Victoria Cross and was killed six months later. So was a member of the staff, George Gilling-Lax. He was a classical scholar for whom Roxburgh had a special affection and who had just taken over a house before war broke out: he could have claimed reservation but declined, writing, 'I have been privileged to enjoy the beauty and freedom of Stowe and it is incumbent upon me to repay the debt and help to preserve these things for others.' In 1941 a topical production of *Coriolanus* was staged: the three principal actors were all killed shortly afterwards. Between Armistice Day 1943 and Armistice Day 1944 no less than seventy Old Stoics perished. A little short of two thousand Old Stoics served in the Forces: one in every seven lost his life. These losses were not as grave as the losses which public schools suffered in the First World War, but they were terrible for a new school and in addition to his grief for them as individuals Roxburgh felt that the heart was being torn out of his corps of old boys, the corps that should sustain the school in years to come.

To those still in the school he thought he owed one particular duty: 'to keep them sane and help them to look beyond the war'; and to give guidance through the Chapel services to 'acute anxieties and urgent fears'. He rose to new heights as a preacher. People remembered especially a sermon that he preached on Armistice Day 1941 which concluded with an allusion to Horace's famous ode. 'A poet once said "It is sweet and noble to die for one's country." He was wrong. It is not sweet; it is bitter. But certainly it is noble.' If Horace was wrong were other Roman virtues in question? Frank Tuohy remembered 'him saying in 1942 "I have just had a most unpleasant experience. A woman telephoned to tell me of the death of her son in action and, I am disgusted to have to say it, she was in a night-club and she was drunk . . ." To me, even then, the drunk mother seemed as sad as anything I could think of . . .' J.F. *per contra* thought of the Roman matron who having lost all her sons in battle said that had she another she would willingly give him to the Republic. The sense of compassion shown by Tuohy and the sense of anguished duty shown by Roxburgh reveal that the sensibility of his boys was now of a different kind belonging to an age different from his own.

The pain at last began to lift. There had been a whole holiday to celebrate the school's coming of age and another in honour of Leonard Cheshire's V.C. The celebration of peace seemed to coincide with some signs of normal Stowe life. In 1945 ten Stoics won entrance awards to Oxford and Cambridge. And the enterprising Nonesuch Club with its Brains Trust and opinion polls conducted with great *éclat* a mock General Election. On this occasion the club's public opinion poll, which gave a narrow victory for the Conservatives, did not reflect the nation's opinion. But Roxburgh was entertained to dinner in the House of Commons by four new Old Stoic members — two Conservative and two Labour — and he moved into a new age.[1] But for him it was an age in which nearly three hundred boys whom he knew personally had died.

He loved boys. No other word conveys the quality of his devotion to them or the extent to which he willingly let them fill his life. In his portrait of Roxburgh at Lancing Evelyn Waugh wrote: 'Most good schoolmasters . . . are homosexual by inclination — how else could they endure their work? — but their interest is diffuse and unacknowledged. J.F.'s passions ran deep': though with characteristic kindness he promptly added, 'I do not think he ever gave them physical release with any of his pupils.'[2] Good schoolmasters are more varied than that. There are many whose first love is not their pupils but the technique of their profession, namely the imparting of knowledge, the delight in getting facts or constructions or ideas across to another mind; these men's calamity comes if they tire of boys or come to loathe them and release their loathing in biting ridicule. There are others who appear to be fond of boys and have a knack of influencing

[1] John Boyd-Carpenter, Conservative M.P. for Kingston; Tufton (later Sir Tufton) Beamish, Conservative M.P. for Lewes; Stephen (later Lord) Taylor, Labour M.P. for Barnet, later Parliamentary Secretary, Commonwealth Relations Office 1964; Stephen Swingler, Labour M.P. for Stafford, later Parliamentary Secretary, Minister of Transport 1964.

[2] Evelyn Waugh, *op. cit.*, p. 160.

and interesting them, but are much less emotionally involved than they would like to think. They have in fact the same kind of affection for them as a District Commissioner in the old days of the Colonial Service had for his native tribe. All good headmasters spend an immense time dealing with boys' individual needs, but few, even great ones, can get to know boys intimately, unless their school is small.

J.F. did not moderate his preoccupation with boys when he left Lancing for Stowe. He extended it. It is true that many good masters are ambivalent and in those who are bachelors the ambivalence must be even stronger. The freshness of Roxburgh's interest in each generation of boys and his delight in their habits, idiosyncracies, high spirits and the whole business of growing up sprang from the emotions they inspired in him. At Lancing he was thought to gather round himself the charming, the tactful, the pleasantly mannered to whom he was drawn by his own charm and urbanity: there he was primarily a sixth-form master who had no cause to throw his net wider than his chosen pupils and the boys in his house. But at Stowe he had a responsibility to all. Using his imagination and sympathy to enter into the lives and experience of every kind of boy he sublimated his emotions triumphantly. He did not respond solely to the charming and attractive: he sought out the shy, the lonely, the scruffy, the ill-adjusted and tried to make their lot happier. He had just as much affection for the unacademic as for the scholar and treated them with his habitual good humour. An Irish M.F.H. recalled: 'When I reached the advanced age of sixteen and a half, J.F. and others decided that I had better go to a crammer. I shall never forget the delightful way he pointed this out: "My dear Harry, I'm afraid Stowe can't teach you any more," he said with a twinkle in his eye.' Every games player knew that J.F. did not pretend to talk Wisden or Twickenham, but they remembered his pleasure when they excelled. Most important of all, he was encouraging to those who did not shine at work or games, boys who pottered about, or kept dogs and ferrets, who hadn't yet found themselves or knew what they liked or wanted to do. A note of an interview with such a boy ran as follows: 'Likes *no* school subject (except Latin a little). Can't bear literature — even *Macbeth* is meaningless to him. Can't learn history. Is bored by geography and floored by maths.

Biology would be intolerable if he tried it. Wants *no* profession except mildly the Army. Abhors the idea of business. Nice boy coming on all round.' The sense of humour and proportion is admirable.

He loved intelligence, skill, enterprise, grace, breeding and beauty. But need was what he responded to. A boy had fallen ill or his parents were abroad, or he was a difficult, intelligent child who had failed to conform in orthodox schools but whom J.F. understood and who was worth understanding — his most intimate friendships with boys arose from situations of this sort. They called specially for his powers of sympathy. 'He always seemed to know the background of one's personal problems without having to look up any papers or consult anyone.' 'The interview was unannounced but he knew me by my Christian name and he knew all the circumstances and answers to my problem.' Twenty years separate these testimonies. He was a listener: few good talkers are. He listened with an alert intelligent expression and had that engaging gift of making you think that your problems alone interested him. Boys felt that his solutions to their troubles were not imposed by a system but fashioned to suit their unique personalities. He would sort out the smallest problems and seemed to worry about how you were getting on. To those who did not like school life his help mattered much. He seemed often to find time to visit sick boys especially if they had been taken to hospital: he would discover the right book on internal combustion engines (not his favourite subject), or send one of his silk handkerchiefs to a boy forbidden to read, or descend with strawberries and gossip, or read aloud for an hour or write this kind of letter in war-time to a boy cheated by an attack of poliomyelitis of his life-long ambition to join the Navy:

. . . It is excellent news that Messrs Biceps and Deltoid are now recovering their senses and beginning to do their jobs again . . . If I did not know your absolute devotion to truth and accuracy I should hesitate to accept the figures you give about pears. As it is I can only congratulate you in reverential amazement. But my own small achievement in growing an apple that weighed 1 lb 6 oz and measured $5\frac{1}{2}''$ across is, of course, barely worth mentioning to a man who grows pears that weigh three pounds each. . . . Goodbye, my dear Andrew, I must break off now and tell Five A what I think of their Certificate chances. As I think nothing of them at all it won't take long to say, but I have got to say it at 5.15 punctually.

But he did not confuse sympathy with softness. A boy's mother died and he was naturally allowed home. But when he seemed to be staying there too long Roxburgh wrote:

The reason I am writing to you again now is that I want to suggest to you that the best thing you can do and the thing that your mother would like you to do is to get back again into the ordinary routine of life as soon as possible — that is as soon as you think it is right to leave your father. This is the correct way to face all disasters — face them, deal with them as far as they can be dealt with, help other people that need help and then get back to your job.

Another boy, reported to him by his housemaster for not co-operating in the house, presented himself indignant and stung by his housemaster's acid tongue, rehearsing his grievances. 'Ah Joey, my dear fellow, I hear you are having trouble with your housemaster,' Roxburgh genially began. He knew of the difficulties; put them from the boy's point of view; then talked of the difficulties that housemasters face and of his confidence in them; discussed whether these differences were fundamental or trivial; and then invited the boy to speak his mind. Instead of detailing injustices with emotion the boy responded to his sympathy, discussed the matter rationally and finally agreed to apologise to his housemaster for troubling him. Schoolboys live in a world in which their masters are for ever telling them that this is right and that is wrong so it is not surprising that they themselves become obsessed by justice and fairness. J.F. would always be moved by an appeal to justice, and boys knew that they would be upheld against masters if he judged them truthful and their case proven: the fact that this made life difficult for the weaker members of the staff he disregarded. Reason not righteousness was Roxburgh's weapon. One day two boys called to tell him that, surprised by the fact that so little water was running over the spillway to the lake opposite the Temple of British Worthies, they had pulled up an iron rod in the sluice gate but could not get it down again: and as a result the lake had disappeared. 'Disappeared!' exclaimed Roxburgh, 'Well you'd better fill it up again.' The boys

spent their spare time mending the whole contraption and returned full of confidence: a mistake had been made, reported and
rectified.

He suffered more than disappointment if he judged that he had
failed with a boy. And he often so judged. Writing to a step-father
about a boy who had to leave because he could not respond to
school routine he said: 'We have failed with him and however the
blame be apportioned between the school and the boy the failure
remains indisputable . . . As a result of our long struggle with
him I have come to feel a real attachment for him.' He could be
outraged by some offences but his reason replaced outrage by
distress, and distress awoke in him the sense of obligation —
particularly to a boy whom he had to expel. On one occasion a
boy had stolen money outside the school and the circumstances
were such that Roxburgh felt he could not be kept. He took so
much trouble in getting him accepted by another public school
that his parents at first appalled and grateful became almost
resentful.

He pitied especially those in trouble for sexual offences, and his
pity had to overcome certain psychological obstructions. Homosexual acts disgusted him and offended his sense of duty. There is
some evidence that this sprang from his days at Charterhouse
where under Rendall's remote rule sex flourished. He insisted that
seats in the Chapel at Stowe should not face each other and that
there should be no specially raised place for a choir as he would
not have the younger boys exposed to rapacious glances. But
reason, not disgust, governed his treatment of sexual practice, and
he modified his tactics to suit each case. One highly honourable
boy who was to be head of the school had been showing signs of
infatuation with small boys: J.F. treated this as a straight case of
discipline, told him to stop at once or lose his promotion. On the
other hand when dealing with an intellectual and highly sexed
boy he launched into an explanation of the psychology of homosexuality and explained that all people had a continuous spectrum
in their nature running from male to female; and that by showing
romantic love for a boy one was increasing the female end of the
spectrum in him. In private he would often make exceedingly
uninhibited remarks. On being told that a particular boy had been
casting looks at another he replied, 'Well, thank God for that: it is

the first constructive idea he has ever had in his life.' He once told Capel Cure that talk of measures to 'provide a solution' for homosexual problems irritated him: there was no solution — other than a school brothel. He welcomed the palliative of a school dance: but while there was no rule against pin-ups his remark on entering a study: 'My dear fellow, must you cover the entire wall with beautiful damsels?' was enough to make the occupants feel that they ought to remove them. If anyone were to observe that the sexual urges are as strong in adolescence as they ever will be he would reply that one of the claims that boarding schools make is to teach chastity and self-control. Those who consider that such an attitude is typical of English hypocrisy should note that at the great Paris *lycée*, Henri Quatre, in the nineteen-fifties, the parent of a boy who had produced for the delight of his fellow students '*un pin-up déshabillable*' was summoned by the Proviseur to be told of the gravity of such conduct; and in such *lycées* the masters would repeat to their pupils the celebrated maxim for success at the Polytechnique: 'Messieurs, les premiers de l'X ne fument pas, ne boivent pas et sont puceaux.' (Gentlemen, those who pass out top of the Polytechnique do not smoke or drink and are virgins.)

Roxburgh taught boys to grow up. He did so partly by representing the world of sophisticated tastes and diction, partly by giving them leisure. But he did so much more by treating seriously almost anything that boys said to him seriously. In one of his talks to the school he urged any boy who wanted to talk about his future career to come and see him at the usual time before supper. A thirteen-and-a-half-year-old went and told him that he wanted to become a schoolmaster. Roxburgh was all attention: discussed his own profession, talked of his own happiness in it, pointed out that it was not a career to grow rich in, never once suggested that it was perhaps a little early to take a final decision. He used to justify his insistence on social conventions, manners and dress by saying that they existed to save people the embarrassment of bothering about such trivial things and he thought that boys matured faster once they mastered the art of being at their ease.

Those little attentions, the note on a birthday, the word of congratulation, the letter in his own hand after the Certificate results,

the unexpected present, the summons when a piece of work had
been sent up to him for commendation, and the twenty minutes of
praise and criticism that followed spent in pointing out an
anachronism and polishing the sentences just as if he were
conducting an individual tutorial produced among the vast proportion of Stoics immense affection. He did not want this to
develop into worship. Affection and worship are tributes to
greatness in a headmaster — and dangerous. They are ways of
dominating boys, of flattering their self-respect yet undermining
the most important of all processes inculcated at school: independence. In an address to parents he begged them not to bring
ferocious powers of organisation to the nursery, cling to their boy
when he was grown up, or overwhelm him with their personality.
He did not wish to govern through hero-worship. Clearly many
would do things simply because he had asked them and would
not do them for others, but he tried to make them think why
it was reasonable to act so. He also in the last analysis kept
his distance. At his funeral an Old Stoic felt, 'It is strange that
you could feel so fond of a person and yet feel that you never
knew him well.' He identified himself in boys' minds with Stowe,
Stowe with liberty and beauty, and life there with being fortunate
and privileged — this was how with all his stress on the individual he produced corporate loyalty of the kind that persuades
old boys to enter their sons for the school.[1]

There was a story current in the masters' common room at
Stowe that at the end of term a group of masters sat round

[1] This process is well illustrated by three communications from David
Niven who wrote to J.F. on leaving: 'I have something that I have been wanting to say for a long time and I decided to say it to you at the end of term but
when the time came I am afraid my heart failed me! You may think it a
colossal piece of cheek, and indeed it is, but please forgive me as it is certainly sincere. I want to congratulate you personally, Sir, on your wonderful achievement in bringing Stowe to what it is . . . And I always wish
I could have done something to help . . . I do hope you are not offended with
what I have written but I could not leave Stowe without expressing my
appreciation and admiration.' Eight years later: 'I am an actor now, God rest
my soul! And I find it much more fun, more interesting and definitely more
lucrative than being a rather inefficient soldier.' Seven years later back in
the army during the war a son was born to him and at once entered for the
school by telegram. 'Both doing well. Father doing even better.'

rivalling each other to write the most blistering report on some vile boy. They despatched the lot smouldering to J.F. who returned them with his own report added: 'He is *persona grata* with us all.' He did on the contrary write frank reports saying for instance that a housemaster's strictures were deserved and that 'his success in science only serves to show it is laziness that makes him fail in other subjects. He is over sixteen and it is time he took himself in hand, realising that life cannot consist in doing only what one pleases. He is a nice fellow, but he is not making anything of himself at all at present — and time is getting on.' One Old Stoic, who in a moment of middle-aged courage re-read his reports, noted that Roxburgh always made 'an appreciation of a developing individual instead of honest appraisals of an unlikeable adolescent'. By the nineteen-twenties parents had become rightly more demanding and were not content to have searing comments served up to them. He therefore tried to impress on his staff that reports were for the benefit of parents: they ought to be constructive and nothing was lost if they were gracious. Masters must not, he told a Masters' Meeting, write 'he does not work well'. 'I suspect,' he added, 'that in this case the master was making a comment on his own work and not on that of the boy. Gentlemen, we *must* take more care. Some masters — no doubt unconsciously — make comments on themselves. One actually wrote in his report, "I must really work harder next term." While fully endorsing the admirable determination on the part of the master concerned it may perhaps not fill the parent with the sort of confidence in our staff that one would like him to have.'

Boys were his life, parents his career. Like most schoolmasters he found unreasonable parents the worst crosses to bear but, although it is an exaggeration to say that before 1914 a parent hoped never to meet his son's headmaster for to do so meant that at the very least the boy was on the point of expulsion, Roxburgh determined to know something about his parents and establish a relationship with them. He did so for the best of reasons: they intrigued him. He once said to a mother on the North Front: 'You see that tree: it is overshadowed on one side by the larger tree and has not developed at all. It is the same with boys. When parents bring their boys here I am as interested in the parents as the boys.' Sometimes his notes were purely snobbish. 'This boy's people did not come over with the Conqueror,' or 'Very well born, very well bred.' At other times they showed that he understood excellently how necessary and how dangerous to their sons parents can be. He pretended to be surprised that so few of them realised that their sons 'lived pretty intensely, having been in the course of the term frequently elated, occasionally distressed and more or less continuously effervescent' and needed rest in the holidays. 'The level of intelligence in a family,' he wrote, 'is reflected with remorseless accuracy in the boys who come out of it.' Parents did not by any means always like him. 'My parents said he was a professional charmer, an actor who lacked sincerity, a shop-walker who was selling his wares.' This reaction was characteristic of those who suspect charm and detest a manner. An officer in the Brigade of Guards decided not to send his son to Stowe because Roxburgh escorted him personally over the school, and a man who did not delegate a task such as that must have a defective knowledge of command and organisation.[1] But on the whole his success was overwhelming and he had a devastating touch with mothers and sisters — remembering their faces, recalling their names, exerting himself with umbrellas on their behalf with an effusion of courtesy which was almost a caricature of his normal spacious manner. His range of interests made him appear capable of discussing anything. 'My mother thought he was wonderful: when she came to see J.F. in my first term they talked about hens.' His fascination was so powerful that it brought retribution. One determined mother on being told that Stowe had no vacancy, gushed: 'Mr Roxburgh, he must come to you; I shan't leave the room till you agree.' 'Dear Lady,' came the immediate reply, 'is that an enticement or a threat?'

Inevitably parents' visits do not form part of the happier memories of a headmaster. Many of them are arranged to air grievances and complaints, and some are emotionally exhausting because parents suffer much distress if they are summoned to be told that their son is in serious trouble. In these interviews a

[1] He was not the first public school headmaster regularly to escort prospective parents over the school and take trouble to impress them. Gray was doing so at Bradfield before the First World War. (A. L. Irvine, *Sixty Years at School*, p. 58.)

headmaster has to be wary. A member of his staff may have made an error of judgment and the parents are out for blood. But if the error is admitted, the school may be presented with a claim for damages and the threat of a lawsuit. More often a parent may be convinced that an error has been made when the school is guilt-less and a headmaster then has to convince an incensed couple to listen to facts and reason. J.F. had a good eye for the parents he could trust. He would sometimes admit an error and disarm them by saying 'I place myself completely in your hands.' The parents were disarmed. But he knew how to send in defence of his staff a bleak though courteous reply to those he thought mis-guided.

I can only say that knowing your son's housemaster as I do I am perfectly certain that whatever he has done has not only been correct but honourable. The use of the word 'vindictive' throughout this long and unhappy correspondence has never ceased to surprise me. But I have not been able to understand your point of view and you have doubtless found mine as difficult to sympathise with. This accounts for the painful quality of the correspondence which I am thankful to think must be nearing its end.

He was really roused by a mother who accused the school of sending her son home knowing that he was ill with an infectious disease and at the same time expressed the hope that her indignant letter would not get the boy into trouble with his housemaster next term. Roxburgh replied that if she thought so ill of Stowe she had the simple remedy of removing her boy. But he was no less ready to help parents. Among many such letters in his files is one communicating with a father who had received a letter of freezing insolence from his son. Roxburgh declined to intervene. 'If I talk to him about the contents of a letter which he wrote to his own parents, isn't there a danger that he will lose confidence in you and never write to you freely again?' Then he proceeded to make practical suggestions.

There is little in these instances that any headmaster could not cap with similar stories of his own, but what set Roxburgh apart was the astonishing number of occasions on which he intervened in boys' lives and the high degree of his accessibility to parents. This posed problems with his staff. 'It is the boys only that really count,' Roxburgh wrote to a prep schoolmaster. 'Parents, masters, school administration count for nothing compared with the boys.' If he gave so much of himself to boys and spared so much time for parents, what had he left for masters?

Chapter VIII

Aftermath

Summing up the power relationships in a public school, John Wilson concluded: 'Generally speaking the headmaster and his staff are on one side of the fence and the boys on the other: but it not infrequently happens with a powerful headmaster that the staff are closer to the boys in all senses than they are to him. "They are all my children," as one headmaster told me.' [1] Roxburgh did not bear out this dictum. He was closer to his boys than to his staff; and this was to lead to difficulties.

Not, of course, in the early years. Then he was working intimately with the masters, partners in a new enterprise, most of them young, practically all bachelors, willing to live a monastic existence in discomfort in which they devoted all their energies to the task. In those days he made himself available to masters for an

[1] John Wilson, *Public Schools and Private Practice*, p. 87.

hour or more five evenings a week. Any master could put his name down for whatever time he might wish. He held memorable though few Masters' Meetings. A master's notes taken during one held in July 1935 survive which show that he interspersed encouragement and admonishment among a mass of routine matters ranging from salaries and reports to methods for preventing cheating in form. Bursarial inspection of masters' bedrooms had revealed 'fundamental ignorance of the basic principles of electricity' and masters must not complain if switches were removed in order to avoid 'the horrors of combustibility'. No, he said in answer to a question, no master can take credit for exam results: the only thing he can take credit for is the personal relationship that exists between him and the boys. Then suddenly he would strike. 'I asked the headmaster of —— "Do you find Sunday afternoon a problem?" He said, "No; the boys sleep; they are so mentally tired." Are we working our fellows hard enough? Are *we* working hard enough? I refer you to the Report of 1932: "Insufficient signs of sustained effort on the part of the boys; they do not respond enough to masters." The key to this is preparation. The key to any educational problem is what the boy does himself. We ought to be more exacting. We must be more exacting to ourselves than we are to the boys. We must not take to despairing in our attitude to backward boys or sets. We should encourage and help by recognising the small successes and efforts of backward boys.' But he used Masters' Meetings principally to allow masters to air their own views and himself to establish genial relations with them. He rarely expounded his educational principles: he expected his staff to follow his example. This, as we shall see, was to make for confusion.

Masters were given uncompromising support against criticism. His correspondence shows again and again how a specific complaint would be treated strictly on its merits. If it was in vague terms and no facts established, it was rebutted unequivocally; if it cited facts, the facts would be checked and, if correct, the correspondent informed. Even when he thought such complaints justified he would not humble the master concerned. He noted them and would then bring them up at an apposite moment when the master would not feel loss of self-respect and the incident itself was dead. Like all sensible high executives he often took the blame himself by insisting that a matter was ultimately his responsibility. If a master blundered he would never reproach him but simply treat the matter as an every-day occurrence that afflicts all men. 'My dear fellow,' he once said to Heckstall-Smith, 'let us consider only the best thing to do next. If I ever thought about the past for any reason other than to find out what is best for the future I shouldn't last three days.' [1] There was never any need, he thought, to blame people; if they are worth keeping they know when they are at fault and all that matters is righting the wrong and in the process educating them.

When masters clashed with boys his approach was different. Boys undoubtedly felt, and were meant to feel, that he would take their part if they had a good cause, and he was not ready to take a master's word unquestioned if a case was referred to him of dispute between a master and a boy. Truth and justice came before a master's *amour propre*. He was right to do so — and could afford to do so — because he was a good judge of boys' truthfulness. Their difficulties and imagined wrongs he could assess with enviable accuracy and he never considered whether his popularity would be affected by his actions. He did not have to: at no time in his career as a schoolmaster was he unable to command respect and gain affection from boys, and he continued to gain it because he was scrupulous not to exploit his gift. And here the impression that he gave to boys and masters alike of having dedicated his life to the profession of schoolmastering came to help him. A master might be irked or wounded by one of his decisions in regard to a boy but he did not think it had been taken from a mean-minded or equivocating or feeble motive or by someone who had sold out. His staff thought of him as an expert in their own job. To work under him was like playing in an orchestra under a maestro — he might be distant and touchy and demand from you more than you thought you could give; but the mastery, the professionalism, the interpretation were of such excellence that you submitted to his spell. He had humour, was never pompous, and handled the terrible trivialities of school life with engaging lightness. Bachelor masters were allowed free laundry which in 1930 was not supposed to exceed 3s. 6d. a week. He was asked to remonstrate with them over their abuse of this privilege. So at a Masters' Meeting

[1] Heckstall-Smith, *Doubtful Schoolmaster*, p. 33.

J.F. began: 'The Bursar — he is really very worried about this — came to me the other day in despair about the laundry bill. He wasn't complaining, poor man, but he has to account for these ridiculous items to his auditors — as though one didn't have to change one's clothes more than once a week. Now let me see' — consulting notes and pulling a long face — 'ah yes, here is Mr X whose laundry comes to 5s. 2d. in the first week of term. Mr Y 7s. 4d. Mr Z 2s. 6d. — I imagine' — this in an audible *sotto voce* — 'he must do a lot of it himself. And then the Bursar mentioned mine. I must admit that I had a trunkful of dirty shirts from an Hellenic Cruise and they seem to have come to' — very impressively — '38s. 5d.'

But the staff's admiration could never have been won by occasional acts of charm. He won their loyalty by the magnetism that he exerted. To some he was a Svengali. They rose on the strength of his wings. Elated they determined to fly for themselves and leave Stowe, but once his hand was removed they fell apart and crashed. Even those who did not submit at the time could not remain untouched. One master who left Stowe in early middle age and did not see eye to eye with Roxburgh wrote to him over the years letters compounded of admiration and reproach, affection and abuse, gratitude and calumny: but he could never stop writing and J.F.'s replies were full of understanding and compassion. Another loyal subordinate, who gave Roxburgh long service but who found him increasingly difficult to work under and finally left, felt that his differences with him were petty compared to J.F.'s qualities as a leader and a man. A few weeks before T. H. White died he wrote an encomium of Roxburgh in which he admitted that, rebellious, proud, insubordinate and suspicious of Roxburgh's pretensions, he had rather disliked him when he was a master. But he later found why he had disliked him.

It was *envy* and it was my own fault . . . I searched about for his weak points hoping to emphasise my own virtues . . . I know, now that I am old myself, why I disliked or envied him. It was because I loved and admired him. I wanted to be his blue-eyed boy as everybody else did. But J.F. had no favourites. He wisely spread the warmth of his heart over a large part of the earth. . . . He was a rarity. If rarity is genius, then he was a genius.

His staff admired him — but they sighed. For the truth was that as a headmaster he was least successful in his relations with his staff; and in the profession that is a serious criticism. In the early days J.F. gave gay, invigorating dinner parties at which he mixed his guests and got to know the young as well as the older masters. These continued well into the 'thirties, but as the staff grew larger and his own burdens too heavy he gradually gave them up and never found a way to replace them. The turn-over in masters impeded his efforts and he was never so intimate with the newcomers. In the 'forties his weariness and distress cut him off from them. His judgment of men was not as good as his judgment of boys: during the war some masters were there only for the period of the emergency, and a few were of dispiriting quality — birds of passage who happened to rest at Stowe on their long flight from job to job. The old freedom for masters to visit him had declined and by then only housemasters and a few seniors had free access. When the war ended and masters returned the familiar scene had changed. In 1937 one master in every three was married: when Roxburgh retired the ratio was exactly the opposite. Between him and the younger members of the staff was a gap of more than thirty years. Those who knew him in the 'twenties were his most uncritical disciples, those of the middle years were more detached though they regarded his foibles with a smile, but those of the last decade saw little of him.

'The staff were certainly last on his agenda with regard to welfare,' one member wrote, and married masters were even lower on it than their bachelor colleagues. Roxburgh never reconciled himself to the need for his staff to marry. House-matrons were a necessity but not wives, and in the 'twenties some of the bachelors on the staff unconsciously adopted Roxburgh's prejudices and implied to their married colleagues that they were really only half time on the job. Roxburgh made no attempt to know wives since then he was overburdened with work much of which he should never have had to do. But even when married masters became the rule rather than the exception he excluded them from his horizon. After the war he was heard to greet the wife of a recently married master whom he was meeting for the third time with the words, 'At last we meet.' He could not help seeing when housemasters were able to marry and retain

their post how greatly their wives helped them, nor the effect that
such wives as Dodie Watt in the art school, or Patience McElwee
in her circle had in helping boys develop. But his indifference to
the difficulties of married masters, many of whom lived through
no fault of theirs some distance from the school sprang from more
sombre reasons than his simple-minded feeling that their useful-
ness had diminished. He was ashamed of their condition and
knew that he was powerless to alter it. One of the savings that had
consciously been made when the school was founded was on
masters' salaries. The Warrington débâcle made it more difficult
to improve them. A young bachelor master living-in could just
make both ends meet. But the married masters lived on a shoe-
string unless they had private means. Roxburgh buried his head
in the sand and almost refused to admit that the problem existed.
After the war, during which the staff had taken salary cuts, some
of the young married masters asked if their salaries could be
paid monthly. J.F.'s nose wrinkled at the mention of this grammar
school custom. 'Gentlemen, have none of you heard of an overdraft at the bank?' Few of them had ever had anything else.

His great gift of talking the language of every boy did not
come to him in dealing with his staff. There were some whose
qualities he never understood and his judgment of them was
distorted by his prejudices. Or perhaps it was that while his prejudices hardly ever affected his relations with boys because he saw
them all as potentially capable of developing in many different
directions, masters were for him formed and unmalleable. He did
not understand every master's idiom and could misjudge the
qualities of those who were not his sort. Tim White did not err
when he said that Roxburgh had no favourites, for Roxburgh
believed familiarity to be incompatible with authority. But he
conspicuously preferred those on the staff of vivacious intelligence; and it was noted that during the war he saw more of John
Davenport than other new masters because he enjoyed his conversation and range of interests. Indeed there was more than a
suspicion in some quarters that he preferred the company of
sophisticated boys to that of their dourer adults. One of his great
admirers on the staff wrote: 'Boys looked on J.F. as a friend but
not, I think, masters. He was always friendly but a little distant
with them. Masters admired, liked and trusted him, but true

friendship did not come into the relationship.' Another underlined this judgment when he wrote, 'In spite of extreme friendliness I never felt quite so intimately at home with J.F. as with his successor.'

The class image of the public school worked upon his own inclinations. Public schoolmasters make an assumption which they greatly value: that although they have chosen to follow a calling which will not make them rich, they talk on equal terms with the parents of the boys they teach — and secretly believe themselves with good cause to be superior to many of them. How, asked Roxburgh, could a man who had an accent and did not have an Oxford or Cambridge degree claim to do so? (The fact that some Stowe parents also had an accent and had never been to a university did not escape him.) He did not deceive himself on this matter. One of the first masters he appointed had a Dublin degree. 'Does not look well for window dressing,' he noted on his file; but he appointed him. On another occasion he noted that an applicant had 'a large nose, a Durham degree and a Cockney accent,' and added with a final flick of the whip, 'He says he would like teaching but has done nothing but Sunday school work so far.' Roxburgh knew, and did not quarrel with, the standards of his world. Window dressing did not trouble him: he enjoyed it. Masters were expected on a ceremonial occasion to add to it. Heckstall-Smith delighted him when he proposed to climb Snowdon on the day that Queen Mary visited Stowe as he did not relish wearing a morning coat; but it was wrong to exclude a master from the ceremony of dedicating the Chapel, when Prince George was present, because he did not possess this ritual garment which only a few years later masses of professional men no longer owned but hired.

Schoolmasters need praise as well as support. They cannot see some building rising, or merger accomplished, or ministerial tangle unravelled as the outcome of their work. Did Roxburgh encourage his staff sufficiently? The evidence conflicts. 'He always showed his joy when a boy won a university scholarship — always,' wrote one of his tutors. A housemaster maintained that he was continually given new heart by J.F.'s 'Well done, you!', and another who had just taken over a house that had hardly won any athletic event for years remembered that he wrote him a note on their first modest triumph. 'He never wrote another note when in later years my house met with far greater success. Of course he was right.' But some of his colleagues were emphatic that he neither praised nor helped his staff enough. 'He was not the man to hand round the kindly word of encouragement,' wrote one of them. 'In one of my army history classes three out of the four got over 93 per cent in the exam and the other about 80 per cent. As this was one of my few academic achievements I hoped . . . but alas, I heard no more.' It is precisely at such unheroic moments that a master longs for the congratulations of a professional who understands precisely what it has meant to achieve such results, the beauty of which those who have never taught cannot appreciate. Younger masters did not always get the help that they needed. Soon after the school started a young master was appointed who had been head boy of his own school. He was to give admirable service as a master for thirty years but in his first term he found to his bewilderment that he was unable to keep order in form. He was at a loss what to do — he had never had any difficulty in keeping order as a prefect. He gave boys lines (the writing out of Latin poetry on specially ruled lined paper that could be obtained only from their housemasters). They warmed to the task of ragging him. He gave them more lines. Their ingenuity rose to new heights. Eventually he gave so many lines that the school ran out of lined paper. At this point he took his problem to Roxburgh. J.F. was unable to help. He could not understand how a good man could fail to keep order and was bereft of suggestions. One of the unfortunate man's colleagues in the end taught him some of the tricks of the trade and saved his career.

With housemasters difficulties were bound to arise. Seven of the eight houses were within two minutes walk of the centre of the main building and the eighth which stood near the Chapel was no more than five minutes away. The houses soon became large, numbering over seventy boys, and few of them were the customary self-contained, independent units in which the housemaster and his family lived on the other side of a baize door. Consequently the housemasters were apprehensive of their ability to supervise and control. Roxburgh's gift of establishing a genuine relationship with every boy that passed through the school meant that he took over work which in other schools was done by a housemaster. He irritated his housemasters by lack of co-ordination over such matters. They felt that he would too readily grant a boy some privilege or permission which his housemaster had decided to refuse; too often make pronouncements to the school without previously informing the housemasters of his intentions. He claimed the right to veto the appointment of house monitors — though he said that he would be surprised if he ever had to exercise it — and to come in on equal terms with a housemaster in choosing his head of house. A headmaster is certain to intervene from time to time and housemasters will want to put certain matters, such as a grave breach of discipline, in his hands; but in the scope of his interference on matters of detail Roxburgh went far beyond what was normal.

And yet if he were to realise his ideals he would have to have gone further still. Some of his housemasters fitted themselves easily to his notions. They might differ with him from time to time but he would listen to and often adopt a suggestion or change of policy. There were others who believed that they were interpreting his ideas but who nevertheless thought it their duty to inform him that while it was one thing to talk to boys as if they were adults they were not in fact adults and could not on all occasions be treated as such. There were others who, frankly disagreeing with his policies, would appeal to him to restrain their more headstrong libertarian colleagues, and visit him sometimes in pairs to put their point of view. He could have helped his housemasters more, and the boys under them, if he had set himself, year in, year out, to explain to them precisely what he wanted their approach to boys to be. He preferred too often to be a court of appeal. Ageless disputes such as the inalienable right of a housemaster to control the boys in his house do not become any fresher with the passage of time. There were men who had been brought up themselves under the old public school ideals and, while genuinely willing to modify them, took their duties seriously and were not prepared to move nearly as far as Roxburgh in giving boys freedom nor to relax the old-style discipline in the house. He occasionally used some devious way to attract their attention to what he considered right and they were doing wrong. For instance a boy of considerable intelligence and scholarly ability when halfway up the school got into trouble with the authorities in his house. Roxburgh sought him out and asked him to help with making the arrangements for some visiting dignitary: a week later he sent him as a reward a splendid crocodile-skin wallet. Such methods did not reconcile the housemaster to his headmaster's point of view — though they did wonders for the boy. Roxburgh heard, sometimes it seemed by telepathy, whether a boy — he might be clever or inarticulate — was being chivied because he was considered in his house conceited or sloppy or dingy or affected or slack. He knew too the pressures and persecutions of schoolboy opinion and recognised that the retribution exacted by prefects or the boy's contemporaries was often excessive and inappropriate in dealing with these growing pains which in some cases could be the first signs of mature individuality emerging. But intervention in individual cases by itself was insufficient. If he wanted to establish a new method of treating boys he had to go beyond personal example.

In this Roxburgh was the victim of a paradox of his own making. He was all too ready to put his apron strings into his staff's hands and some became so used to his advice and intervention that they were accustomed to leave him to take decisions. A chief executive can in fact unwittingly geld his subordinates if he is too accessible, too ready to give his opinion, too expectant to be consulted: his staff discover that it is not worth their while doing anything on their own account without putting it up to their chief first. Eventually the dynamic of the enterprise rests entirely upon him. But Roxburgh would not assume the mantle of the traditional autocratic headmaster, who, though he demands obedience, loyalty, willingness to help, and generates a little fear among his staff, also fulfils the role of a father figure. Onto him masters discharge their anxieties and he is often well-liked because the staff put all decisions into his hands and do not have to perform the disturbing act of reasoning and questioning. On the contrary Roxburgh could never be content with giving orders but demanded rationality. This imposes a strain both on the headmaster and his staff. Rational discussion is more civilised. Even if it is time-consuming and emotionally exhausting, to debate issues face to face on equal terms calmly and coolly in an institution is a finer ideal than the sharp command. Roxburgh tried it, but in the end it frayed his nerves. He liked approval and could be visibly put out if it was withheld, and he did not appreciate that some men need to chew over a problem and deliberately withhold judgment on a scheme until they have ruminated. He interpreted hesitancy sometimes as lack of good will. He was also handicapped by the fact that his mind worked fast and accurately; those of some of his colleagues did not. The very strength of his personality and the admiration that his staff felt for his achievement spelt danger. A master would consult him, receive approval for some specific proposal and interpret this as general approval of the way in which according to his own lights he was carrying out Roxburgh's policy. Then Roxburgh would do something which showed that the master had mistaken what the great man's policy was — worse still when he supported somebody else whose attitude was baldly opposed to all that the master held dear — and the shock was all the greater. There was more contention than was inevitable between the traditionalists and the radicals on the staff because each believed that he was interpreting Roxburgh's ideals correctly but none could be sure where Roxburgh himself would put the emphasis. All his masters were agreed upon the objective, no two could agree how to attain it. This made for excellence at the start, for tension later and for difficulty after he retired.

The highly personal nature of his rule offended his peers who did not regard him as one of their leaders. There are some headmasters who are the natural choice as spokesmen for their profession. While having a feel for the direction in which events are moving, they are too shrewd to push solutions which are much in advance of opinion among their colleagues: that means in practice pushing with the finger-tips. Roxburgh was not regarded as a sound man — he was a little too outspoken about the defects of the public schools, and the powerful impact on the boys made by his charismatic régime seemed too much a condemnation of the role of headmasters elsewhere. He was no committee man. Someone has to hammer out agreements with the Ministry about pensions or find common ground between the schools on matters concerning which each educationalist is convinced that he alone has found the appropriate solution; but Roxburgh refused to leave a task that he was doing supremely well and move on to what have unkindly been described as spheres of higher uselessness.[1] 'Naturally enough,' wrote a friend, 'men of his inspiration and stature are individualists: he did not take kindly to organisation and methods and I doubt whether he had much affection for the Headmasters' Conference.'

Something has to be sacrificed in every scheme of education. Roxburgh sacrificed his influence upon his staff. In a perfect world every member of it would have followed his methods, but this could have been achieved only if he had spent as many hours advising and encouraging masters as he spent upon the boys. There were too few hours in the day. A public school headmaster has to work through his colleagues and hope that they, and especially his housemasters, will convey to the boys what he values. In the long run it is the only way to influence a school. Ideally when the school numbered 500 he should have devoted less time to his boys and more time to his staff. He should no doubt consciously and firmly have put behind him the early years when the prestige and position of the school depended inevitably upon his own personality and effort, and have begun to delegate and spread his power of persuasion upon those who were in the future to carry out his purpose. Instead he preferred to carry on doing triumphantly what he had learnt at Lancing and perfected at Stowe. This was a fault; but it is given to few men to make full use of the gifts they have, and to fewer still to continue to develop new talents.

Writing to the Governors after the war to urge a rise in salary for his much valued secretary R. E. Lucas, Roxburgh concluded his letter by saying, 'Finally his tact in dealing with masters both as a colleague and as representing myself is remarkable and helps to make up my own deficiencies in that department.' He had in fact at that time caused some offence by saying at a Masters' Meeting that the school had been carried on by 'the middle aged and mediocre', not a phrase that showed much appreciation of all the extra duties and grinding work that his colleagues had

---

[1] He even spoke of the work of being a headmaster as inferior to that of a teacher, describing himself in 1931 as 'a fallen angel who has given up work that demands a man's highest qualities for work that demands only toil and tact and the qualities of a good clerk'.

endured, while those who had been away on war duties were returning refreshed from the change. His individual apologies for the phrase were not well received — except by those who had the insight to realise that Roxburgh had himself in mind when he spoke. He thought himself now inadequate and expressed in private his opinion that he was running-down. He began to make frequent clandestine visits to Harley Street and worried about his health. He entered the post-war years depressed and convinced that Stowe had fallen a long way from the goals which he had set and which were in sight when war had come. 'It was a young school (only sixteen) when the greatest war in history hit it,' he told the school in a sermon in the summer of 1946. 'Of course it went backwards. It is now just beginning to go forwards again. How fast and how far it will go forward depends upon what loyalty you show to it, what you do to raise its standards in work and games and how far you restore to it the enthusiasm, the drive for achievement, the spirit of unselfishness, the sense of duty and the fine feeling of honour which were once its inspiration and which became perhaps a little dimmed during the years of the war.' On this last point he was somewhat reassured. Some boys behaved obstreperously at Bletchley station and J.F. demanded to know names and threatened to beat the culprits. To his surprise thirty came to report themselves. In fact things were beginning to pick up. The first masters began to return in the autumn that the war ended. In January 1946 an Old Stoic dinner had been held in London and oversubscribed: Roxburgh must have known that they came to see him as much as each other. A retrospective exhibition of Old Stoic art mounted by Robin and Dodie Watt was a reminder of what could be achieved. Leslie Huggins resumed his subscription concerts, the London Philharmonic again performed and an ambitious production of *St Joan* was staged. But Roxburgh was dissatisfied. In 1948 he returned twice to his theme. One of the claims that the public schools make for their system is that they teach boys to 'care'. Boys are taught to take it for granted that a job is more than an occupation defined in terms of contractual obligations. Their masters do not work a fixed number of hours and then knock off: they belong to a community and serve it by turning up at all sorts of voluntary activities although in terms of contract they are not obliged to do so. Once individuals in a community care they put more into their society than they take out of it. Roxburgh tried to get over in a sermon how much can be achieved if only a few do so. 'All people on many subjects and many people on all subjects are simply indifferent when left to themselves. But they may be moved to think or act by the influence of a few individuals who have convictions and the courage of them — individuals who *care*. So if ever you are in a position in which you and perhaps a few friends feel that the community you are in ought to change its ways of thinking or acting, do not say to yourselves, "What do we amount to?" Why, you amount to an army if you *care*. If you are the few who care among the many who don't, then you are in a triumphant position — in the same position as the great reformers who have moved the world in the past.'

He was worried by the external situation which faced the public schools. During the war long discussions and negotiations had taken place leading up to the publication of the Fleming Report[1] which envisaged the public schools offering a number of places to local authorities on condition that the latter paid the fees. In *Eleutheros* he had advocated broadening the base of public school entry and in 1940 had written to Sir Percy Nunn:[2] 'I myself have urged that the Public Schools should be thrown open to merit quite irrespective of birth.' [3] But Roxburgh did not play much part in the long negotiations between the schools and the education authorities. Like many public school headmasters of his generation he was astonishingly ignorant of what happened to children under the State system. Gracefully presiding once at a

[1] *The Public Schools and the General Educational System*, 1944.

[2] Sir Percy Nunn, Professor of Education, London University 1916–36.

[3] In 1926 Roxburgh had been nervous of Norwood's scheme to bring poor boys into the public school system. (See *The Spectator*, CXXXVII, Nos 5133 and 5134, 13 and 20 November 1926, pp. 847 and 890.) In *Eleutheros* (London, 1930), pp. 82–3, he was ready to accept a few: cf. J. F. Roxburgh, 'The Public Schools and the Future' in *The Headmaster Speaks* (London, 1936), pp. 219–235. But, although he usually expressed the orthodox fear of socialist confiscation or abolition and of the bureaucratic influence of the Board of Education, a schoolmaster in 1941 wrote in his diary the account of an evening spent on a visit to Roxburgh at Stowe and reported that he was 'a surprising radical on the Public Schools question: he holds that they ought to be handed over lock stock and barrel to the State, and apparently said so to the horror of the Headmaster of Eton at a recent meeting'.

meeting held in Berkhamsted between officials from the Board of Education and local authorities and representatives of the public schools he asked quite early on in the proceedings: 'At what age do . . . er . . . they begin their education?' An hour or so later he slipped in almost as an aside, 'When in fact do they go to their . . . er . . . next school?' Finally, so negligently as if he had always known it, he said, 'How old are most of them when they leave?' 'Fourteen.' 'Dear me!' No one at that meeting doubted his desire to help but he was not a natural choice for negotiations at the national level. Roxburgh had no difficulty in persuading his Governors to offer places under the Fleming scheme but the local authorities refused to fill them.

During the last years of the war he had put forward to the Governors a scheme that Stowe should open its own prep school for boys from eleven to thirteen years of age so that boys in the State system who would leave their elementary school at eleven could have two years of prep school experience to enable them to cope with a public school curriculum and accustom them to life in a boarding school. Early in 1945 the Wicken Estate, a few miles from Stowe, was considered for a junior school; Roxburgh suggested a terminal fee of £60 a year; and a lease was recommended to the Central Committee of the Allied Schools. Later in the month an estimated budget for a junior school was submitted by Pickard-Cambridge to Norwood as Chairman of the Central Committee and at the end of November Wicken Park was taken over. But the failure to implement the Fleming scheme on the scale that the public schools had hoped dished the plan. Wicken was given over to girls and became a preparatory school for Westonbirt. A further proposal that Stowe should take over Akeley Wood preparatory school also came to nothing. Roxburgh felt frustrated and baffled.

He was baffled because he could not see what the future held in store. No one could. No one predicted that the public schools were on the verge of a period in which waiting lists bulged and every place was to be oversubscribed. In Roxburgh's last years as a headmaster the outlook was gloomy. The Labour administration, though it made no move against the public schools, could hardly be described as friendly or even neutral; it was difficult to see how the professional classes could afford for long to pay the ever rising fees in time of inflation; and how were schools to renovate their antiquated equipment when fee income was continually falling below running costs? It was only after he retired that it became evident that the public schools so far from withering away were again to grow in number and size. The rise in the birth rate that began in the last years of the war, the prosperity which the Conservative administrations of the nineteen-fifties brought in particular to the upper and middle classes engaged in business, the ability of many parents to pay public school fees out of capital appreciation and by other methods, the rebuilding of the public schools' laboratories with the help of an immense fund raised by industry, and the success of appeals made to their alumni — these all lay in the future. Roxburgh could not get accustomed to the economics of inflation. He had been used to a stable fee that needed little change over the years. The notion that the school fee would be put up once in the five-year career of every boy in the school, and indeed might even have to be put up twice, was not one that he took to easily. He was astonished by the way that a sound surplus in 1946 became in 1947 a sizeable deficit. He was depressed by the increasing difficulty in paying fees that faced professional men whose incomes lagged behind the rise in prices. Barristers, civil servants, doctors, dons, army officers, clergymen — the cultivated *rentier*, the man of letters or the country gentleman — had been among the parents whom he had valued in the creation of Stowe. Now many of these were no longer able to afford the fees and their sons were not there to leaven the intake·

He was slow to realise the change that was bound to occur in the status of his staff. The housing shortage and the rise in prices made it difficult for young masters to find a house and themselves finance the purchase. The Legal and General again came to the rescue by building or purchasing houses on behalf of Stowe and renting them to the school which in turn gave service tenancies to the masters. They were in the end to acquire for the school fifteen of such properties. Stowe was again paying interest on outstanding mortgages and loans but the Legal and General fixed the rate at the very low figure of 2·5 per cent. The war had naturally put a strain on the finances of the Allied Schools as a whole. Westonbirt and Harrogate had been requisitioned and Felixstowe evacuated and when the buildings of these schools were released they had all suffered damage; but government compensation was paid at the values of 1939 and in the meantime building costs had risen by a factor of three. Stowe, which benefited as it did during the war from the support of the other schools in the group, had to be content with its share of whatever resources were available; and in the immediate post-war period of rationing and controls the return to the standards that Roxburgh considered minimal was slow.

Roxburgh was working as hard as ever with all the full-time devotion that a bachelor can afford, but he was working at the same things. Ideally he should have taken a term off and gone on a busman's holiday to gain some new ideas and impressions in other schools and other countries. But in the post-war period this was difficult and in any case he would have thought such an excursion soft. A visiting headmaster some fifteen years his junior, who had been preaching in Chapel, sitting at supper with him and one of his colleagues referred to the change of date of the annual meeting of the Headmasters' Conference. In previous years it had been held in the holidays but now it had been transferred to early term-time, and the visitor approved on the grounds that headmasters need what little holiday they can get. But to Roxburgh the change seemed self-indulgent. He retorted with some acerbity and was nettled for the rest of the meal. He had always prescribed the need for change and did so still, but he no longer understood the framework in which change was to be set. He had lived in a world in which a man saved part of his income, savings kept their value and work was defined as one's routine occupation. To count a conference in which one jawed with one's colleagues as work, to expect one's fare to such a conference to count as expenses, still more to be paid to take a compulsory holiday were unpleasant absurdities. And yet both he and the school would have benefited had he gone out to look at what was happening elsewhere. During the war the Stowe community had grown in on itself and Roxburgh feared that there were not enough fresh ideas about. He told the school in 1948 that 'our standards of achievement in work and games fell during the war, and though they are rising again they are not rising fast enough: there is not the old tingle in the air — the tingle of effort and achievement'. He should, for instance, have rationalised the salary scale of his staff which had become appallingly tangled. In the difficult times he could not obtain overall increases in salaries and he had been in the habit of making treaties with individual masters. When pressed by one to better his situation, he would single out some special responsibility for which the master could get a small additional payment and in rectifying injustices produced in the long run further inequities. Then again he should have noticed that by this time nearly all schools had instituted limited tenure for housemasters, usually fixed at fifteen years. This practice had arisen partly because it becomes harder to keep the old resilience and hawk-eyed concern for what is going on in one's house; and partly because housemasterships are the main means of promotion in a school and stepping stone to a headmastership elsewhere. Unless there is a regular turn-over, promotion among the staff is blocked and good young men will not apply to join when they cannot be assured that vacancies in the houses will occur within a reasonable term of years. This was a reform integral to what he was trying to achieve but he failed to institute it. Even his most solid admirers among the staff felt that, as one of them put it, he 'allowed too many outstanding personalities to leave or perhaps I should say that he didn't do enough to deter them from leaving'. On the other hand he still had a good eye for undesirable change. In 1948 an idiotic new regulation came into force which imposed a minimum age of sixteen upon School Certificate candidates. Roxburgh wrote to *The Times* with fine asperity.

Sir, Mr Maiden would not have found an ally in Dr Johnson, whom Boswell reports as saying: 'I am always for getting a boy forward in his learning.' But surely the real question at issue is whether the age at which a boy should take an examination ought to be decided by those who teach him and know him or laid down by a government department. In any case, the enforcement of minimum ages always produces hard cases — and will continue to do so until parents arrange for all boys to be born in the same month of the year.[1]

One major step was at last taken. He had never appointed a Second Master; Ivor Cross had for many years been recognised as the senior member of the staff and when Cross left during the war to start his own school in Wales, Haworth became doyen of

[1] *The Times*, 27 July 1948.

the masters. But when Haworth retired in 1947 Roxburgh realised
that the time had come when he must appoint an official deputy.
There were two obvious candidates, Capel Cure who had been a
housemaster since 1931 and was his special friend on whom he
relied in particular for counsel and support; and 'Fritz' Clifford
who had also been long a housemaster and who had commanded
the Corps for ten years with much distinction. He appointed
Clifford partly because he recognised that he brought another
kind of experience to bear upon affairs and would represent
points of view which might differ from his own as well as being
able loyally to carry out his wishes.

Had he been ten years younger and still been headmaster when
the shortages and austerities of the post-war period were only
memories, there is no doubt that he would have put such matters
to rights. He was in a cruel situation. Until the prosperity of the
school was restored he could not raise the salaries of his staff and
improve their living conditions and thus again attract more men
— for as ever he was able to attract some — of the kind that had
given the school impetus before the war. He knew a good deal of
what was at fault but he was powerless to remedy it. Stowe was
entering a new age. In 1948 he appointed the first Old Stoic to
serve on the staff and the following year two Old Stoics' sons
became the first of their kind to win scholarships to the school.
Conversely a famous character among the masters, C. W. G.
Ratcliffe, noted for his mordant tongue, followed other of his
earliest associates into retirement, and the Watts decided to
return to Canada. Recognising that in 1948 Roxburgh would reach
sixty, the normal retiring age for public school headmasters, the
Governors had asked him in the previous year to stay on. It was
an awkward time for a change. Many good schoolmasters had just
returned from the war. Either they had at once been appointed to
headmasterships in place of men well beyond the retiring age; or
they had not yet re-established themselves; or they had taken over
a house in their school and did not feel that it would be honourable to throw it up at once for a headmastership. Roxburgh's
name and personality were already restoring the entry to Stowe
now that times were becoming more normal. Some hoped that he
would consent to serve for several more years.

But his reply was unequivocal. He told the Governors that he would stay on for one more year after he was sixty and would then retire. By now he was able to afford to do so. At one time his generosity to others and his expenditure not only on himself but on the school had been such that it looked as if he might be embarrassed on retirement. In 1927 the Governors for the first time had given him some allowance towards the expenses that he was bound to meet in the fulfilment of his job but it was long before he received a realistic allowance. (It was fixed in 1940 at £1,500 for his household staff and expenses.) As late as 1938 his lawyer wrote him:

You will become fifty this year . . . and the question of how you will live after retirement must be faced without further delay . . . Your endowment policies added to the small amount of capital you already possess will be quite insufficient to provide you with a proper livelihood when your salary ceases . . . no pension attached to your present post.

The last was remedied that year and a pension of £350 a year on retirement at sixty was granted him. He was still on occasions raising money by realising securities and cashing insurance policies. The war, by limiting his spending, improved his situation as did a small legacy from his mother who had occasionally helped him with gifts and advances of capital. At the end of the war he was able to write to his bank: 'At the moment when this large and long-outstanding overdraft is at last being paid off, I feel I must express my appreciation to you for the patience and consideration which has been shown to me at all times by this Bank.' Thus although he could hardly be called well-to-do, he could contemplate retirement without immediate worry.

But this would never have been a decisive factor with him. The clue is to be found on the shelves of his library. In a copy of C. Maxwell's *The Wisdom of Dr Johnson* which J.F. must have been reading shortly before his retirement (it was published in 1948) the following quotation from *The Rambler* is heavily scored in the margin:

He that is himself weary will soon weary the public. Let him there-fore lay down his employment whatever it may be who can no longer exert his former activity or attention; let him not endeavour to struggle with censure or obstinately infest the stage until a general hiss commands him to depart.

He knew himself to be weary but he was making one last effort before he left the stage. In 1949 he brought the school numbers back to what they had been before the war and Stowe again numbered over 500 boys. The school gained in that year the record number of eleven Oxford and Cambridge scholarships and exhibitions. Very fittingly, in his last term at the school, the War Memorial in the Chapel to the 270 Old Stoics who had been killed was dedicated. Roxburgh had an impressive gift for the conduct of important occasions and gave all he knew to the preparation of this last tribute to men who had meant so much to him. There was an awkward hitch. The Archbishop of Canterbury, himself a former headmaster of a public school, was due to join Roxburgh and the five other Bishops at lunch. But he made a late start from London, his chauffeur took a wrong turning, he stopped like a Good Samaritan to give assistance at a road accident, and was delayed for nearly an hour and a half. For the first time on such an occasion J.F. looked flustered. In the end all was well and the Archbishop arrived in time for the Service and in his address spoke of 'the headmaster of that young School, who had so nobly and creatively guided it through the twenty-six years of its existence, had welcomed each one of these to the school and had watched him progress year by year.' The Chaplain recalled that when all the guests had departed 'J.F. with his unfailing courtesy, despite his tiredness and great emotional strain, nevertheless took the trouble to write me a short note that evening thanking me for all I had done. I had done little enough but the gesture was typical.'

In the last months life was full of intimations of mortality. His portrait was painted by James Gunn: the artist delighted him, the portrait did not. The masters subscribed £200 and gave him a painting of the South Front. The prefects, mystified as to what to choose, settled on a Crown Derby dinner service which, as one of them said, 'I don't suppose he can have had any use for in his retirement'; and J.F. much touched replied that he could not let the occasion go by without commemorating it in the same way — and handed out munificent book tokens to them all. The Governors recorded at their last meeting their 'gratitude and admiration for the work which during twenty-six years he had done for the school of which he was virtually the creator and the unfailing courage, optimism and practical wisdom in face of difficulties and his constant personal interest in his boys during their school life and afterwards'. Four days earlier in balmy summer weather more than a thousand Old Stoics had gathered at Stowe to salute him. Before tea John Boyd-Carpenter made a lively and affectionate speech and Roxburgh was presented by his Old Boys with a Sunbeam-Talbot Ninety, a clock specially designed to reproduce the unique Stowe chimes of forty-three strokes, a £700 cheque placed to his account at a travel agency to induce him to take a holiday, and a cheque for £5,000, which was added to later, for him to do with as he wished — his wish being to give it to the school to build new workshops.

Finally there came the last Sunday. Boys have a cool appreciation of drama and one of his prefects who too was leaving that term recalled the closing days:

One was conscious that last week that this was J.F.'s last Assembly, last lesson, last Chapel — particularly that last Chapel. Being Prefect of Chapel, I sat right at the back by the swing doors, so I could not see J.F. clearly. We wondered what emotion he must be feeling and showing, he who had created the place we lived in and loved. It was almost unbearable to think that he was going. I think he read the lesson and it sounded quite normal: no emotion betrayed there. Then right at the end he led the procession of masters down the aisle in his usual way. Surely now we should see some sign. Slowly, perhaps a bit slower than usual, the familiar figure came nearer. The slight stoop, hands clasping the lapels of his gown, mortar-board firmly clutched in one hand, the greying hair parted in the middle, the perfectly knotted tie curving forward in its usual elegant way — all looked quite normal. He was looking down at the aisle ahead of him as he approached those of us at the back. I had opened the swing doors and bolted them back in place. As he came up to us by the door he looked up and straight out of the doors. I can only describe the look on his face as radiant; no trace of sadness, no tiredness; simply an expression of pride, achievement, triumph. I don't think I ever saw him again, except for the sight of his slim figure walking alone back to the South Front a few moments after he had left the Chapel. That look on his face has remained with me ever since.

So term ended, and so ended Roxburgh's long headmastership. He had talked with a new kind of informality at his last prefects' dinner about the move to his house at Great Brickhill and the furniture he would have to sell and he now faced the desolating experience of choosing what to keep and pack, and setting his papers in order. 'I am,' he wrote from Brickhill in August, 'responsible at Stowe until the end of this month, though actually sleeping here while my Stowe rooms are being dismantled. After that I shall remain within reach until the School and Higher Certificate results come in for my last act as HM will be to send them out to the boys.' Once again he despatched the results with the customary notes of congratulation and encouragement. After that, save for one brief visit to stand by the grave in the church-yard at Stowe Church when Leslie Huggins was buried in 1952, he was never to set foot on Stowe ground again.

Chapter IX

The Man Himself

What animated this teacher, what lay behind the sympathetic manner, the elaborate courtesy and effervescent affectation, what inspired that exceptional devotion from those that were around him and the considerable suspicion among those who were not? Was his manner a mask concealing inner frivolity and emptiness? People noticed that his public addresses contained a great deal about learning and beauty and service to the community but did not extol the Higher Values nor dwell reverently on the sustaining Faith. Headmasters who preached the cardinal virtues looked askance and asked why he would not stand up and be counted as a witness to Christianity; occasionally parents and strangers judged that behind the courtesy lay the values of a snob; more rarely boys condemned him for being insincere. What then were his qualities and how did he convey his beliefs?

It is often assumed that an expansive personality must be a mask which conceals an inner life of labyrinthine complexity quite different from the public face. This is an error. There are human beings who wear masks but Roxburgh was not one of them. Like many others whose manners and idiosyncrasies impress themselves indelibly upon their contemporaries' memory he was all of a piece and his outward attributes reflected his inner integrity. His character shone through his appearance. The hats from Scott's, the classically tailored suits, the baroque ties and gorgeous silk handkerchiefs, the watch chain with the little revolving seal, the alert expression, the affable 'My dear fellow . . .', were all part of a *persona* that had been moulded and chased by an artist so as to express his own talents. T. H. White described him as a 'tall, wonderfully tailored gentleman, lean, clean shaven, hair apparently cut that morning, soigné, looking a bit like a noble, middle-aged Jeune Premier'. He did his best to impose his own standards upon the school. He besought the school to wear waistcoats on Speech Day. He did not require hair to be cropped but it must be brushed: 'My dear Basset, what is the French for a hair-brush?' An outbreak of coloured golf-umbrellas or pastel shade pullovers did not worry him, but a boy without a tie-pin would be handed one with a request not to appear half-naked. (To Roxburgh's chagrin the Prince of Wales arrived at Stowe on a warm breezy summer's day with tie fluttering: he got him to wear one.) Whatever else he did, he impressed: and boys like their headmaster to be somewhat larger than life.

They noticed too that *he* was impressed. J.F. had more than his share of personal vanity. So have most good-looking men. 'I have heard it said (and I choose to believe),' wrote a Stoic who was devoted to him, 'that he parted his hair just off-centre precisely to offset the slight crookedness of the line of his nose.' Another of his close friends observed that he had 'a horror of growing old and of looking old: in the last two years at Stowe he would often be seen making a conscious effort to compose his facial muscles to a younger look'. A spasm of pain appeared on his face at the sight of his passport photograph; and he referred to his portrait as 'that libellous square-yard'. After the early years at Stowe he always wore a suit and once apologised to two masters who found him *en déshabillé* wearing grey flannel trousers while pruning a rose. On one occasion vanity and courtesy strove for the mastery. Leaving the Capel Cures for a long train journey he found his kind hostess pressing a packet of sandwiches upon him. He could not risk being seen vulgarly masticating sandwiches: neither could he offend such thoughtfulness. A day or two later came a letter. Could Ursula kindly post him his mackintosh? — he had foolishly left it behind. There in its pocket was the packet of sandwiches.

Whatever he did in public he liked to do with masterly ease. He was a graceful skater but skating on the lakes in the first cold winter of the war he fell heavily: he handed his skates to the boy who had picked him up saying that he was too old and should have known better. Each year the whole school answered a general knowledge paper set by a committee of masters. J.F. did the paper and always came top with over ninety per cent. One year Ian Clarke, who had married a young and gifted wife coming of a famous Scots academic family, rang him up on some matter of business and at the end asked insouciantly, 'By the way how many did you get for the General Knowledge paper?' 'Ninety-three,' said Roxburgh. 'Margaret got ninety-four,' was the swift reply. The line went dead. But J.F. had the last word — a bunch of violets for a prize. He was touchy if his name was spelt wrongly, touchier still if his professional judgment was questioned by those who he thought had no right or qualifications to question it, and he did not take kindly to even the mildest criticism of Stowe by his one-time pupils. He could be petty and say pettish things to his colleagues when his vanity was offended. He was angered by a woman novelist of the kind that never published less than one book a year, lampooning him as a headmaster who 'never lets the parents get a word in edgeways . . . and gets rid of them by sending them off on a conducted tour'. He swore that he would never let her son enter Stowe. 'I always felt,' wrote a thoughtful observer among Stoics of the earlier period, 'that the main motive of his behaviour was vanity — and here I must say I think I was dead wrong; no one could have done what he did from such a motive however sublimated.'

Vanity alone certainly could not account for his generosity nor even for his extravagance. In February 1925 he wrote to his lawyer (who was also his cousin), 'I have always had an overdraft every term since we started and the bulk of my salary has always gone in paying staff.[1] This does not seem to be a very satisfactory arrangement though of course I do not deny that I am a bit extravagant.' There was indeed no denying it. He spent prodigally on others but not to exert power over them nor to bind them to him in the fear of not being loved. Each Head of the School received on leaving gold cuff-links, engraved with the Stowe crest and the receiver's monogram, and silver cigarette boxes were showered as wedding presents on many of his pupils. He took out policies for his score of godchildren so that each should receive £100 on his or her twenty-first birthday. It was the same with his staff: half a dozen champagne to a sick colleague transported personally as a pick-me-up; a car hired at his expense for his secretary to save her cycling after an illness; his own petrol ration in war-time to fetch an oil stove for a newly married master without cooking facilities. Each gesture in itself what anyone might have done but these were only three from a legion of such services. He also gave help secretly to a number of old people who were in difficulties. Many of his gifts were spontaneous to meet a need or to encourage. His own self-indulgence was harmless; clothes were his affectation, silver, glass, china and furniture his delight. He liked to travel in comfort. Much of his income went in hospitality (for it was not until the war that the Governors gave him any entertainment allowance) — and there undoubtedly he got pleasure from producing a procession of wines whether for distinguished guests or young colleagues, and in displaying his pieces and his own sensitivity towards them. Once when Archbishop Temple was lunching with him and asked for orangeade, the waiter poured the fluid into one of his celebrated pigeon's blood wine-glasses. J.F. expostulated: 'My dear Archbishop, you can't, you positively can't, drink orangeade out of a red wine-glass.' He liked his guests to admire his blue Bristol, the Venetian champagne glasses or his Sheraton desk, or to spot the painting of the Temple of Vesta which had been attributed to Poussin. He cultivated patrician tastes.

It was the cultivation of these tastes as much as his obvious awareness of social distinctions that made some dismiss him as a

[1] He had at that time to maintain at his own expense two secretaries, a housekeeper and a chauffeur-gardener.

snob. To be known as a *cognoscente* who indulges his taste for the elegant does not endear a man to the academic profession whose members are in general too hard-pressed financially to express themselves in this way and who distrust the sensuality of the visual arts. They disapproved of his delight in social niceties. He was not always tactful in expressing it. When the Chapel stalls were being embellished with the arms, personal, collective or vicarious, of their donors, he wrote to Warrington, who was not armigerous: 'It would do no harm to invent a motto if you cannot track down your real one. I should like to invent a Latin motto indicating that you have lit educational torches all over the country. Something on these lines could probably be composed if a new one has to be put together.' Warrington's reply has not been preserved. Fellow members of his profession whispered that he put the superficial before the fundamental. Their patience was indeed tried when Stowe had five royal visits in the first fifteen years. But great personages enjoy seeing places that are being talked about and making their own judgments; and it was Roxburgh's reputation at Stowe that made the invitations attractive. He seemed to have invisible antennae that warned him of the appearance at Stowe of any important person. Within a few minutes J.F. would emerge on the North Front, hat and stick in hand, circle the field, walk past the distinguished visitor, then as if for no reason glance back, register first astonishment, then delight, and approach with his captivating smile . . . But with all his arts he did not turn his back on his profession, nor try to move in worldly society, nor spend his holidays hob-nobbing with the successful and powerful and accepting invitations to spacious country houses. He was without pretensions.

The élite of his dreams was, unlike the Edwardian *beau monde*, one in which taste counted as much as birth or money, and from this sprang his impatience with boorishness, the unkempt and the deviant. He saw society in Victorian terms: it was the duty of the élite to set standards and elevate their inferiors. But he thought that the élite gained even more in carrying out its responsibilities than those they helped. At a concert in December 1927 to raise funds for Stowe's newly opened London Boys' Club, called the Pineapple from the old pub which formed its first premises, Roxburgh said that although the club 'might be of some service to working boys in Marylebone, it would be of greater service to us, by affording us a means of understanding conditions of life in the slums; and since comprehension was the first step towards betterment, the Club might in the future help us to face the slum problem, to the honour of our generation'. He used to visit the Club boys when they had their annual camp in the grounds at Stowe and when he retired they gave him wholly unprompted an engraved pewter mug as a present. He had a touch of natural courtesy towards the school's staff. He would stop, stand aside and sweep off his hat to allow a house matron to pass and he was not one to slink past garrulous retainers for fear that they would detain him. Public schools are fortunate in that they evoke a peculiarly strong loyalty from their servants who identify themselves with the place and are content to work for lower wages than they can get elsewhere. They have the feeling of belonging to a family; matrons and secretaries revel in the family gossip; and porters and handymen brighten when the school wins at football. But while the Bursar is their chief, much depends on the masters, and a conversable and considerate headmaster is a boon. Like the lord of the manor, J.F. had the right word for the estate workers, or the steward, or the lab. assistants, or his housekeeper who spoke of 'his faultless good manners and deep gratitude for the smallest service'. He was observed on one occasion when a char scrubbing the stairs made way for him. 'With a courtly gesture he raised his mortar-board and bowed. No queen could have been acknowledged more gracefully.'

But his graciousness had limits. In the years between the wars there was a bevy of waiters and maids at the school, casual labour that was paid off at the end of each term and had to live during the holidays on what they had saved or find another job, men and girls who were at the lowest end of the employment scale, the men often unemployed miners from the Durham coalfields and the girls Irish immigrants. Some may consider that they were lucky enough to have a roof over their heads, but they lived at Stowe in squalid conditions, with little freedom and without, as the staff now has, a welfare officer. One day Stephen Taylor, who later worked for many years at the Pineapple, and thanks to this work in a boys' club became like Attlee before him a socialist, heard J.F. telling off some of the waiters for playing football in the Power House Yard, where they were out of sight, surrounded by boilers and electrical plant and could hardly be said to be embarrassing the school. Poor fellows: all around them were large playing fields but they had nowhere to play. They had few graces and were desperately poor, unlike the upper servants whom J.F. greeted so cordially: they did not seem to him to inhabit the world he lived in. On another occasion the master in charge of boxing allowed the maids to form part of the audience one year at the school boxing competitions. He received a note from Rox-burgh, expressing as he always did his delight at the spirit shown by the boys and the way the affair had been organised but pro-testing at the indelicacy of allowing the maids to watch such con-tests. Had he been less concerned with appearances he might have reflected that the maids in the circumstances of their lives were subject to far more brutalising influences than boxing. He assumed as an axiom of life that people should keep to their stations. He disapproved of boys fraternising with the servants. An Old Stoic priest who knew him and who himself lived with his curate, a tramp, and a collection of down and outs and Borstal boys, observed that J.F. would have seen the point of 'living among one's people, but I'm not sure that he would have understood trying to live, to some extent, as they do: he would have thought that a lowering of standards'. His priorities were not those of the social worker; he felt uncomfortable meeting on equal terms people from other classes; an accent grated on his ears. Despite his attempts to see that Stoics did not leave the school unaware of the gravity of the social issues in the country and despite his own conviction that too little was being done to improve the lot of the unemployed, he could not face the realities of the times when he found them on his own doorstep. He had good principles, but people matter more than principles.

Social class — the way in which people treat other people and are in turn reciprocally treated by them — has absorbed the energies of English novelists for over two centuries. As every half-century sees the barriers and divisions between classes gradually diminishing, we find the assumptions of the preceding half-century intolerably snobbish. It is easy not to quarrel with the code of behaviour that was axiomatic to a mid-Victorian noble-man, because his age has vanished; but it is far more difficult to regard dispassionately the assumptions of a young Edwardian Liberal who supported Lloyd George's Insurance Act but regarded the ruling élite as a circle to which admittance could be gained only by producing a card marked beauty or brains or birth or wealth, as well as evidence that the holder has assimilated all the values, habits, customs, ways of speech and behaviour of the élite itself. To Roxburgh it seemed that there was always certain to be an élite marked off clearly from the rest of society by the fact that they led the lives of gentlemen and others did not. He was well aware that the public schools have always educated those aspiring to enter this class as well as the sons of those who already belonged to it and once a boy was at Stowe he made no distinctions; but it was noticeable that under his management of the entry two of the houses seemed to become the natural habitat of boys from the north of England. He believed that certain social distinctions which he made were for the good of the school's development as well as agreeable to him. English-speaking boys from the Dominions and Colonies were naturally welcome. So were Americans. The first, Ambrose Short, arrived in 1933; got J.F. to allow the institution of a weekly dancing class; and organised the first School Dance in the following summer. American boys were greatly to his taste. But he would not admit coloured boys. In 1928 he refused admission to the sons of a Maharajah, confessed himself 'illiberal' but hoped that the Governors would not press him. Later when asked by the new Secretary of the Allied Schools, 'What is your view on the Colour question?' Roxburgh replied: 'Schools which have open dormitories and not (as at Eton and Harrow) separate rooms ought not in my opinion to receive coloured boys.' What curious sexual prejudice was here at work? Or did he imagine that as such boys might be more physically mature trouble would ensue? Or was it an ingenious excuse? But in one respect his prejudice was straightforward. Canning, the Headmaster of Canford, had written about numbers at his school: 'I am filling up slowly but with the most unexpectedly exalted scions.' Roxburgh replied: 'I am glad to hear that your School list will soon resemble an extract from Debrett. I know some Schools whose lists are like the hock pages in a Wine List.' He accepted boys of Jewish descent, though, as is customary in those public schools that are religious foundations, within the scope of an unspoken quota. But when Hitler's persecution began, he did not doubt where his duty lay. Just before the war he besought some senior boys to 'Keep "bloody" for something that really deserves it such as the way the Nazis treat the Jews'. He relaxed the rule against foreigners though he insisted on interviewing all candidates personally. One of them, Peter Sichel, recalled that interview, his future at stake, he himself all washed and shining, pathetically anxious to please and perhaps a little too forward, being put at his ease, sized up in half an hour and told with good humour that his looks and his name might be subjected to some ridicule unless both were slightly changed. He should part his hair on the side instead of wearing it *en brosse* and should anglicise the pronunciation of his name to Sitchell. To these boys and their parents Roxburgh was especially considerate and sympathetic. Two years after his retirement a German refugee was Head of the School: he was killed in action in Korea.

The more fanciful Stowe intellectuals used to detect in him a touch or two of his Lancing pupil's creation, Dr Fagan of Llanabba Castle. If a boy felt doubts about Roxburgh's scale of values he was likely to have those doubts reinforced on the day before he left Stowe when the headmaster gave a talk to leavers. It was an odd performance. Perhaps because his dislike of the emotional and his sense of the appropriate forbad him to say anything that could be construed as sentimental or uplifting, he concentrated on giving worldly advice. To give young men worldly advice is sensible — so long as it is really worldly. He began with a mnemonic: the four L's, Language, Letters, Love, L.S.D., complicated at a later date by the addition of Laws, Labour and Level. The wisdom of the mnemonic consisted in remembering the following rules for life: restrain your language; answer letters the same day; keep your financial resources in such good order that a wedding present can be despatched to whatever friend was about to commit the classic act of folly; and above all if you fell in love yourself before twenty-five, take a single ticket to the North Pole and *be very careful what you write to women* . . . 'Gentlemen, whatever else you may have to do with women — however great the temptation, whatever the provocation — never, gentlemen, I implore you, I entreat you, never write to them. Women always keep letters, never destroy them, always know

175

when to produce them.' The Edwardian world of temptation for young men that this address conjured up was intriguing. There floated into the air the wraith of the designing tobacconist's daughter, the plight of the Prisoner of Zenda and other foolish princes, trapped into morganatic marriages by too passionate avowals, the Fabergé trifle to grace a friend's table — at any moment you expected him to embark on a minute analysis on the etiquette of visiting cards. It was as astonishing as the time when he burst out while a form was wrestling with a passage about the predatory habits of Roman mistresses with 'Gentlemen, they're not worth it: they're like coffee — they smell better than they taste'. He had little experience of women and none of sex. It was impossible to imagine anyone unleashing vivacities about bed still less broaching dirty stories in his presence.[1] He was prudish; and at times you could discern beneath the surface something prissy and spidery.

But it was this hatred of indelicacy and search for what was fitting and orderly that formed his courtesy. An extremely clever Stowe boy in the 'forties thought him insincere and wrote: 'We were sceptical, we admired sincerity and plain speaking, we were reading Orwell.' The mention of that name provokes a contrast — Orwell who so bleakly and devastatingly deflated both the conservative and the socialist ideologies of the times, whose honesty made him declass himself, work at the meanest jobs, and sleep in the flop-houses, was someone whose annihilating vision was completely out of focus with Roxburgh's practical, pragmatic, unalarmed approach to life. If you were looking for frank views boldly and nakedly expressed and designed to provoke even franker replies, J.F. was not a model. There were times when he would say things to spare people's feelings or to avoid the effort of disagreement when nothing important was at stake; and people who took his words in earnest and at face value could be disconcerted. Often his interlocutor read more into what he said than in fact he had said, because his manner was so friendly.

[1] His dislike of earthy as well as bawdy language made him make one exception to his rule that there should be no private Stowe language. He ordained that lavatories should be called 'Egypt' (the Rugby term, for instance, is *topos*) as the first ones had been sited near the Egyptian entry which the Marquis of Buckingham had constructed beneath the North Front portico.

Sometimes he gave a false impression by what he omitted to say. Omission is, of course, a device practised by those who have constantly to write testimonials. His testimonials to tutors of colleges about his boys were examples of how to blend advocacy with truthfulness, and he always respected the recipient, when he knew him, as well as the individual about whom he was writing. He was less scrupulous towards impersonal institutions. An official of the Board of Education took him to task for writing a glowing testimonial about a man who turned out to be fatally unsuitable and was not best pleased when Roxburgh replied: 'My dear fellow, I never knew Whitehall took any notice of those things.' He took pains to pour oil on troubled waters. One of his Heads of School reading the lesson on the first day of term instead of turning to the noble first chapter of Joshua turned in error to the first chapter of Judges and found himself retailing how the Israelites sliced off with relish the thumbs, great toes and other attributes of some heathen king. After the service he hurried to the vestry to apologise to the Chaplain and heard J.F. saying: 'I can't believe he did it on purpose.' Roxburgh knew, like other men who are by nature polite, that he was sometimes accused of insincerity and in an address he gave at Felixstowe Ladies College in 1930 he made his own apologia: 'Politeness is necessary, false politeness is abominable; but it is the falseness we should get rid of, not the politeness. When we say we are glad to see someone, let us make ourselves glad to see him. Lie like knaves and there is no forgiveness, but lie like knights and the lie becomes true before it passes our lips.' A new boy once had experience of such a lie. Venturing hesitantly upon the ice for almost the first time on skates, he slipped right in his headmaster's path and sent him sprawling. Roxburgh hauled him to his feet at once with 'My dear fellow, I am so sorry. How very clumsy of me!' The innumerable stories of his courtesy, forethought and consideration obscure the fact that he was a man with the power of quick decision, who was ready to say unwelcome things to boys or colleagues. He spoke the truth to boys even when it did not flatter him. Heckstall-Smith tells the story of a cunning boy asking his housemaster for permission to watch a Test Match in London, who refused on the grounds that the headmaster would not allow it or his parents approve. Might he go if he got leave from parents and headmaster? Yes. He then approached J.F. who refused on the grounds that his housemaster would not allow it or his parents approve. Might he go if he got leave from both? 'No, you may not.' 'Why not, sir?' 'I can't think why not at the moment, but I'm sure there must be a reason.' This special kind of honesty, not invariably evident among schoolmasters, impressed Heckstall-Smith, who once told Roxburgh that he was so polite that he couldn't believe him when he paid him a compliment. 'He looked astonished, swallowed once, and then said something quite rude, which struck me as the exact truth. After this I had no difficulty.'[1]

He was far more than a nice man. His tolerance was not an easy way out: it was a respect for the individual. For instance he would make the effort to understand a boy's mumbled incoherences when others would have brushed them off as stupidity. His disinclination to lecture boys and to appeal to their moral sense was not indifference: it was a hatred of cant. A boy thought it his duty to oppose some of the senior prefects who were being disloyal to their position in the school, and met with much unpleasantness. Having annihilated the prefects, J.F. sent for him.

I was told that being right didn't entitle me to either happiness or an easy path. I was to guard against turning myself into a self-righteous prig. The spirit of his advice to me, expounded at some length, was that it is very hard to live down a quarrel in which one is right — one had nothing to regret. Being wrong leaves more room for manœuvre! I was most impressed by the seeming contrariness of this: I had been sure until then that all I had to worry about was being right . . . At the time I was somewhat shocked that J.F.'s sympathy took such an unexpected form. I have been grateful ever since.

In the feverish 'thirties schoolboys formed passionate opinions about politics: they might be pacifists, communists, fascists, they might jeer at the League, or they might support Esmond Romilly at Wellington publishing his anti-public school magazine, *Out of Bounds*. Headmasters began to be faced with ticklish problems of freedom of conscience and political independence and not all of them steered a morally distinguished course between youthful rebelliousness, priggishness and exaggeration on the one hand

[1] Heckstall-Smith, *Doubtful Schoolmaster*, p. 29.

and patriotic pressure from legions of Old Boys on the other. Roxburgh's political views at this time were those of a moderate conservative and he did not agree with the views of the minority who refused on pacifist grounds to join the O.T.C. or who improbably regarded the Corps as a tool of capitalist aggression. But he ensured that there should be provision for those who did not want to join the O.T.C. He insisted that they should join the Scouts or perform some other activity no less exacting; and he would listen with an open mind to any who came to him.

When I was about sixteen [one of his pupils recollected] I went through a period of rather agonising reassessment of my whole approach to life and seriously doubted many of the precepts and dogmas that had governed my behaviour hitherto. I think it was started by my introduction to the scientific method. In any event, I finally decided that among other things I wanted to resign from the O.T.C. and spend some time working with the gardeners and foresters on the estate. After much trepidation I sought an interview with J.F. I knew that I would find it very hard to express these thoughts, being naturally reticent, but was soon put at relative ease by the initial 'My dear fellow', and by J.F.'s magnanimous and open approach to my problems. He did not seem to scorn what were undoubtedly unusual views, although I am sure that he did not agree with all of them. I came away deeply grateful to him and his liberality. I was allowed to resign from the O.T.C. without fuss and to spend an hour or two each week working with and getting to know some of the estate workers. During my later years at Stowe I developed a philosophy which I still greatly value and which has served me well. If it had not been for J.F., it might well have been repressed.

On another occasion a fourteen-year-old boy came to him bitterly indignant that his reading of Plato's *Republic* was being disturbed by his obligations as a fag. J.F. did not excuse him fagging: but he let it be known in his house that reading the *Republic* was a highly important undertaking and that, subject to duties obligatory on all boys of his age, he was to be given every opportunity to do so. During the war an Old Stoic inveighed to J.F. that a contemporary of his was a conscientious objector. Roxburgh himself believed that conscientious objectors were mistaken; but 'he took me gently to task for this and pointed out the necessity for respecting other people's principles and being loyal to one's own'. It was part of his sensitivity to what others felt and suffered that he hated to listen to derogatory remarks about people. Scandal did not amuse him. 'He bestowed praise and criticism with equally devastating effect,' said one Stoic, 'but I never heard him blame anyone.' He did in fact frequently blame himself in public and in private — and, as happens sometimes, his honesty and humility disarmed his critics.

Headmasters fulfil a social role that is also fulfilled by judges and clergymen: they are the guardians of the system of higher values and are expected to praise and expound the virtues. They differ in the virtues that they emphasise. Roxburgh differed in that he emphasised the graces: delicacy, generosity and what Castiglione called *sprezzatura*, a natural spontaneity of manner, which together with magnanimity was the apex of the Renaissance ideal. In doing so he could have appealed to Erasmus's *De Civilitate* or to a very different authority, Dr Johnson, who said, 'Every man of any education would rather be called a rascal than accused of deficiency in *the graces*.'[1] To praise these particular qualities was then unusual and it was sometimes assumed that he did not care about bravery, strenuousness, modesty and other virtues that had for generations been upheld in the public schools. This was not so. Because he was unusual as a headmaster people forgot how deep in him lay the traditional virtues. It was the same with his self-control and rationality. They made one forget that he was a man of strong emotions. And some of those emotions he channeled into his religion.

About his religion hung a veil of mystery and suspicion. There was a well-known story at Lancing that the successor to his Chapel stall found Roxburgh's copy of Omar Khayyám which he had forgotten to rescue when he left. Pained disapproval had been expressed in some quarters that *Eleutheros*, a book purporting to elucidate what the public schools stood for, contained no word about God. In the controversy over the Chapel cross he treated the matter in public as a matter of policy, reiterating that Stowe would be harmed if it got the reputation of being extremist in religion; but whether the absence or presence of a cross meant anything to him personally was obscure. He was often accused

[1] Boswell's *Life of Johnson*, May 1776, ed. L. F. Powell (London and New York, 1934), III, p. 54.

of religious indifference, yet anyone who has read his sermons alone cannot doubt that this charge was false. Why were there doubts?

Roxburgh grew up at a time when church-going was declining yet when religious controversy remained exceedingly pungent. In the Church of England Evangelicalism had lost ground but its revivals and missions still generated enthusiasm; and on the other wing the extreme Anglo-Catholics were at their most provocative in mocking Protestantism, satirising the Modernists for whittling away so much of traditional dogma that nothing was left and using every device to introduce Romanising practices to make effective their claim that the Anglican Church was not heretical but an integral part of the Holy Catholic Church. Stirring Roman Catholic apologists, such as Fr Martindale or Belloc, were at the height of their fame, and new churches such as The Christian Scientists, or movements such as Spiritualism gathered adherents. The contentious atmosphere, the sense of capturing or defending certain spiritual positions and the passionate adherence to one or other ecclesiastical party inspired some young men with a new sense of Christian mission.

Roxburgh was not so inspired. He found such controversy odious. The issues over which Church parties disputed seemed to him to be unrelated to the spiritual problems that ought to be occupying men's minds. He thought religion was almost wholly to do with individuals: the ecumenical mission of the Church meant little to him. So did theology. As a liberal to whom reason was important, he might have been expected to lean to Modernism, or to have been attracted to theologians who provided explanations of the graver perplexities of the Christian faith. But Roxburgh did not regard theology as a bulwark of the faith in which to instruct the young: the acrid controversies of the times suggested to him rather that it severed the Christian from his God and from other Christians. Theology for him was summed up in three words. 'St John,' he said in a sermon, 'uttered that final and crowning statement of the Christian faith — *God is Love.*' When he was a housemaster at Lancing he wrote a letter to Ursula Capel Cure on the eve of her Confirmation and though the language he used to a twelve-year-old girl was simple it expressed the simplicity of his own beliefs.

I am awfully glad to hear that you are going to be Confirmed on the same day as our fellows here — (there are eight in Sanderson's) — and I shall be thinking a lot about you as well as about them. You will like being a Senior Member of our Society, instead of just a Junior Member as you have been so far. By 'our Society' I mean the Church, of course, but I always think of it as a Society because it really is just like lots of ordinary societies — societies for 'preventing cruelty to animals' and societies 'for promoting the study of Greek' and all sorts of societies for all sorts of purposes — only much more wonderful and founded by a much more wonderful Person than any ordinary societies. I think the Church is just a great big *Society for the Promotion of Love*, and all that you will have to do, now that you are becoming a senior member of it, is to love as many people as you can as hard as you can, and to love the Founder of the Society more than anyone. Because the Society has only got two rules and they are as simple as anything. *Rule One* is 'Love God', and *Rule Two* is 'Love Everyone Else' . . .

Religion in his eyes, therefore, sprang from two simple needs: the need to love other people and the need to ask God for help to do so. A sermon on Palm Sunday 1932 shows that beside these two needs everything else for him was secondary. The sermon begins with the assumption that the supreme reality is mind and that God is the ultimate mind. We cannot comprehend this Mind but we can conceive it through the life of Christ, because before us stands the historical fact of Christ's teaching as the highest morality yet propounded. 'Christianity reveals the moral nature of the universe at the level of human life.' Man has need for help in his struggle against indolence, self-indulgence, hate, cruelty and cowardice. 'The first contact between the struggling human soul and the Divine Soul . . . is made when man, burdened with anxiety or just feeling his own hopeless deficiencies, goes humbly to his God and finds *not* the Mind which made the world, *not* the abstract principle of goodness, beauty and truth, and *not* the Absolute of the philosophers, but simply a friend and helper. That is the point where true religion begins.' He was in fact a Low Churchman.

The Low Church has never been the community to inspire lyrical memoirs. Most of the vigour and fervour in the High and

Low parties in the Church of England of the Victorian age came on the one side from the Tractarians and Ritualists, and on the other from the Evangelicals. But the large majority of the clergy and laity stood apart from these embattled partisans and adhered to two camps disparagingly called by the activists the High and Dry and the Low and Slow. By the nineteen-twenties the Low Churchman was often one who hid his religious light under a bushel. 'What doth the Lord require of thee, but to do justly, and to love mercy, and to walk humbly with thy God?' was the modest, kindly text which for many Low Churchmen summed up their duties. In what sense the Bible was the Word of God, what the relation was between the Passion of Christ and man's reconciliation with God, how God had dealt with and would deal with the whole human race, were only three of the inexplicable, inextricable and incomprehensible questions that theology strove to answer. But what made Christianity — and therefore life — intelligible was not theology, and still less the Church as an authoritative body, but the life of Jesus as portrayed in the Gospels. The Low Churchman turned to Jesus as his Master and his Friend. He talked to him in his silent prayers and hoped, in talking, to find him.

Time and again Roxburgh returned in his sermons to his belief that Christ's life and example alone make life intelligible. We can never expect that any academic study will teach us how to live. That is learnt only through our own efforts to discipline ourselves. He practised self-discipline himself and preached often on the text 'He that keepeth the law, happy is he'. Like St Paul he envisaged law as a liberator; he thought of the spiritual life as something that flourishes only if the laws which guide it are self-made; and he saw Gethsemane as the supreme example of dominion over self. But self-discipline is too hard a task for human beings. That is why the human soul must be recharged from the source of all goodness. We can recharge it and discover the Will of God by studying the life of Christ especially as portrayed by St Luke; and by prayer. Then and then only could man learn to love.

He interpreted Christian love in sermons to the school as kindness, consideration, sympathy, delicacy of feeling, unwillingness to wound. He once told the Parents' Association that 'the most fruitful source of unhappiness at school is not the legalised tyranny of the prefects but the persecution of a boy by others of his own age or a little older'. He knew that this form of persecution is almost impossible for masters or even prefects to stop, and he therefore frequently in sermons reverted to this theme. Christian love meant to him feeling and action, action and feeling. 'There is something more difficult than to believe in Christianity, and that is to act on it.' When he preached at Charterhouse he reiterated 'the first thing is to try Christianity as a practical rule of life. The rest will follow . . . Few people can believe in it until they have tried to practise it.' Or again: 'You do not need to wait till you have studied Christian theology before you can start being a Christian.' Always the end is action. Most of his sermons were moral discourses giving practical advice — 'think for yourself', 'be strenuous, virtuous, companionable, tolerant and loyal', 'practise liking other people', 'it is not the things that happen to you that matter; it is what you do about them'. Just after the General Strike in 1926 came another exhortation, 'disagree as much as you can with as much as you can': he warned against the danger of 'thinking by infection' and listed specifically sixteen statements to illustrate the social and economic problems of the day upon which knowledge should be sought and opinions formed. If thinking made a boy turn away from Christianity it was to be regretted: but he wanted his boys to think out their faith for themselves.

He gave himself strict rules in writing his sermons. The message was to be simple and so was the language in which he gave it. He paid tremendous attention to this rule. He would address notes to himself — here is one attached to a sermon in 1930: 'You must be shorter and have it better fixed in your head. You must have good clear catch-words — not too many, they are needed only at the junctions — especially near the end when you may get worked up and find the pulpit spinning round and no clue to help you, as tonight.' Sometimes he is satisfied: 'They listened' is scribbled on one; but often he was not, and the note is attached 'Will not do again, not appreciated' or 'I was most disappointed with this.' Many of the typescripts are revised, sometimes with whole pages re-written, sometimes with a change of emphasis or a substitution of words and phrases. It is true that the standard of preaching by visitors did not make it difficult for him to shine in comparison, but by any standard he was an admirable preacher. He had always been ready to perform the duties of a Christian schoolmaster. At Lancing he had given Confirmation talks to the members of his house and he headed his notes: *Pro eis me sanctifico*. Nor did he shrink from speaking about the central Christian doctrines. At Easter 1929 he preached on Immortality, of the aspiration of the spirit reaching out to God — the Christian hope (the hope, that is, of immortality, of 'work to do beyond the grave'). 'The Christian hope depends upon the belief that by prayer to God and by work for God a man can become, as it were, filled with the spirit of God, and that the spirit of God is the spirit of life which is stronger in the end than death.'[1]

How then could there have been any doubt concerning his beliefs? How could some boys when they left believe that he managed to preach once a term without ever mentioning the name of God? There are two reasons. He did not believe himself fit to evangelise; and he detested unction.

The public schools are nearly all religious foundations, but the

---

[1] It is even just conceivable that he contemplated taking Orders. When in 1941 the Bishop of Oxford required that all Lay Preachers should be registered and licensed, Roxburgh wrote that he was reluctant to sign a form attesting adherence to the Thirty-Nine Articles and said 'Indeed if I had been willing to declare assent to the Articles I should not have decided some years ago that I would not endeavour to take Orders.' There are many guises in which his admirers saw J.F. — as a diplomat or a pro-consul or a barrister; but they did not picture him as a clergyman. And yet, although his politeness could make him dissemble, this statement was on too serious a subject and it was made in a private letter. He was a man who would do anything for the benefit of his boys and at one time it may have seemed to him that a difficulty that had arisen in the religious life of the school could only be solved by himself taking Orders while the chaplaincy was vacant. In 1933 the Chaplain had resigned; the religious needs of the school as seen by Roxburgh and as seen by the first governing body were so different as to make the choice of a chaplain difficult; both the Governors' minutes and Roxburgh's correspondence show the difficulty there was in finding a successor; and as he himself put it in mid-search 'those that were good would not come and those that would come were not good'. In the end two years later a successor was found, but these may have been the years that he referred to in his letter to the Bishop.

degree to which boys are instructed in the professed faith differs from school to school. The Roman Catholic schools are meticulous in grounding their boys in both the liturgy and the apologetics of their Faith so that they emerge instructed in the elements of theology to a degree unknown in Anglican schools. Many of their masters are priests who hope that boys will be influenced by the teaching of those who have plainly dedicated their lives to God; and the schools accept boys only from Catholic families where they have been brought up in a Catholic atmosphere. The Church of England public schools after the First World War had to expect that a proportion of their entrants would come from homes that were indifferent to religion or perhaps agnostic; and they also had to contend with growing disbelief in Christianity among the boys themselves, which was no more than a reflection of what was happening in society at large. Their chaplains, therefore, had a different task from those in the Roman Catholic schools. The schools gave religious instruction. It took the form of Holy Communion on Sundays and compulsory Chapel (at that time once a day and twice on Sundays); morning prayer, house prayers; voluntary services; Scripture lessons in form (usually once or twice a week); and special instruction at Confirmation. Masters in Holy Orders and housemasters were there to aid any boy who was in religious difficulty — the Chaplain naturally having a special responsibility for initiating religious activities. But opinions would always vary on the prominence that religion should be given in the life of the school; and that meant in practice how far the headmaster and his staff taught subjects or made the school look at issues from an explicitly Christian standpoint. The deeply religious were always likely to criticise headmasters for not emphasising Christianity enough. Roxburgh was certainly so criticised.

To an Old Stoic schoolmaster teaching at another school who contrasted certain things at Stowe favourably to his present experience but found religious education at Stowe wanting, Roxburgh replied:

What you say about religion hits me hard because I know it to be true. I don't think I had better try to explain in a letter what my ideas are about religion in schools. I hope you won't think it absurd if I say only that I think too much religious teaching is worse than too little.

I have had experience of too much. But that doesn't mean that we have enough here. The lack of it is due to my personal inadequacy. . . . I could not conceivably do the kind of thing that your Headmaster does so admirably. I lack the conviction and certainty with which he speaks, and of course (like most people) I fall one hundred miles below him in moral force.

'I think too much religious teaching is worse than too little . . .' That was a conclusion which he had come to and on which he acted. On another occasion he said in a speech to parents:

Few boys are intensely religious and those who are do not always carry their religion into manhood. . . . The best foundation for a religious manhood is a religion suitable to boyhood; and, remember, that cannot be the same as your religion. . . . If a boy is to have a religion which he will carry through life (or rather which will carry him through life) it will be a religion which he has found for himself. You cannot find it for him. . . . You can set him on the road towards finding it: that is all.

A letter exists in reply to one from Archdeacon Ritchie, who often preached at the school and who had asked whether Roxburgh was satisfied that boys understood 'the relevance of Christianity to the world's situation and where and how God comes into the scheme of things and what is the purpose of life'. Roxburgh surveyed the whole of religious education at Stowe, not claiming nor conceding too much, but concluding that he could give no definite reply because however much formal instruction there might be what really influenced boys was the tone of the place and the Christian qualifications of the staff. But he was not prepared to infuse the teaching with religion. He would not, for instance, deliver the typical public school sermon of the day which sneered at agnostics and implied that those who could not receive the Christian faith in its entirety were vapid egoists. He did not doubt that at Stowe some boys would lose their faith and that others would find it. He would set an example — he communicated every Sunday — but no more. To him that service meant Communion rather than the Eucharistic sacrifice. 'I have,' he wrote, 'the profoundest belief in the quiet Early Service to which small young scholars and large old footballers alike find their way unbidden in the dim light and sacrifice an hour of well-earned bed in an honest and sometimes passionate attempt to find and follow their Lord.'

Roxburgh never tried to convey the impression that religion suffused all his thoughts. It palpably did not. There are saintly men and women of whom this is true, and there are rather more who by using unction imply that it does so though in fact it does not. Every creed whether religious or political uses shorthand phrases, clichés and compressed arguments that become the standard fare to comfort the converted. At Lancing he had spent his time trying to get his Sixth form to avoid clichés when they wrote paragraphs for him; and as a great deal of pious talk and writing employs just such trite phrases he found unction doubly displeasing. That was why he would have no sentimental hymns. He gave his Chaplains a free hand but his manner was anything but ecclesiastical. Even after the Warrington régime was over he thought loyalty was due to the school's Evangelical foundation, and he once took it upon himself to request the bishop not to wear cope and mitre at Confirmation, although he said that he had no objection to these robes when the bishop was marrying an Old Stoic in the Chapel. The Chaplain innocently asked why. 'J.F. answered in his most urbane manner patting me on the shoulder, "After all, a wedding is a joyful occasion". I was left wondering what sort of an occasion a Confirmation was.' A notice in J.F.'s hand to the effect that the bishop was to officiate at some service of dedication appeared on the Masters' notice board with the characteristic exhortation: 'I hope that as many masters as possible will make it convenient to be present at this harmless little ceremony.'[1] J.F. enjoyed being naughty to the clergy. 'You don't mind, do you, if I tell you that the little anchor thing that you have on the neck of your stole is apt to slip round.' The 'anchor thing' was the priest's cross. He was a religious, but not a spiritual man.

Indeed we have to go back a century before Roxburgh's time to find a representative figure to express the comedy which he found in churchiness. Sydney Smith was a clergyman and also one of the most amusing Englishmen who has ever lived. When he talked grave men fell into paroxyms of hilarity and literally

[1] Heckstall-Smith, *op. cit.*, p. 29.

rolled on the carpet exhausted with laughter. It was Smith who said of a bishop that he deserved to be preached to death by wild curates and that his own idea of Heaven was eating *paté de fois gras* to the sound of trumpets; who told an alarmed lady that the heat of the previous day had been so dreadful that there was nothing left for it but to take off his flesh and sit in his bones; and who wondered how a bishop could marry — for 'How can he flirt? The most he can say is "I will see you in the vestry after service." ' Sydney Smith scandalised those who deplored that a clergyman should have so little reverence. And indeed he was without reverence. He disliked the enthusiasm of the Methodists, referred to the Oxford Movement as Newmania and was satirical about his profession. 'An ounce of mother wit is worth a pound of clergy.'[1] And yet this rationalist in theology who campaigned for Catholic Emancipation and championed the poor, packed his sermons with practical religion, wrote acute pastoralia, and radiated goodness through his world. He too was a Low Churchman. There was something of the spirit of Sydney Smith in Roxburgh. J.F. did not invariably speak in hushed tones about religion and the clergy and gave his irony free rein when he met what he thought was obscurantism in religion. He admired G. K. Chesterton for bringing cheerfulness and gaiety into Christianity and for his ringing attacks on respectability and the Establishment. He once pained his sophisticated Sixth Form on a Sunday evening by quoting Chesterton's verses about 'all the easy speeches that comfort cruel men' and interspersing the quotation with exclamations of 'Bravo, Chesterton!' Like Sydney Smith his conception of Christianity omitted vast tracts that are included in that word; and like him he thought that in some cases it was all the better for that.

If religion was not the mainspring of his life was it perhaps friendship? The longer he remained a headmaster the vaster grew the number of those who thought of him as a friend. But in fact he had few intimate friends. Belonging to a generation decimated in the First World War he had not many of his own age, and living at Stowe for so many weeks during the year he found difficulty in keeping up with those he had. His new friendships similarly suffered. Muriel Currey, for instance, was often taken

[1] Hesketh Pearson, *The Smith of Smiths* (London, 1934), p. 231.

abroad by her assignments and their meetings dwindled to an occasional lunch in London or Oxford: the war led their paths apart. There were always some members of the staff at Stowe with whom he could relax and he found particular happiness and freedom in Capel Cure's company — all the more apparent when sparks flew between them as they could. But in the holidays he needed to get away from his colleagues and when he curtailed his excursions he began to suffer the loneliness of the busy man. He formed intimate friendships with very few of his former pupils. Cholmeley Harrison and Christopher Barlow among the early Stoics held a special place in his affections and he found Toby O'Brien in particular intellectually congenial. To them he showed glimpses of his private life; and later with a number, such as Roland Oliver and Wayland Young, he carried on a considerable correspondence after they had left. He saw these friends intermittently but not as much as they would have liked or he needed. Good teachers are always giving; they enjoy doing so: that is why they become teachers. Roxburgh gave prodigiously and imparted to hundreds a sense of their own potentialities. But the obverse of giving is receiving, and that Roxburgh did not do. He could not receive love to anything like the extent that he gave it. This was sad. He was too sensitive to be self-sufficient. The emotional reserve, common to many Scotsmen, had been reinforced by his own self-discipline which he imposed when his hopes of marriage faded. This was the scar which his passion for Sonia left.

He had also become the prisoner of his own image. The reputation which he had built with each successive generation of boys had to be maintained. To each he had to give the same attention while at the same time maintaining interest in those that had left. He could not, as others can, retire gracefully from a maze of acquaintances and cultivate the intimate friendship of a few. He could never shed acquaintances, and before him stretched entry lists for future years of boys to whom he felt as strong a sense of duty as to his former pupils. After his illness in the early nineteen-thirties he had no longer the strength to maintain a private life. Affability of the kind that he practised is terribly destructive of the nerves: it leaves no residue of strength to meet the demands of intimate friendship. At Lancing when he was young he had deliberately experimented to see how he could make the most effective impression upon schoolboys by exploiting all his talents. The genie whom he had summoned up now had him in his power. Roxburgh's constant preoccupation with the young did not of itself cut him off from adult company: his tastes and intelligence were too highly developed for that to occur. But his entire devotion to Stowe and its affairs, and to Stoics past and present and their affairs, in the end curtailed his ability, and even his desire, to preserve for himself an inner life. But it is not in any of us to exploit more than a fraction of the possibilities of life. He would have thought that his private life was of small account and that its sacrifice was immaterial.

It was sacrificed to the mainspring of his life. That was work. It is often assumed nowadays that compulsive industry is the symptom of a subconscious desire to escape from life: submerged beneath a mountain of correspondence and interviews the psyche can take refuge from the emotionally demanding relationships of love and friendship. But in J.F. industry was part of his heredity and upbringing. His father had died of overwork, and within him was clamped a gyroscope which swung him relentlessly on to the course of work and duty. Throughout his life we have seen occurrences when Scottish industry and puritan duty were mellowed but reinforced by the Roman virtues which he had learnt to admire in his reading of the classics. Everyone remembered his social graces: few considered the severity of his self-discipline. He kept everything in control, good qualities as well as bad, his friendships and his snobbery; and he was not a man of mild feeling — his rare outbursts showed the strength of his emotions. With his self-discipline went a scathing criticism of his own abilities. He knew what he did well but he judged that he did most other things not nearly well enough. And thus when he retired and his work was done he did not believe that he had much more to offer.

Chapter X

Retirement & Death

Those who live in public apartments are at the mercy of visitors. As early as 1935 Roxburgh had looked for a place to be used as an occasional retreat and to which he might eventually retire. He explored Penn and Jordans but in the following year he found what he wanted at Great Brickhill, a few miles south of Bletchley. There he bought a plot of land at the top of a hill with a view which swept straight across country to the line of the Chilterns, and planned to build a house worthy of the site. He laid out the terrace, bought more land to preserve the view and began to develop a garden. All this was done with the familiar care and precision. The bricks of the garden wall were hand-made to ensure that they should be of the right colour and in 1939 he took the lease of a cottage in Brickhill to use as a base while he brought the garden acreage under control and designed his house. He dreamt of the days when he would play host to Old Stoics in a house of modest size but of some distinction, large enough to contain an adequate staff and enable him to continue living in something like the style that he had enjoyed at Stowe.

The dream was shattered by the war. In the post-war years when the country was repairing the damage from air raids and six years of dilapidation it would have been impossible to obtain a licence to build a house of the size that he had in mind and he soon realised that he must modify his plans. He hit on the sensible compromise of building a gardener's cottage to which he could retire while waiting for the day when he would be able to build the main house. So in 1947 he measured out the site in person and himself cut the first turf having chosen the type of brick he wanted with the help of an Old Stoic who scoured the south of England and the Midlands as far as Shrewsbury to provide samples. The Garden Cottage was small and when he left Stowe he had to sell many of his belongings and cram the rest into it. The life of hospitality of the type that he had in mind was no longer possible.

The months immediately following his retirement were, however, largely spent away from Brickhill. There was a short visit to Paris; and a stay in Ireland with his old friend Cholmeley Harrison idling on the beach and reading some of his old favourites — Catullus and the French lyric poets among them. Then in the autumn he set out on the cruise financed by the Old Stoics' subscriptions. He went to South Africa and arriving at Durban at 4.30 in the morning found himself greeted by a small company of Old Stoics who had not only got up at this discouraging hour but had contrived to manufacture a sort of flag of the Stowe colours which they displayed at the dockside. He never forgot that welcome. He thought of it as some kind of proof that what he had done at Stowe was really remembered with affection. In Johannesburg Old Stoics and their wives gave him lunch at the Inanda Club and paid him a tribute which pleased him, telling him how grateful they were 'for the spirit of tolerance, plain ordinary tolerance for other people and ideas' which they would always think of as part of J.F.'s Stowe. The tour took him to Kenya, too briefly for him to meet more than a few of his former pupils there, but he was at least able to spend an afternoon with one of them in his home near Nairobi, and with another to attend a polo match which, as his host said, 'he endured in his usual well-mannered style'. But he was lonely on the trip: he said he missed having someone to whom he could say: 'Isn't that marvellous?'

When he at last returned to Brickhill he began with relief to work. Ever since he had gone to Stowe he had grown roses in his garden there and during the war had been grafting and cross-fertilising them. He became an expert. He spent long hours of planning and cultivation with Charles Franklin who had been his gardener since 1937 and had become his friend. He was ready for any work and pushed himself beyond his physical strength, gardening in his oldest clothes and defying the weather in, of all garments for him, a duffle-coat. He had reason to be proud of the products of his grafting and his growing. He used to show; and at the Woburn Show of 1951 he carried off eleven prizes for his roses — he had a particular fondness for yellow roses — his sweet peas, his gooseberries and his tomatoes. 'Schoolmastering, if you like it, is the finest thing in the world — but, my dear fellow, I really do think that I am a better rose gardener than ever I was schoolmaster.' It was Horace on his Sabine Farm.

He sometimes travelled — to Scotland for instance where his Aunt Anna still lived. He went to France each spring — he was at Chartres as late as 1953. He returned to his first love, photography, and now interested himself in colour processes: he photographed architectural features such as Linslade spire and also his prize fruit and flowers. His style of photography remained of its era: it did not cross his mind to develop his film himself, that was work for the chemist. Some Old Stoics thought that on his retirement he would become an important figure in determining the nation's educational policy or occupying himself with some of the problems that the public schools were facing. But he had no inclination to do so. 'Administration of whatever kind will not fill the place of my Stoics,' he had told one who asked him what he intended to do on retirement, and he was emphatic that if he took on work it was to be with people rather than with affairs. He still did some committee work — he took part in the business of the Friends of Stowe — but his doctors would not allow him to do much. On another matter he had the most rigid views. He would not return to Stowe nor involve himself in Old Stoic functions. He would hear no Stowe news nor write to those there: once only he asked his former secretary to send him news of the university scholarship results. There were many reasons why he cut himself off completely from the place. He was determined not to embarrass his successor Eric Reynolds; he knew the dangers of a Lanchester tradition — the petrification of a régime that is associated with the name and idea of a particular headmaster such as Arnold; and he could not have borne the emotional strain which renewed contact would have imposed upon him.

Old Stoics naturally visited him on their way to and from Stowe and he still corresponded with many of them especially when they sought his advice or help. Sometimes to his mortification he forgot a name. To one to whom this happened he said mournfully: 'Derry, *never* retire.' Those who came to see him were sometimes shocked that his life had contracted into such a little span. 'I used,' wrote one Old Stoic who lived near him during those years, 'I used to see him sometimes, when nearly always we would walk round his lovely garden on the hill-top, and would feel the aching gap left in the walls for the house that would never be built. I never enjoyed those meetings for one sensed that he was not happy there. It was oppressive to him, and it seemed to affect his alertness and interest in everything else.' 'Here was the neat little lodge near the entrance,' wrote another; 'there was his big garden descending in shallow terraces towards the view; and full of roses; and immaculately kept. And here in the middle was the gap where his own house ought to have been . . . so the formal garden was aligned on an absence, and he was living on the edge of it.' Naturally his friends were dismayed to see his activities reduced to reading the lesson in Brickhill church and acting as host to the British Legion collecting shillings at the gate for entry to his garden; and many judged that retirement was killing him. Recalling a dinner given to him by Old Stoics in Edinburgh six months before he retired one of his hosts recorded that he had been impressed by J.F.'s acceptance of finality regarding his life at Brickhill. 'It was as if his whole motive power was due to be removed, and in fact I think that with the inspiration of Stowe gone he lost any reason for continued existence.' But the truth was that even before he retired his health was beginning to fail. His strength never recovered and as time went by he found himself able to do less and less. By 1953, though not yet sixty-five, he was writing 'For some time now I have neither given nor accepted invitations of any kind — not even to afternoon tea! I am told that I shall be all right "in the Summer" but the Summer has not yet come, and . . . I go to ground from 2 p.m. onwards.' In the preceding years he found all too soon that any social contacts outside his most intimate circle tired him. There was no sign of mental decline but he was unable to cope with any un-expected demand. His memory was still prodigious but it began to fall short of its once fabulous power and he was also embar-rassed by slight deafness. Hating to do less well anything that he had done once superlatively, he came to resent unheralded visits and could be brusque to those who dropped in to see him un-announced. He had his pride: that somebody might get less from him than he expected was unendurable. Friends who saw him in those days and were saddened by the sight of a man apparently with few resources did not realise that the activity which he had wisely sought — teaching in a prep school for half a morning — exhausted him. The energy still left to him went into this and into his garden. His physique allowed him to do less and less and, four years after he had retired, so far was he from being a fit man again that the black-outs, which had first afflicted him at the times of the Warrington crisis, became more frequent.

If sickness was stealing upon him, it came at the gallop for another. Early in 1953 it became evident that Capel Cure, who was still in his early fifties, was stricken with cancer and the end came with appalling swiftness. He bore gruelling medical treat-ment during the summer and had to go home: a few days after term ended he died. Although remaining independent and in no way aping J.F.'s manner or his habits, Capel had modelled his life on him. Like him he had remained a bachelor and devoted his life entirely to Stowe. He had always meant much to J.F. who throughout his headmastership turned to him instinctively in time of trouble as his letter to Mrs Capel Cure shows:

> . . . As each day passes I come to realise a little more clearly what has gone out of my life. Ever since I left Stowe and we only met at intervals, I used to say to myself regularly 'How will Eddie like that?', or 'I must ask Capel about that', or 'tell Capel about that' — and I find myself doing so still. An old friend has just

written to me: 'I never met him, but I have known through you
how much you depended on his judgment.' Indeed I did. I could
not have carried on at Stowe during the bad years without having
him to consult and pour out to, nor, towards the end when I was
unfit and doing badly, without his encouragement. Of course he
was a remarkable schoolmaster and did wonderful things for his
House and his Form and the School. But everyone else will tell
you that. I am thinking selfishly of what he did for me and what
he was to me and how much he has meant to me even since the
Stowe days. And when I think of that, I can begin to guess a
little of what this disaster means for you, my dear friend. It will
take all your courage — the well-known Capel courage! — to bear
it. But I believe you will be able to when you think how much
that son of yours did for English schoolboys for thirty years and
what numbers of young people are at this moment better men —
more generous-minded, more honourable, more modest and truer
lovers of what is beautiful, besides being wiser and more efficient
— through contact with him. That reflexion helps me too, though
in my selfish moments I think more about the effect he had on an
elderly schoolmaster than on young schoolboys!

Once more my love to you — and a handshake . . . Don't let
me lose touch with you . . .

His dream of building the house of his desire finally faded.
Secretively in order to attract no notice or sympathy he sold the
main plot of land which contained his beautiful garden and the
Atlantic cedars which on 11 November in each year of the war he
had planted to commemorate the Old Stoics whose names he had
read out on that day at the service in Stowe Chapel. His new plan
was to enlarge and alter Garden Cottage. The winter passed and
in 1954 he celebrated his sixty-sixth birthday. The morning after,
on 6 May, the workmen, who were still on the site as the altera-
tions had not been wholly completed, noticed that they had not
seen him at the ordinary hour and they heard his bath running for
an unusually long time. They called Franklin who found that he
had collapsed into the bath. He had been struck by coronary
thrombosis and it was this that killed him: he had not drowned
for no water was found in his lungs.

Such was the end of this much-loved man; and as they read of
his death pupils and colleagues who had been touched by his spell

felt miserable that something that had once been a part of them had ceased to exist. What had he achieved?

Perhaps the greatest educationalists are those who have the good fortune to do their life's work in an institution which by the accident of history is going to be the instrument for change making its influence felt right through society. That is why Arnold is the epitome of headmasters. Roxburgh was not quite as fortunate. He worked in the period between the Balfour and the Butler Acts. The Balfour Act of 1902, passed only ten years before Roxburgh became a schoolmaster, laid the foundations of state secondary education in Britain. But although for years afterwards the public schools were to dominate adolescent education, the Butler Act, passed five years before Roxburgh retired, was an act of recognition that the state system had come of age. The maintained grammar and secondary modern schools, which were then established, became the recognised mainstream of the country's secondary education and the public schools a tributary. The public schools during Roxburgh's lifetime had certainly trained a high proportion of the nation's leaders as any analysis of the composition of Cabinets, Parliament, the Civil Service, the City, the Armed Forces and management will show. But by the early nineteen sixties it was not only clear that this proportion would fall, but the question also began to be asked, even in the public schools themselves, whether future leaders would be successful if they had been isolated from their contemporaries and lacked any sense of community with them. Among public school headmasters grew a feeling that under the changed structure of society their schools had been deprived of their old functions and responsibilities. Anxious not to be dammed or diverted when the mainstream flowed past them they welcomed schemes to integrate the public schools into the state system which went far beyond the Fleming scheme. But all this occurred years after Roxburgh was dead. There were in fact two debates concerning the public schools in his time. The debate on the class structure and image of the public schools which became the crucial debate of the future; and the transformation of the public school ethos to which Roxburgh devoted his life. It is interesting that on these issues he came under fire from both flanks and his achievement was denigrated by two social groups which rarely find themselves in alliance: the radicals who hated the ethos of the public schools but even more the class distinction which they preserved and who dismissed him as a snob; and the *bien-pensant* wing of the Establishment for whom he was too showy, too lacking in piety towards the old public school unction, too modern and subversive.

Roxburgh's educational ideal was the child of his youth in Edwardian England. It did not herald a new public school epoch. So far from representing something new in English education he was the final flowering of the old public school tradition — self-sufficient and inward-looking, cultivating the manners and morality of a governing élite. To-day the atmosphere which his ideals breathed, like the soil of the pre-1914 English society in which they were grounded, has vanished. His emphasis on elegance of mind and taste — all the trappings from his own sartorial conspicuousness to the patrician embellishments and pursuits which he encouraged boys to develop — will appear to some to have been a delusion even at the time when he became a headmaster. It is also possible to argue that he was caught in a dilemma of his own making. A public school then differed from a boarding school by virtue of its assertion that it *was* a public school. It automatically built into its structure certain received traditions: a Christian tradition, a curriculum geared to Oxford and Cambridge entry, competition between houses, corporal punishment, fagging — the stressing of religious, social and moral, as well as intellectual, possibilities in the lives of the boys within the well-known public school framework. He was determined to work within this framework, because he wanted Stowe to succeed in a particular way and appreciated that it could not so succeed unless he conformed to the pattern. Yet to work so closely within the framework meant that some of his most important ideas could not be realised as he would have wished. Many other objections could be brought against his intentions and achievements, so that it is all the more important to see him accurately in relation to his times and to isolate what he himself considered to be of prime importance in the public schools in his day.

His main achievement was, perhaps, to shift from his pedestal the father-figure of the public schools. Dr Arnold was not the source of Roxburgh's inspiration. He looked instead to the son of that great headmaster, Matthew Arnold, for guidance. Roxburgh wanted to civilise what Matthew Arnold called the Barbarians, the upper class public schoolboys, and to give them a sense that in their hands lay the cultural standards and welfare of the country. Everybody was to get not only the opportunity but positive encouragement to love the arts. That was not so common then as now. He did much to reduce that well-publicised division in the inter-war period between the aesthete and the athlete: both flourished, and of course at times each was satirical about the other, but there was tolerance and respect for those who chose to paint or go bird's nesting or write poetry or devote their spare time to toxophily or architectural church-crawls. In Norwood's time at Marlborough in the 'twenties a school magazine was produced satirising games and the public school spirit and bearing the motto 'Upon Philistia will I triumph'. Norwood suppressed it and preached a sermon upon intellectual arrogance. Such an incident was unthinkable at Roxburgh's Stowe. Roxburgh set out to humanise public school life and bring greater kindness and understanding among boys. Of course there were at Stowe, as at all schools, sadistic prefects, persecuting cliques, unimaginative subordinates, and unhappy boys. Stowe had its full share of public school crime and it would be grotesque to pretend that the pattern of behaviour that Roxburgh set was printed upon his boys who lived the characteristic life of schoolboys of their time. Some of the maladjusted, difficult, sensitive creatures still continued to suffer in the intense community life of a public school. But Roxburgh's Stowe was designed to help them and did so by enabling them to preserve their individuality. Their analogues from other schools were astonished at the university to find that these Stoics had not detested their schooldays as they had. The difference in atmosphere was always noticed. Griffith Williams, who was in a position in the Ministry of Education to make comparisons, wrote after Roxburgh's death:

Consider what the Public Schools were like before 1914. There were of course great human personalities like Talboys of Wellington. But in the main the staffs consisted of dignified remote figures, often with high ideals and scholarly gifts but with little sympathy for boys and an unreasoning suspicion of undue familiarity. Sometimes a young man would appear like a flash of lightning, but he seldom stayed long and the schools reverted to type. Stowe and J.F. revolutionised all that. He came at a critical period in the history of the Public School and the lessons he taught have now become part of the national stock in trade. . . . He will rank among the twelve great Headmasters of the past hundred and fifty years.

In the late nineteen-thirties young headmasters of a different type began to be appointed such as Robert Longden[1] or Robert Birley, and a new generation who had been affected by the mood of personal freedom which flourished at Oxford and Cambridge between the wars came to the front. They would have done so if Roxburgh had never existed but his example made their appointment easier because he had already made himself felt and known as a new type of headmaster.

Just as he made sensitive moral distinctions in judging behaviour, knowing that part of the revolt against the public school code had arisen because virtue had become identified with good form and excessive loyalty to the corporate body, so he happily accepted a loss of efficiency in the interest of freedom. 'Some day,' he concluded in a letter to an old pupil, 'perhaps this place will have an efficient headmaster. I hope it won't, because if it does its character will entirely change. But the possibility cannot be excluded from our vision of the future.' A fellow-headmaster once sneered that Roxburgh's Stowe was an exotic creation founded on frivolous superficialities — 'All the luxuries but none of the necessities,' — so although a school's success cannot be measured statistically some facts about the more conventional achievements should be recorded. During his headmastership this new school won 123 awards to Oxford and Cambridge. In the war one in every eight serving was decorated and of the 279 decorations 228 were for gallantry in the field. If team games are regarded as an index the school won as many matches at cricket as it lost: at rugger, if the war years are excepted, when Roxburgh's policy of encouraging boys to go to the university at seventeen brought a series of monotonous losses in a game where age and weight tell, Stowe won three-fifths of its matches. But the bandying about of figures proves little and this record may possibly have been

[1] Robert Longden, Student of Christ Church 1929–37, Master of Wellington 1937–40.

surpassed by other new schools. Roxburgh not merely created a school: he succeeded in giving it status. In that indefinable, almost unspeakable, hierarchy in which the public schools are ranked he made Stowe a school that could be mentioned in the same breath with other more famous and ancient institutions. That was certainly one of his ambitions and he achieved it. But his far more important ambition he also achieved: to influence boys by his teaching in class and to make many of them happy.

How many did his personality touch? The biographers of headmasters table their undeniable virtues and then blandly assume that by process of osmosis these virtues became implanted in the hearts of all the boys in the school. It is a convenient but inaccurate theory. It was impossible to be at Stowe for more than a term and not sense Roxburgh's spirit because he would have taught you and greeted you. But there were certainly many who never troubled their heads to discover what he was at; who when they left were able to give the stock imitation of his manner and little else. Yet equally it was impossible for a man of his distinctiveness of character not to influence a great number of his boys. There will be some who will judge that the impact of a personality such as his would have been bound to be deplorable. That is possible. Any strongly defined personality is bound to impinge in a multitude of ways, often in ways which can hardly be foreseen. Headmasters of a stamp different from his — upright, high-minded moralists who consciously set before boys an austere set of values — may exert over some a fine influence, but they also breed prigs and amoralists in almost equal proportion, because few of us are able to transmute precepts and example into the everyday business of living. Roxburgh deliberately relaxed the moral temperature of the public school in his time. In this he was wise. The public schools of the inter-war years were still laying the accent on the stern, unyielding Victorian ideals and appealing to the virtues which had supposedly inspired the officer class in the First World War. The gap was growing wider between the culture which these schools purveyed and the culture of the 'twenties and 'thirties. The emphasis on rectitude and fortitude was maladjusted to the freer life which boys enjoyed within the family and to the iconoclastic, experimental, deflationary spirit which the First World War engendered. Roxburgh did not ally himself specifically with any one tendency. He believed in freedom to choose and freedom to criticise. He also sensed that the discrepancy between the old public school way of life and the lives which boys lived at home was growing wider. He countered this through his worldliness. His worldliness was refreshing, so rare in a pedagogue. There came a time when you wondered whether it was false. Laurence Whistler once compared him to a great baroque church in Rome, in front an imposing eloquent stone façade but at the sides brickwork with holes left by the scaffolding, not a fraudulent building for it fulfilled its function as a church, but giving something of a false impression. But his worldliness, his invitation to acquire sophistication and to grow up, was not the centre of his influence. At the centre lay his affection. Whoever rejected his values, or failed to respond to his teaching, knew that J.F. retained, and would continue to retain, affection and respect for him as an individual. He allowed neither system nor theory nor any abstraction to come between himself and the boys in his school. The force of his charm for ever returned because he cared for you as an individual and not as a unit on a conveyor belt handing on a torch mechanically in the spirit of *Vitaï Lampada*. In his last years he became the prisoner of this devotion and of his legend and he wore himself out trying to retain for every Stoic the memory of being treated as a unique creature; but whatever the limitations that this imposed upon his other activities as a headmaster, it always served as a reminder that education is to do primarily with people and not with schemes. That was why he was such a perennial topic among his former pupils. Others observed with amused surprise that when two or three of them met they would often chat about him just as a century before among Rugbeians Arnold's name would hardly fail to be mentioned. Like the Cossacks in Gogol's story, rowing swiftly down the Dnieper when their chief Taras Bulba has gone to his death, 'they talked of their Commander'.

Recalling the old days with Patrick Hunter during his last term at Stowe, in that summer of 1949, Roxburgh said: 'I hope that it is as a schoolmaster that I shall be remembered. If I am not remembered as that, I would rather not be remembered at all.'[1] He had always thought of himself as a teacher — and in his retirement he could not endure to be parted from his profession. In the spring of 1950, back from his cruise round Africa, he decided that he was fit enough to teach in a preparatory school. He was a formidable candidate for a junior post among men much junior to him. The first school to which he applied politely declined his offer, and it was with some diffidence that the Rev. T. A. Flynn, headmaster of The Old Ride near Little Horwood, accepted him. Roxburgh had insisted that there should be limiting clauses in the terms of appointment. He was to have no official responsibility; no contact with parents; and no entanglement in school affairs. What he had come to do was to teach — to round off his career as he had begun it. He had always said that he could not understand boys below the age of adolescence, but now he was prepared to learn 'the new technique of teaching these squeakers'. He taught in the morning for only two hours but it was the saving of him. In 1951 a year after starting at The Old Ride he wrote, 'Meanwhile, I will only say this, having recovered my health and become desperately anxious to find a job (and a job concerned with *people*, preferably young) I have taken to prep-school-mastering. Every day in term time I go off from my cottage and teach in a prep school ten miles away. It is grand fun and I simply could not do without it.' Two years later the work was clearly all that he could do but he preferred to give up almost everything else rather than stop teaching.

In the spring of 1950 then, the masters and boys awaited his arrival with lively expectation: his reputation had preceded him and the boys at least knew that he drove a car exceedingly fast. The Old Ride was approached by a long straight drive, inadequately surfaced, and visible for all its length from some of the school's windows. Down this he would bucket towards mid-morning, the small boys glued to the seconds hands of their watches hoping for a new record. He would pull up sharp under the chestnut tree, climb from the car before the dust had settled and slam the car door (for one who could not bear to hear paper crumpled in form it was odd that he slammed doors mercilessly). He then strode

[1] It is as a schoolmaster that he is remembered by the inscription in the Roxburgh Hall that was built in his memory. See page 210.

across the yard swinging his small suitcase — one of the same suitcases in which at Stowe he had kept the school books which he showered round the form. If now and then he arrived in a taxi it was understood that there had been 'another accident'. He drank coffee with the staff in the library and then taught between break and lunch. The suitcases now sometimes contained fruit from his garden — if, for instance, a boy in his form had a birthday. Once again the far-famed silk handkerchiefs became a by-word. One day he was challenged on the spur of the moment to produce ten silk handkerchiefs on the spot or bring next day a punnet of strawberries. He had no need to bring the strawberries: four came from his pockets, two from his sleeves, two from both of his suitcases. Once again there rose the same chorus of testimony to his powers as a teacher. 'He could teach me more in a week than most in a term.' Again the same quality in his teaching was noted by his pupils — 'that fine refusal to believe that you would be capable of such poor form, so that you dared not disappoint'. Then as they came back one summer term they were told that he had died. He left five pounds in his will to each of those he had taught during his last term.

During the last ten years of his life Roxburgh described himself as finished and 'doing badly'; and to those who knew him he appeared in retirement a wraith of his former self. Of course his colleagues at The Old Ride enjoyed, as the headmaster put it in the letter he wrote to *The Times*, his 'good-humoured and amusing company' but how did he appear to someone who had never previously known him? Perhaps the most moving of all testimonies to J.F. came from the youngest of his colleagues[1] at that prep school who knew him solely in the days when he was done for.

The news that J.F. was to join us as a part-time member of the staff naturally recalled his legend to us: the man of elegance and wit, who had reigned as heir to the Dukes of Buckingham and Chandos, reviving at Stowe, and personifying in himself, so many of the eighteenth-century graces; the confirmed misogynist, whose charm no mother could resist; the scholar whose presence had awed his colleagues of the Headmasters' Conference; most of all, of course, the Headmaster who had made Stowe, by living Stowe's motto. We wondered if it were

[1] R. H. Horne, Headmaster of Richmond Lodge Preparatory School.

possible that such a man could work profitably and happily with young barbarians of preparatory school age — and with us, who would be his colleagues, all much younger, less well qualified, than he. For myself, I found that I, at the age of 21, had J.F. attached to my department — Classics and English — as my subordinate. The ludicrous quality of this situation did little to abate my terror at the prospect of such formidable assistance.

Our fears and worries were completely groundless; his legend had told us much that was true; it had not revealed to us his immense kindness, his overruling love of boys and of scholarship, or the humility which we ought to have realised was bound to be a characteristic of such a man.

It would be untrue to say that J.F. was universally successful as a Preparatory Schoolmaster. I do not know how long it had been since he had tried to teach a form of duller boys — certainly, though he and they always held each other in great affection and esteem, his attempts at The Old Ride to teach boys of average or below-average ability were often academically disastrous. But with the prospective scholars, his genius flowered. Under his guidance our Sixth Form learned to appreciate the finer things of life — English poetry, French painting, ecclesiastic architecture — to an extent seen in too few Preparatory Schools. Under his tutelage, too, they learned what is meant by scholarship, and the excellence of his teaching of French, Greek and English to our prospective scholars was shown both in our scholarship results and his pupils' fidelity to his precepts: as for their reaction to him, I can perhaps summarise it by saying that we had to introduce a rule forbidding the sporting of coloured silk handkerchiefs — a quantity of which had appeared to overflow from the breast pockets of their owners, in the approved J.F. style.

Small boys, though easily misled for a short while, are impossible to deceive for long: if J.F. had merely appeared and dazzled them with a degree of 'presence', urbanity and scholarship previously unknown to them, they would soon have seen through such a façade. In fact, their loyalty to him never wavered, because they knew that transcending the persona which delighted and amused us all was a steady and burning love for them, and for the ideas of scholarship. The material evidence of this love — no boy's birthday, in holiday or term-time, ever forgotten, the shower of little presents, — were merely tokens, but tokens which gave proof of the real trouble and thought which he gave to the needs of every individual boy.

We on the staff saw other facets of his nature: more, perhaps, than the boys, we could appreciate the presence, and dignity, the fastidious-ness, and the clarity of mind which gave him so much of his greatness: impossible for J.F. to be in a room without one's knowing it: impossible, too, for a group of which he was a member to have any other centre. Though he must have yearned again and again to advise us, to correct us, to lead us, — no doubt sometimes to shake us! — he never ventured an opinion on school matters without being asked. His manners and methods as a colleague were perfect.

I doubt if J.F. will live in history as anything so dull as a Great Educationalist: I doubt if he had 'Views on Education': — I think that he would have laughed at the laboratory techniques so often applied to the so-called Science of Teaching: he knew that education was not a science at all, but an art; in this art, he laboured constantly to increase his already golden talent. He did not merely believe, he knew, and silently taught us his colleagues, that the good schoolmaster lived his life by three rules: his own life should symbolise his teaching, he should know and love what he teaches, and, most of all, he should love, and work for, every individual boy under his care.

His funeral service, crowded with friends and pupils, was held in the Chapel and fell by chance on the anniversary of the foundation of the school. Stowe's splendour and beauty which had meant so much to him seemed doubly touching on that bright spring day. His ashes lie beneath the stones of the sanctuary.

Notes

Chapter II

p. 21. Alexander Balfour had set up as a trader in Liverpool with Stephen Williamson in 1851 and in due course created the firm of Balfour, Williamson & Co. Archibald Roxburgh went out to the subsidiary company, Williamson, Balfour in Chile. This firm financed a school for children of the English artisan community and Archibald Roxburgh was on the committee.

p. 21. After a brief period on her return from Chile in lodgings at Weston-super-Mare where her brother-in-law lived, Janet Roxburgh settled at Selby Holme, Mossley Hill, Liverpool, for six years and then moved to 15 Kirby Park.

p. 33. The Roxburghs rented a farm house, Ballintomb, at Dulnain Bridge: later Joanna Cathcart bought her own house Ach-na-Bhealaidh. The Campbell boys, Edward and Jack, inherited their father's legal practice and became Roxburgh's solicitors.

Chapter III

p. 48. It was hard to think of J.F. as a games player later in life but he did in fact play games often at Lancing. 'There was a scratch team got up by Dick [Harris] on Thursday,' he wrote in a letter to his mother in 1912. 'I was pressed into service and we had a jolly game beating the 2nd easily. It is great fun playing soccer even badly.' In the holidays he played golf and found the game 'the best distraction in the world'.

Chapter IV

p. 67. The five hand-picked boys were D. F. Wilson, N. A. C. Croft, H. E. Robinson, The Hon. G. C. S. P. Butler, all from Lancing; and A. G. Bowie who was a boy at Eastbourne where Ivor Cross had been teaching.

p. 74. The format of Stowe's school magazine also influenced that of a good many similar productions. *The Stoic* which was edited by boys and guided in its first years by Ivor Cross bore the imprint of Roxburgh's personality. *The Graphic* described it as 'a spacious quarterly with meadowy margins' and *The Spectator* as 'a very attractive production'. The quality of the photographs, the choice of print and the cover with Roman capitals on a plain white background, designed by Cross's architect brother, broke away from the dingy productions of the Victorian era.

Chapter VII

p. 124. Roxburgh made an excellent after-dinner speech always carefully prepared. He kept a small note book in which he wrote down jokes which were current or events from the evening newspapers of the night on which he was speaking which he could twist to allude to Stowe gossip. As with his sermons he jotted down how they were received. He did not care much for this kind of humour and was invariably self-critical. After the London Old Stoic dinner of 1945 he noted: 'Own speech covered much the usual ground and must not be repeated. Old jokes are no good now. Must do something a bit fresh.'

p. 124. It should be mentioned that among his outside activities was Freemasonry but he appears to have been a mason only in a formal sense. He first attended a Masonic function in October 1927 as Gisborough's protégé. In the following May he attended a fiftieth anniversary meeting in London of the Royal Arch Chapter and took a guest from Buckingham; thereafter he went spasmodically and without real comprehension to local meetings of his lodge. In May 1930 he confessed 'I regret to say that I am the worst of Masons . . .' and clearly remained so, for eight years later he wrote, 'I have not been to a Masonic meeting of your kind now for many years. I have found it quite impossible to keep up my interest in things Masonic while carrying the ever increasing burden of Stowe.' In the early months of the war he resigned from the St Mary's Chapter.

Chapter X

p. 203. The inscription in the Roxburgh Hall, built in his memory and in part from money which he and Huggins bequeathed to the school, surmounts the proscenium and was composed by Patrick Hunter — who also provided the translation given below:

MAGISTER SAPIENTISSIMUS
ERUDITISSIMUS DILECTISSIMUS
SCHOLAE STOICAE PRINCEPS ET CREATOR
SUI SEMPER OBLITUS ALIORUM STUDIOSUS
DISCIPULOS
HUMANITATE ALUIT COMITATE EXCOLUIT
DILIGENTIA EDUCAVIT

Here was a master whom his pupils loved,
Cultured and wise;
Who shaped a school and watched his new-born Stowe
To fullness rise.
Always to others' needs he gave himself,
Always himself forgot,
Although his boys will not;
So courteously he fashioned them, so kindly fed,
And so devotedly to knowledge led.

Index

Y.